17

Philosophers and God

Philosophers and God

At the frontiers of faith and reason

Edited by

*John Cornwell and
Michael McGhee*

continuum

Continuum
The Tower Building, 11 York Road, London SE1 7NX
80 Maiden Lane, Suite 704, New York, NY 10038

www.continuumbooks.com

First published 2009.

British Library Cataloguing-in-Publication Data
A catalogue record for this book is available from the British Library.

ISBN 978-0-8470-6548-3

Designed and typeset by Kenneth Burnley, Wirral, Cheshire

Printed and bound in Great Britain by the MPG Books Group

Contents

vi   *Contents*

*This book is dedicated to the memory of
the late Peter Lipton
1954–2007*

Notes on Contributors

John Cornwell is Director of the Science and Human Dimension Project at Jesus College, Cambridge. He is the author of *The Power to Harm* (Penguin, 1998), *The Pope in Winter* (Penguin, 2005) and *Hitler's Scientists* (Viking Adult, 2003). He has edited a number of collections of essays in philosophy of science, including *Nature's Imagination* (Oxford University Press, 1995), *Consciousness and Human Identity* (Oxford University Press, 1998) and *Explanations* (Oxford University Press, 2004).

Michael McGhee is Senior Fellow in the Department of Philosophy at the University of Liverpool. He is the author of *Transformations of Mind: Philosophy as Spiritual Practice* (Cambridge University Press, 2000) and co-editor of *Contemporary Buddhism: An Interdisciplinary Journal*. He edited *Philosophy, Religion and the Spiritual Life* (Cambridge University Press, 2002).

Peter Lipton
The late Peter Lipton (9 October 1954–25 November 2007) was the first Hans Rausing Professor of the History and Philosophy of Science in the University of Cambridge from 1997 to 2007, and head of his department from 1996 until his death. He was author of *Inference to the Best Explanation* (1991, second edition 2004).

Stephen R. L. Clark is Professor of Philosophy at the University of Liverpool. His most recent publications are *Biology and Christian Ethics* (Cambridge University Press, 2000), *G. K. Chesterton: Thinking Backwards, Looking Forwards* (Templeton Foundation Press, 2006) and *Understanding Faith* (Imprint Academic, 2009).

Nicholas Lash is Emeritus Norris-Hulse Professor of Divinity in the University of Cambridge. His many books include *Theology on Dover Beach* (Wipf and Stock, 2005), *Theology on the Way to Emmaus* (Wipf and Stock, 2005), *Easter in Ordinary* (University of Notre Dame Press, 1990), and most recently *Theology for Pilgrims* (Darton, Longman and Todd, 2008). He is a Fellow of Clare Hall, Cambridge.

David E. Cooper is Professor of Philosophy (Emeritus) at Durham University. He has been a Visiting Professor at universities in the USA, Canada, Germany, Malta and Sri Lanka. His most recent books are *The Measure of Things: Humanism, Humility and Mystery* (Oxford University Press, 2002), *Meaning* (Acumen Publishing, 2003), *Buddhism, Virtue and Environment* (with Simon P. James, Ashgate, 2005), and *A Philosophy of Gardens* (Oxford University Press, 2006).

Daphne Hampson is Professor Emerita of Divinity in the University of St Andrews and an affiliate of the Department of Theology at Oxford University. She is the author of *Theology and Feminism* (Blackwell, 1990), *After Christianity* (SCM Press, 1996/2002), editor of *Swallowing a Fishbone?: Feminist Theologians Debate Christianity* (SPCK Publishing, 1996) and, reflecting a further field of interest, of *Christian Contradictions: The Structures of Lutheran and Catholic Thought* (Cambridge University Press, 2001).

Janet Martin Soskice is University Reader in Philosophical Theology at the University of Cambridge and a Fellow of Jesus College. She is a past-President of the Catholic Theological Association of Great Britain and is currently President of the Society for the Study of Theology. Dr Soskice is the author of *Metaphor and Religious Language* (Oxford University Press, 1984) and *The Kindness of God* (Oxford University Press, 2008), and *Sisters of Sinai: How Two Lady Adventurers Found the Hidden Gospels* (Chatto and Knopf, 2009).

Francis X. Clooney, SJ, is a Roman Catholic priest and a member of the Society of Jesus. He has taught at Harvard Divinity School since 2005. Fr Clooney is the author of numerous articles and books, including *Hindu God, Christian God* (Oxford University Press, 2001), and *Divine Mother, Blessed Mother: Hindu Goddesses and the Virgin Mary* (Oxford University Press, 2005). He has just published two books: *Beyond Compare: St Francis and Sri Vedanta Desika on Loving Surrender to God* (Georgetown University Press, 2008), and *The Truth, the Way, the Life: Christian Commentary on the Three Holy Mantras of the Srivaisnava Hindus* (Peeters Publishing [Leuven], 2008).

Morny Joy is a University Professor in the Department of Religious Studies at the University of Calgary. She has an MA from the University of Ottawa (1973) and a PhD from McGill (1981). Morny's principal areas of research are philosophy and religion, especially Continental philosophy. Morny has written and co-edited a number of books and has written many articles in the area of women, philosophy and religion. Her most recent publication is *Divine Love: Luce Irigaray, Women, Gender and Religion* (University of Manchester Press, 2007).

Anthony Kenny was ordained a Roman Catholic priest after studying at the English College in Rome and was for four years a curate in Liverpool. In 1963 he was laicized at his own request and from that time pursued an academic career as a philosopher. He became Master of Balliol College, Oxford, and later Warden of Rhodes House. He has been President of the British Academy and Chairman of the British Library, and is now retired. He is married, with two sons and three granddaughters.

Clare Carlisle is Lecturer in Philosophy at the University of Liverpool. She is the author of three books on Kierkegaard, and the translator of Félix Ravaisson's *Of Habit*.

James P. Mackey is currently Visiting Professor at the School of Religions and Theology, Trinity College, the University of Dublin; Thomas Chalmers Professor of Theology (Emeritus), the University of Edinburgh; and Founding Editor of *Studies in World Christianity*. Recent publications: *Christianity and Creation* (Continuum, 2006); *The Scientist and the Theologian: On the Origin and End of Creation* (Columba Press, 2001); *Jesus of Nazareth: The Life, the Faith, and the Future of the Prophet* (Columba Press, 2008).

Pamela Sue Anderson is Reader in Philosophy of Religion, University of Oxford, and Fellow in Philosophy, Regent's Park College, Oxford. She is author of *Ricoeur and Kant* (Scholars Press, 1993); *A Feminist Philosophy of Religion* (Blackwell, 1998); co-edited with Beverley Clack, *Feminist Philosophy of Religion: Critical Readings* (Routledge, 2004); has an edited volume, *New Topics in Feminist Philosophy of Religion: Contestation and Transcendence Incarnate* (Springer, 2009); and has published numerous articles informed by a range of Continental philosophers, especially Kant, Paul Ricoeur, Luce Irigaray, Julia Kristeva and Michele Le Doeuff. Her current project is a monograph, *Goodness, God and Gender: A Thoughtful Love of Life*.

Richard Norman is Emeritus Professor of Moral Philosophy at the University of Kent. His published books include *The Moral Philosophers* (Oxford University Press, 1988) and *On Humanism* (Routledge, 2004). He is a Vice-President of the British Humanist Association.

Anthony O'Hear is Professor of Philosophy at the University of Buckingham, Director of the Royal Institute of Philosophy, and Editor of *Philosophy*. His books include *Beyond Evolution* (Oxford University Press, 1997), *Philosophy in the New Century* (Continuum, 2001), *The Great Books* (Icon Books, 2007) and *The Landscape of Humanity* (Imprint Academic, 2008).

Gordon Graham is Henry Luce III Professor of Philosophy and the Arts at Princeton Theological Seminary. He was formerly Regius Professor of Moral Philosophy at the University of Aberdeen. His most recent book is *The Re-enchantment of the World: Art versus Religion* (Oxford University Press, 2007).

Simon Oliver is Senior Lecturer in Systematic Theology and Director of the Centre for Faith, Reason and Ethics at the University of Wales, Lampeter. Recent publications include *Philosophy, God and Motion* (Routledge, 2005) and *Creation's Ends: Teleology, Ethics and the Natural* (forthcoming).

Harriet A. Harris is a member of the Faculty of Theology at the University of Oxford, and Chaplain of Wadham College Oxford. Her publications include *Fundamentalism and Evangelicals* (Oxford University Press, 1998, 2008), *Faith and Philosophical Analysis* which she co-edited with Chris Insole (Ashgate, 2005), and the Lent book, *Faith Without Hostages* (SPCK, 2004).

Preface

John Cornwell

Director, Science and Human Dimension Project,
Jesus College, Cambridge

The idea for this collection of essays was originally suggested by the late Professor Peter Lipton, to whom it is dedicated; it was further shaped in workshop sessions under the auspices of the Jesus College, Cambridge, Science and Human Dimension Project.

In the summer of 2007 Oxford University Press published a book entitled *Philosophers Without Gods*. The philosopher Professor Louise Anthony had elicited contributions from 20 British and American philosophers, united in their conviction that philosophy favours atheism. The collection also gives the impression of reacting to a sense of mild persecution, especially those who live and work in the United States. Professor Anthony claims in her Introduction that we live in a cultural climate in which sceptics and atheists are viewed with suspicion. 'We are presumed', she writes, 'to be arrogant, devoid of moral sentiments, and insensitive to a wide variety of human goods.' She goes on: 'This volume, written by philosophers who have abjured religious faith as philosophers, is meant to contribute to a more just understanding of those who have rejected religious belief.'

The collection constitutes sporadic, personal and autobiographical soundings in the contemporary seas of atheism, rather than a systematic thesis or a concerted anti-religion campaign. None of the contributors are casual atheists. Yet while they hold senior posts in philosophy departments, the cumulative impression of their approach is hardly philosophical in a technical sense. While some of the authors are knowledgeable about Judaism, Catholicism, Evangelical Protestantism and Eastern Orthodox Christianity, they betray scant appreciation of what it is that philosophers of religion do.

Among some familiar questions, they discuss: Dostoyevsky's 'If God is dead then everything is permitted'; the possibility of morality without religion; God's monstrous evil as evidenced by scripture; the claim that belief has 'pathological features'. Professor Georges Rey, for example, argues that religious beliefs are not so much believed as avowed, and Jonathan Adler, who concurs, discusses why fanaticism is so frequently grounded in religious belief. Adler thence argues that religious faith is at odds with ordinary norms of knowledge, norms that serve to block extremist inferences in ordinary circumstances.

Surprisingly the volume has only one brief discussion of humanism – by Louise Anthony herself: 'I have no trouble calling myself an atheist,' she writes, 'but if I had to choose a designation, analogous to Catholic or Christian, that might convey something about my positive commitments, I would choose humanist. I would connect myself with thinkers like Aristotle, Descartes, Hume, Kant, and Marx, who were awed and inspired by human capacities: for thought, for creation, and for sympathy. As they appreciated, our value as persons does not depend upon and cannot be secured by patronage of any external being. It emanates from within. Human dignity is not, and should not be thought to be, hostage to any myth.'

There is more sorrow than anger in the collection. Several authors acknowledge the loss suffered when faith dissolves. Just three express what one might term evangelical or militant atheism. Professor Edwin Curley urges atheists to abandon their quietism when religion is invoked in defence of immoral social policies. Louise Anthony indicts what she calls dogmatic religions, like Catholicism, for 'lionizing', as she puts it, 'the irrational acceptance of preposterous claims'. Professor Simon Blackburn, of the University of Cambridge, in a chapter entitled 'Religion and Respect', deplores the way the mere designation of a belief as religious is held by many to immunize it from all criticism.

Which brings us to the origins of our book. 'Some years ago, without realizing what it might mean,' writes Professor Blackburn, 'I accepted a dinner invitation from a Jewish colleague on a Friday night. During the course of the meal, some kind of observance was put in train, and it turned out that I was expected to play along – put on a hat, or some such. I demurred, saying that I felt uncomfortable doing something that might be the expression of some belief that I do not hold, or of joining a "fellowship" with which I felt no special community-feeling beyond whatever I feel for human beings in general.'

Professor Blackburn writes that the 'evening was strained after that'. He continues: 'Had my host stood up and asked me to toast the Hale-Bopp hopefuls, or to break bread in token of fellowship with them, I would have been just as embarrassed and indeed angry.'

Those of us who knew the late Peter Lipton, and had been privileged to be invited to the Friday night Jewish suppers hosted by him and his wife Diana, would have recognized the circumstance in which Professor Blackburn found himself (although there is no suggestion that he had been required to wear a 'hat, or some such', or in any way been discomforted, at the Liptons' table). Yet it was only to be expected that Peter, who was then head of the Department of History and Philosophy of Science in the University of Cambridge, and a colleague of Professor Blackburn's, would be intrigued by the dilemma so described and its consequent reflections.

Peter and I at first discussed Simon Blackburn's chapter, and the *Philosophers Without Gods* book, in the context of the so-called 'new atheist' surge. We had been intrigued by Richard Dawkins' claim that questions as to the existence or non-existence of God were the business of scientists to the exclusion of all other disciplines. Where did that leave philosophy? I should mention, at this point, that Peter and I had worked together on some seven conferences, and three books, arising from the activities of the Jesus College project. He was enthusiastic about considering a counter-volume, if not a counter-blast, that would challenge not only Richard Dawkins' contention about scientists, but the impression conveyed by the contributors to *Philosophers Without Gods* that contemporary philosophy leads to atheism. So we came to envisage a collection involving an assortment of philosophers and philosophers of religion, spanning a variety of positions of faith and indeed agnosticism, which Dawkins had characterized as merely 'namby-pamby atheism'.

Peter, moreover, drew my attention to the second part of Simon Blackburn's chapter. Here Blackburn appeals to what he describes as 'postmodernist writings on religion' in order to define the term 'onto-religion'. 'Onto-theology makes existence claims', he writes. 'It takes religious language in the same spirit in which people calling themselves scientific realists take science. It makes claims about what exists, and these claims are more or less reasonable and convincing, and when they are true they point to explanation of the way things are in one respect or another. Onto-theology believes that there is, literally, a three-decker universe.'

Yet onto-theology, he declares, is now old hat in sophisticated circles. Instead we should 'see religion in the light of poetry, symbol, myth, practice, emotion, and attitude, or in general, a stance toward the ordinary world, the everyday world around us'. He goes on, 'Let us call this interpretation of religious practice the expressive interpretation.' Like the other anti-realist or anti-representational theories, it could be offered in a number of different ways. But, he continues, 'we might call expressive theology the minimal unconfused revision of the confused state of mind of the person in the pew'.

Then he comments: 'However we take it, expressive theology makes it harder to be an atheist. In the days of onto-theology we knew what went on when someone claimed that God exists, and we knew how to argue that there is not the slightest reason to believe it. But once all that is dismissed as old hat, the plot thickens. If someone thinks that the events depicted in the Harry Potter films really happened, or are the kind of events that really happen, we can hope to mobilize observation and science and human testimony to disabuse them. But if someone claims that the movies express emotions and dreams that it is good that people have, it is harder to mount resistance. Nobody wants to disallow uplifting fiction.'

Peter Lipton's interest in the second half of Blackburn's chapter arose precisely because his own position in relation to religion might be described in terms of Blackburn's 'expressive theology'. What is more, Peter had written a personal essay on the topic, entitled 'Science Religion, and the Immersion Theory', a shortened version of which had been published in the *Jewish Quarterly* (Spring 2007). Peter agreed that in a volume answering *Philosophers Without Gods*, his own essay offered a response to Blackburn's critique of expressive theology.

Not long after this Peter died, and my friend Michael McGhee, then head of the Department of Philosophy at Liverpool University, agreed to become joint editor. Michael has been responsible in the main for the task of choosing our contributors, eliciting their contributions and editing them. He also co-directed our philosophy workshop sessions in Cambridge in September of 2008, a process described with lighthearted charity by one of the participants as being reminiscent of 'herding cats'. This is an instance where I can say without the least exaggeration that this book would not have seen the light of day without Michael McGhee's unflagging efforts.

Michael and I are immensely grateful to all our contributors, and to Robin Baird-Smith who was prompt in his enthusiasm to become our publisher. We also express our gratitude to the Master and Fellows of Jesus College, Cambridge, for creating ideal auspices for this project, to John Wilkins for advice, and to Crispin Rope for his unique vision and generosity.

Introduction

Michael McGhee

To begin on a personal note, I was glad to accept John Cornwell's invitation to continue the project that he had begun with the late Peter Lipton. It seemed a timely one in the current climate of public controversy and confusion about religion, religious belief and spirituality. I did want, however, slightly to broaden the scope of their original project by making some connection with non-theistic traditions, and I wanted to include a humanist presence and make space for other forms of religious scepticism. I had found much of interest in the collection mentioned in John's Preface, *Philosophers Without Gods: Meditations on Atheism and the Secular Life*, and was sympathetic to his and Peter Lipton's idea of a 'counter-volume' that would challenge the impression that contemporary philosophy leads to 'atheism'. The impression may be false, but it is a longstanding one, widely and casually held, particularly and not unexpectedly among philosophers themselves – and it goes, usually, with a failure to appreciate the multiple perspectives available within both religious and non-religious views of life, a multiplicity that blurs or even overlaps the edges of that distinction itself. However, I was also struck by two things: first by the fact that the contributors to the book were based mainly in the US, and second by their general approach – irenic, personal and exploratory, in the service of 'humanizing' atheism/secularism and defending it against misrepresentation. The approach offered a model for the present volume, that it should be similarly irenic, personal and exploratory, in seeking, on a slightly broader canvas, to examine the nature of the conceptual space between secular humanism, atheism, theism and non-theism.

As for the geographical fact I have just referred to, it is plain enough that it is also in this case a cultural one and it is not surprising that in a country where the failure of a President-Elect to go to church draws adverse comment in the media, philosophers proposing a secular position should find their situation a dialectically delicate one – whereas in the UK the situation is rather the reverse.

John Cornwell finds the *mot juste* when he refers to the 'new atheist' *surge* in this country. The spectacle has not been a pretty or improving one, mostly because the 'debate' has tended more towards polemic than towards philosophy and has been ill-tempered rather than robust. The trouble is that polemicists trade certainties like pugilists trade punches, and they have an eager audience who want their side to prevail, their prior views to be confirmed – to secure them, perhaps, against the private doubts behind the public profession of certitude, whether this is the 'aggressive secularism' complained of by 'people of faith' in the UK or the religious conservatism in the US that is suspicious of secular humanism. But, whatever is in the ascendant, the general tendency of polemic is to deal in exclusive opposi-tions, to polarize, to defend and entrench a position rather than to take risks or explore. Thus 'religion' or 'faith' becomes, from a hostile perspec-tive, a single, undifferentiated and negative entity – aspects which are the legitimate object of criticism become the thing itself; and seen through hostile 'religious' eyes an equally undifferentiated secularism has poisoned the wells of public and private morality, has led to casual relativism and fos-tered a spirit of selfishness. But these polarized attitudes blunt discernment, inhibit our sense of the creative possibilities, deaden the imagination – and, crucially, are remote from the spirit of philosophical inquiry, which seeks not victory, but understanding, testing ideas through dialogue.

In these essays, then, leading philosophers and theologians have responded to an invitation to reflect upon their attitudes to religion in an irenic and non-polemical spirit that was honest to experience and rose above the rancour and narrowness of recent public debates. Our hope as editors was that contributors should be willing to subject their own religious views (or their views about religion), and the formation of those views, to a philo-sophically motivated self-examination. The result is a fascinating and nuanced diversity of engaged and creative responses to, as well as *conceptions* of, our religious traditions. There are many voices here – humanist, agnos-tic, feminist, Buddhist, Jewish, Christian, post-Christian – and many *tones* of voice – passionate, personal, defiant, meditative, exasperated, patient, scep-tical, cool. Taken in the round, these attractively written and approachable essays provide an encouraging picture of the creative and fertile state of philosophical theology and, more widely, the philosophy of religion.

In his posthumously published essay, 'Science and Religion: The Immer-sion Solution', Peter Lipton sets out to suggest how work in the philosophy of science might be applied in the philosophy of religion. Writing as at once a scientific realist and a progressive Jew, and confronting the apparent paradox of this interior juxtaposition, he explores the relationship between science and religion with what he calls a personal edge, in the belief that his 'cognitive predicament' (the familiar tensions and contradictions between science and religion) is widely shared. Lipton seems to be reflecting here on the observations by Simon Blackburn mentioned in the Preface, in which Blackburn confronts a surely problematic dichotomy between an 'onto-theology' that appears to be the traditional natural theology associated with classical theism, and an 'expressivism' that seems to read the poetry, symbolism and metaphor of scripture as though it applied, like 'uplifting fiction', exclusively to our human condition and aspirations. The problematic assumption here – presumably of the post-modern religious writers he refers to rather than of Blackburn himself – is that the symbolism, the metaphorical language, *either* discloses some aspect of the (discredited) God of the philosophers *or* some aspect of our human condition, whereas there is a third alternative, one entirely familiar to philosophers of religion and theologians whether they are theists or not, that the metaphorical language is intended to disclose the nature of the relationship between humanity and the God of religion. In any event, Lipton's own position is somewhat more nuanced than the dichotomy could allow. Thus although he takes an 'anti-realist' view of religious claims, he refuses to reduce either the biblical text to metaphor, or the *application* of the metaphor to the human condition. He distinguishes in a familiar way between cognitive *claims* or content and *beliefs* about those claims or content and, in the light of this distinction makes a related and further distinction between the strategies of what he calls 'adjustments of content' and 'adjustments of atti-tude' in the face of cognitive tensions and contradictions, as between, for instance, the scientist's sub-atomic table and the table of common sense which we set for breakfast. In the case of his anti-realism about religion it is to be understood as an adjustment of *attitude* towards religious claims, rather than the kind of adjustment of content which typically, and, he thinks, mistakenly, reduces them to metaphorical references to human nature or to expressions of value, etc. Part of the point is to 'preserve literal content' and not misrepresent it as something else. But he also wants to remind us that 'religion' is not *reducible* to doctrine – it also encompasses a distinctive form of *life*. Lipton suggests that literal content in science as well as in religion can be preserved through the 'constructive empiricism' cham-pioned by Bas van Fraassen, one of the components of which, in the case of science, is *immersion* in the theory, that is to say, an imaginative entry into the world of that theory which amounts to 'acceptance' rather than global 'belief'. In the case of religion the analogous activity would be immersion in the world of the religious text and participation, with the community of one's co-religionists, in the life of religious thought and practice; and 'acceptance' of the religious texts is constituted by one's believing what there is good, independent reason to believe, and by committing oneself to using them as a means of thinking about the world and one's own life. It is not an accident, perhaps, that Lipton refers approvingly to the work of another philosopher of science, Richard Braithwaite, who, he thinks, would have been satisfied with the immersion solution. Lipton concedes, though, that 'many religious people would have difficulty seeing the point or value of religion without belief in God'.

In 'What has Plotinus' One to do with God?', Stephen Clark makes a profound and moving contribution to our understanding of the contemporary relevance of the great neo-Platonist and of his significance for the history of Christianity. He ends his essay with words that are uncannily (and ironically) close to Lipton's: 'Believing in God is putting our trust in a certain way of seeing, and seeking to live out of that insight.' The *closeness* lies in the way in which for both of them a 'way of seeing' is connected with *life*. Talk of 'ways of seeing' is easily misunderstood: it is sometimes assumed, though perhaps never quite explicitly, that one can don or doff 'ways of seeing' as though they were items of clothing or, if we do think of them in terms of that metaphor, we should insist that we grow into them only slowly, so that the rider added by Clark, in which he quotes Plotinus, is important – it refers us to the conditions under which a way of seeing becomes available in the first place: 'It does no good at all to say "Look to God", unless one also teaches how one is to look: Plotinus made every effort to teach us.' The *irony* of the apparent convergence of Clark's and Lipton's thinking lies in the different significance that 'believing in God' seems to have for these two philosophers. For Clark and many others, the expression 'belief in God' is not to be construed according to the logic of scientific belief, even by analogy. It involves a different concept of 'belief'. Thus Clark opens his essay in terms that seem diametrically opposed to the anti-realism explored by Lipton, and his remarks bring us to a recurrent theme of this collection: what constitutes a proper understanding of the traditional doctrine of God, and has it been properly grasped by anti-religious secularists? 'God is not', Clark writes, 'a thing to be named or described, and "belief in God" is not like a belief in extraterrestial intelligences, or fairies, or the Loch Ness Monster. What is called "the One", or "the Good", or "the Centre", must be posited if there is to be any genuine explanation of the things that are – and such an explanation cannot itself be constituted by any of the things that are.'

Clark's amiable reference to Loch Ness echoes an expression used by the Catholic theologian Nicholas Lash in his essay, 'Thinking, Attending, Praying'. What Lash calls Loch Ness theology is the 'story . . . of plucky little *homo sapiens* striding out into the great unknown, anxiously seeking for some evidence that somewhere out there in all this darkness, deity may be discerned'. Part of Lash's point is that this involves a confused conception of

God that is, nevertheless, the shared premise of much misconceived debate between believers and non-believers. Lash draws attention to the constant shifts that mark the history of our concepts, and pays particular attention to the history of the term 'religion', one outcome of which history, he concludes, 'is that Christianity – an ineluctably public fact with distinctive memories, practices and institutions – has become, with bewildering rapidity, widely unintelligible in our culture'. If Christians want to understand themselves and be understood by others, he suggests, then they need to stop thinking of themselves as 'belonging to a "religion"': they should, rather, conceive themselves as belonging to a *school*, one whose pedagogy, shared by other such schools, he tells us, 'has the twofold purpose – however differently conceived and executed in the different traditions – of weaning us from our idolatry and purifying our desire'.

Not all such 'schools of pedagogy' are conceived in theistic terms, however, and not all philosophers of religion are disposed to think, as Clark does, in terms of an *explanation* of the things that are. Thus in his 'Mystery, World and Religion' David E. Cooper describes the path that led him to think that 'reality as it "anyway" is, independently of human perspective, is mysterious'. He construes 'mystery' as 'what cannot . . . be conceptualized or literally articulated' and the role of what he calls a sense of mystery is to provide 'a measure for the leading of our lives, something for these to answer to'. But if it is to play this role it is 'essential that one is offered intimations of, and an attunement to, the mysterious which enables the faith that lives led in certain ways do answer to, are consonant with, the way of things'. Cooper here offers an alternative picture of 'faith' to the theistic one, a picture which is not, however, unrelated to Lash's notion of discipleship. It derives from the Buddhist notion of *saddha*, confidence or trust: 'an intelligent, reflective confidence in the wisdom of a great thinker and in the path he follows and teaches'. But what is it to live a life that is consonant with or attuned to the way things are? Cooper draws on Nietzsche and Heidegger here: 'This world is not simply a human world, unthinkable in isolation from us, but at the same time a realization of, a coming forth of, something to which we can strive to answer and measure up.'

These reflections on the 'world', and Lash's adverse comments on seeking out God, both find some echo in Daphne Hampson's fine essay 'Searching for God?' in which she insists on the significance of Heidegger's famous lecture, *What is Metaphysics?* '(T)he answer to the question as to what is *meta phusis*, beyond nature, is "Nichts", nothing.' She remarks of Heidegger, 'that in and through the world he finds a premonition of being', and traces out the background of his thinking not only in Nietzsche and Hegel, but also in Luther, whose conception of 'transcendence' was not Greek but Hebrew. God is 'the Other in our midst' and the movement is always from

God to us and not the other way around: 'our lives hid with Christ in God we are as never before thrown into the world'. Hampson writes as a post-Christian and this historical background is prefatory to the expression of her concern that 'the philosophy of religion as practised in the Anglo-Saxon tradition has run into the sand' and to her judgement that we need to abandon the (problematically gendered) Abrahamic myths. In which case, how should we conceive God? 'We should see the world as the scene of our activity and the place of our discernment of what I shall call a "dimension" to reality which is God.' And what is decisively problematic about Christianity is its 'particularity', about the incarnation or the resurrection, or the uniqueness of its scripture.

Hampson refers in her sceptical reflections about Christianity to her conversations with another contributor to this collection, Janet Soskice. In her own essay, 'Love and Reason', Soskice bears reflective witness to her Christian faith and in fact seems to concur with both Hampson and Lash that the direction of movement is from God to us, and does so in a way that raises again the issue discussed by Hampson of the nature and implications of divine transcendence. Soskice talks of how her faith came from a dramatic religious experience: 'I found myself to be surrounded by a presence of love, a love so real and so personal that I could not doubt it', and goes on to say that she felt herself to have been addressed 'by One to Whom I could speak'. She relates this sense of being addressed to Paul Ricoeur's reflections on listening and *hubris* and this leads her, through a consideration of the significance of the 'Word' in the opening of John's Gospel, to an account of Augustine and Philo, and of what it means to be a Christian philosopher, on the basis of which she concludes, as have many other believers, that the representations of that belief by such writers as Richard Dawkins are remote from its lived reality.

Fr Francis X. Clooney, SJ, bears witness to his Catholic faith in a radically different way, describing the nature of the risk to faith and identity of his scholarly, but necessarily personal, explorations of the Hindu religious traditions. What Clooney proposed to himself as an Indologist who was also a Catholic priest was the venture of stepping beyond his commitment to ways of thinking, speaking and acting that were intimate to his Christian way of thinking about and encountering God. This enterprise is reminiscent in some ways of Lipton's description of immersion, and it would no doubt be salutary and informative if it were more generally essayed. Clooney discusses the practice of 'inculturation' adopted by his Jesuit forebears, Francis Xavier and Roberto de Nobili, but sees the contemporary challenge as requiring more than external adaptation if inter-religious learning is to be meaningful, a challenge he describes as a risk of heart and mind given over to a new religious possibility.

In concert with Hampson and other women religious thinkers, Morny Joy would presumably want to say that there were gender-based limits to the possibility of immersion when so much religion, whether Eastern or Western, is the product of the male imagination. She starts her essay, 'In Search of Wisdom', with the remark: 'I am loath to identify myself with any form of institutional religion. The reason for this is that I have found, with a few minor exceptions, that both in their official policies and attitudes towards women, institutional forms of religion leave much to be desired.' She prefers to describe her position in terms of the search for wisdom, and the work (in progress) of her essay is to spell out what this means both theoretically and existentially. She draws inspiration from Hadot, Ricoeur, Arendt and Grace Jantzen – for instance from Hadot's account of how the ancient philosophical schools were 'more intent on inculcating a disciplined mode of existence, rather than endorsing a particular doctrine or set of conceptual truths'. In her brief account of the development of Hadot's thinking she remarks that he 'presents two . . . practical qualities or modes of living, derived from ancient philosophy, that are characteristic of a person who seeks to progress on the path to wisdom'. One of these is that of living in accordance with nature, and the other that of living with a focus on the present. The idea of 'living in accordance with nature' echoes David Cooper's talk of a life 'attuned to the way things are' and faces the same challenge: what *is* it to do this? Joy reports Hadot as describing it as 'a discipline whereby one sought to establish a form of coherence and balance in oneself that, at the same time, coincides with that of the larger cosmic dimension'. It also requires a commitment to contributing to the well-being of the whole. Grace Jantzen had written of the origins of violence and of 'the deep misogyny of western culture' and had turned to Arendt's notion of 'natality', as Ricoeur had done – in her case to provide an alternative vision of women and embodied life that promoted the value and beauty of life in this world.

One of the questions that Peter Lipton's essay may leave the reader with is whether he is an agnostic or an atheist, while Nicholas Lash has sought to describe a nescience about God that doesn't amount to agnosticism. But what *is* agnosticism? According to Sir Anthony Kenny, Richard Dawkins, who has been the moderately sized mammal in the room for several contributors, is mistaken in his opinion that it is a wet form of atheism, and in his essay 'Agnosticism and Atheism', Kenny sets out to show that agnosticism is epistemically and morally preferable to atheism. In the case of the Olympian gods, Kenny says, we are all atheists, though this doesn't mean that we cannot learn from and enjoy Ancient Greek literature. Kenny declares himself to be an atheist also in respect of the God of traditional Judeo-Christian natural theology, 'a being endowed with omnipotence, omniscience and supreme benevolence'. Having concluded long since in his well-known *The God of the Philosophers* that there can be no such thing as the God of scholastic or rationalist philosophy, Kenny remarks that 'Whatever truth is contained in the Judeo-Christian scriptures is presented to us not literally, but metaphorically'. The God of scholastic or rationalist philosophy is presumably not what is presented literally in the Judeo-Christian scriptures. A more obvious candidate for that position would be the God of naïve realism. But if whatever truth might be contained in the scriptures is a truth presented metaphorically, the question arises whether it is about human beings or about a divine being that is not the God of the philosophers. In any event, in that book Kenny 'left open the question whether it is possible to conceive, and believe in, a God defined in less absolute terms' and in that sense he is not an atheist but has remained an agnostic – specifically, agnostic about whether there is or is not an intelligent designer of the universe. In what follows he examines the arguments for and against the existence of such a being and concludes with his well-known remark about how it is possible for an agnostic to pray: 'Some find something comic in the idea of an agnostic praying to a God whose existence he doubts. It is surely no more unreasonable than the act of a man adrift in the ocean, trapped in a cave, or stranded on a mountainside, who cries for help though he may never be heard or fires a signal which may never be seen.'

The significance or otherwise of knowing or not knowing whether there is a God depends upon the appropriateness to the religious context of the standard of knowledge appealed to. It is striking how close, then, Kenny's image of the agnostic's prayer – like the cry for help of a man adrift in the ocean – comes to Lash's remark that 'in praying we *address* the dark, sometimes to the point of crying to the silence which surrounds us as the voice of God'. Lash adds that 'the paradigm of our experience remains the Garden of Gethsemane'. In the poignantly expressed conclusion of her essay, 'Ideals Without Idealism', Clare Carlisle refers to Kierkegaard's thought that 'in order to pray, there must be a God', and remarks that he 'immediately adds that (in other words) "there must be a self plus possibility". Here, a "self" is conceived as determinate, limited, whilst its "possibility" transcends its limitations and yet is in some way related to it.' Carlisle has been discussing the 'spiritual ideals' set before us by Kierkegaard, 'poet of the religious', 'ideals of purity of heart; love of the neighbour; radiant self-transparency; truthfulness to oneself, to another person, or to God'. These are ideals desired by the 'restless heart' and, she tells us, Kierkegaard 'refuses to compromise on their purity – while insisting also that they are impossible to attain'. Carlisle suggests that 'there is something "religious" about the structure of the ideals in question: on the one hand an absolute impossibility, tied to an interpretation of the human condition as such; and on the other hand an absolute demand, an irresistible claim exerted by these ideals that admits of no compromise'. She believes that a similar logic is to be found in Buddhist teaching and that it may be shared by other traditions.

Carlisle points out Kierkegaard's willingness to talk of the limitations of the human condition in terms of 'original sin', a notion central to the concerns of James P. Mackey in his essay, 'The God of the Prophet Jesus of Nazareth', where he puts to one side the rationalist, scholastic, philosopher's God and makes a sharp distinction between two conceptions of the God of religion that reflect precisely the human condition, the spiritual state of his hearers: 'as any careful reader of what Christians call the New Testament can see, the picture of God painted in the life, death and teaching of the seer Jesus, was tampered with, and it was reduced to their measure and sometimes corrupted, even from the very outset of his public mission, by the closest and most trusted of his followers who called themselves "sons of the prophets"'. Mackey throws down a striking challenge to secular humanists whose critiques of religion are well made, he thinks, against the *unregenerate* God of original sin, of a self-aggrandizing religion, but which fail to appreciate the profound humanism of the God of Jesus the Prophet and are therefore left with a problem of human evil that can only be overcome through a fidelity to the ideal made manifest in the life and death of Jesus – of refusing to return evil for evil.

In my own contribution, 'Humanism and Spirituality: or How to be a Good Atheist', I reflect on what would constitute a just assessment of religion by secular humanists, and on what they can honourably retrieve as genuine wisdom from the religious texts and language of the traditions. Another shift away from the centrality of 'belief' and towards a social (rather than private, 'Cartesian') notion of spirituality is offered by Pamela Sue Anderson in her essay, 'A Turn to Spiritual Virtues in Philosophy of Religion: "The Thoughtful Love of Life"'. The virtues she refers to are love, trust, respect and hope, and what Anderson proposes is a turn that aims 'at transforming both the focus and the conceptual scheme in contemporary philosophy of religion'. Anderson sets this proposed change of direction for the philosophy of religion in a broad and also detailed discussion of the historical context that explains its necessity, offering an absorbing discussion of Kant, and drawing on the ancient conception of philosophy, on insights from feminist epistemology, and from recent writing on spirituality by John Cottingham and Robert Solomon, to the end of working out 'a revised form of practical rationality for philosophy of religion which has a critical role to play. To educate our emotions and passions is to motivate reason, especially in meditation on living a life and not merely on death or immortality.'

In his eloquent essay, 'Secularism and Shared Values', Richard Norman, who writes as a humanist, corrects some confusions in recent public reflections by prominent churchmen about the dangers of secularism, suggesting that different definitions have been conflated. He is himself concerned to explore, defend and spell out the implications for public policy of a secularism defined 'as a normative view about society: the view that social and political institutions should be independent of religion or religious institutions'. The position can be summarized as the view that there should be no privileged place for religion(s) in the public life of society. This sense is often run together, he says, with a second normative view, of secularism as an individual way of life, by which he means 'a view of the world and a way of life based entirely on non-religious beliefs and values'. Commitment to secularism in the first sense does not depend upon commitment to secularism in the second, and, in a discussion of the history of some of the tensions between them, and of the sources for necessary shared values, in which he invokes Richard Hooker and the Putney debates of 1647, he concludes that in a multicultural society 'Christianity – the Christian churches and individual Christians – are, like other faiths, welcome to play a continuing part in shared public life, but it should not be a privileged role, not an exclusive or entrenched role'.

There are intriguing comparisons to be made between Norman's reflections and those of Anthony O'Hear in his essay, 'Religion in Public Life'. O'Hear seeks to defend a pluralist view of society but sees a clear role for religion in the public life of such a society, even though the churches are the preserve of minorities, a role quite distinct from that of the secular power or sovereign, and one conceived, ironically, by medieval Christian thinkers such as Hildebrand and Dante. 'While each of us might want to defend a particular view of life as being the right one or the best (for all, even), I believe that no one has such a comprehensive monopoly of wisdom as to have the right to impose that view on everyone else; this follows in part from a belief in human fallibility, which can be expressed in either secular or religious terms.'

Gordon Graham's essay, 'Religion and Theology', recalls us to Lipton's insistence that religion encompasses a way of life and is not to be reduced to the set of its doctrines. But there is a further question about the proper understanding of the relationship between them, and Graham is concerned to query the common assumption about the relationship between belief and practice that leads us to think that what is *fundamentally* at issue between secularists and believers is a difference of belief – as though their different ways of life were simply grounded in and explained by different theories. Graham also inserts into the discussion the important idea that faith is not properly to be thought of as 'a belief' but is rather a matter of an attitude. Thus, for instance, 'Christianity is related to, but not to be equated with, believing the theological doctrines characteristic of Christianity.' So, religion is primarily 'a way of living life, letting it be shaped by a desire to avoid idolatry, venerate the sacred, and protect it from desecration'. However, where does this leave the secularist who might also want to appeal to absolute or sacred values? Graham ends his essay with a challenge: 'Anyone who wishes to retain sacred value while abandoning the supernatural, must therefore explain what it is that enables the sacred to *require* veneration, to *forbid* desecration and so on.'

In 'Wisdom and Belief in Theology and Philosophy' Simon Oliver writes perceptively about the relationship between philosophy of religion and theology, satirically highlighting as a preliminary those popular secularist distortions of 'religious belief' as blind, dogmatic and inflexible, and the misunderstandings of even well-meaning philosophers who work with a rationalistic model of God and belief that answers to little or nothing in the tradition. Oliver is eloquent about his discovery of a very different view of God, knowledge and belief in early Christian thought: 'The traditional reticence of Christian theology is born of the sense that our knowledge is a dim reflection of truth which, although faint, is not thereby "off the mark" and untrustworthy.' He goes on to discuss Plato's *Symposium* and Nicholas of Cusa's *De Sapientia* with a view to exploring how this more traditional theology and philosophy might inform our understanding of religious belief.

Finally, in 'Provocation', Harriet A. Harris offers a reflective and personal evocation of her own experience of the 'dynamics' of faith in relation to the tasks of reason, and of its changing character as she moves through her life. She distinguishes between the 'triggers' of faith and its 'seeming grounds', and finds both of these to be fleeting. Faith is, rather, provoked, and there is a sense of restlessness in its absence, and the provocation is to think and speak truthfully, and to unite integrity of thought and integrity of action. Reflecting on those who are raised in communities of faith, she draws an analogy with being brought up in a musical family and being educated musically: 'whether or not people take to music . . . or reject the musical heritage of their up-bringing seems not ultimately to be determined by the musicality (or lack of musicality) of that up-bringing'. In common with other contributors, Harris does not see an opposition between faith and reason, or see either as static, but sees reason as taken up in the development of faith, in the sense that learning practices of confession, learning to live as one who is forgiven and forgiving, transforms our ways of being in the world. Reason itself is subject to this shaping, but also its critic . . .

1

Science and Religion:
The Immersion Solution

PETER LIPTON

Introduction: two ways to handle contradictions

This essay focuses on the cognitive tension between science and religion, in particular on the contradictions between some of the claims of current science and some of the claims in religious texts. My aim is to suggest how some work in the philosophy of science may help to manage this tension. Thus I will attempt to apply some work in the philosophy of science to the philosophy of religion, following the traditional gambit of trying to stretch the little that one does understand to cover what one does not understand.

My own views on science and religion are hardly views from nowhere. My scientific perspective is that of a hopeful realist. Scientific realism is the view that science, though fallible through and through, is in the truth business, attempting to find out about a world independent of ourselves, and it is the view that business is, on the whole, going pretty well. My religious perspective is that of a progressive Jew.

The problem I am worrying in this essay is my own problem. I take my other philosophical problems seriously too, but for me the question of the relationship between science and religion has a personal edge I do not feel in my other philosophical obsessions with the likes of the problems of induction or the content of *ceteris paribus* laws. My reply to a charge of self-indulgence would be that my cognitive predicament is, I believe, widely shared.

How do we manage contradictions? The White Queen famously gave Alice excellent advice:

'I can't believe *that*,' said Alice.

'Can't you?' the Queen said in a pitying tone. 'Try again. Draw a long breath and shut your eyes.'

Alice laughed. 'There's no use trying,' she said, 'One can't believe impossible things.'

'I dare say you haven't had much practice,' said the Queen. 'When I was your age I always did it for half an hour a day. Why, sometimes I believed as many as six impossible things before breakfast.'

The White Queen has nothing on me. I believe many more than six impossible things before breakfast and I do it effortlessly, since my beliefs include many contradictions I have not noticed. Some of them are obvious in retrospect. When I lived in rural northwest Massachusetts, I preferred one route walking to my office and another route coming home, believing in each case that I was taking the shortest route. For an unconscionable time, I failed to put these beliefs together and so failed to deploy my sophisticated geometrical knowledge that the length of a path does not depend on the direction travelled. It is, however, more challenging to believe contradictions once you are made aware of them. Few of us aspire to the White Queen's level of cognitive control in such cases, but there are plenty of other options available. Ignoring the contradiction very often works. Another option is to find a way of compartmentalizing beliefs, effectively preventing contradictory beliefs from coming into contact with each other. But suppose that we wish squarely to face up to a contradiction and manage it directly? In many cases we will try to show that the contradiction is only apparent. One of the maxims in the professional philosopher's toolkit is: confronted with a contradiction, make a distinction that will dissolve it. *In extremis*, however, we might just face the music and give up some of our claims or our beliefs to restore consistency.

When claims form contradictions it is impossible for them all to be correct. Consistency is of course no guarantee of truth, but it is a necessary condition. In this essay I am particularly interested in the choice between two strategies for managing contradictions so as to restore consistency, especially as those contradictions arise between science and religion. This choice is between *adjusting content* and *adjusting attitude*. Adjusting content means giving up some claims. Adjusting attitude means keeping the claims but changing one's epistemic attitude toward at least some of them. It is the second strategy that I am going to favour in the particular context of science and religion. The general contrast between these strategies can be brought out in the context of the astronomer Arthur Eddington's memorable discussion of his two tables:

I . . . have drawn up my chairs to my two tables. Two tables! Yes; there are duplicates of every object about me – two tables, two chairs, two pens . . . One of them has been familiar to me from earliest years . . . It has extension; it is comparatively permanent; it is coloured; above all it is substantial . . . Table No. 2 is my scientific table . . . It does not belong to the world previously mentioned . . . My scientific table is mostly empti-ness. Sparsely scattered in that emptiness are numerous electric charges rushing about with great speed; but their combined bulk amounts to less than a billionth of the bulk of the table itself. Notwithstanding its strange construction it turns out to be an entirely efficient table. It supports my writing paper as satisfactorily as table No. 1; for when I lay the paper on it the little electric particles with their headlong speed keep on hitting the underside, so that the paper is maintained in shuttlecock fashion at a nearly steady level.

My subject is the tension between science and religion, not between science and commonsense, but Eddington's tables help to clarify the contrast between the two ways of managing contradictions, the contrast between adjusting content, and leaving content alone but adjusting attitude. In the case of my strange beliefs about walking to and from my office, you will be pleased to hear that I reacted to the contradiction by adjusting content: I simply gave up the claim that one route was the shorter in one direction and the other route was shorter in the other direction (though I never did work out which route was the shorter). In the case of the two tables, to adjust content would be to give up on some of the claims of science, of everyday life or both, insofar as there are genuine contradictions between them. But unlike the case of the two routes, in the case of the two tables adjusting content is not the natural option. In particular, we are not going simply to give up our claims about the everyday table.

Unlike the White Queen perhaps, we just can't do it. But however deeply we are immersed in our everyday view of the world, we may admit that certain parts of it systematically attribute more than is really there, and these parts are a kind of projection of our own experience that may con-tradict the scientific story which we take to be closer to the truth about the table. If this is the line we take, then we might nevertheless continue to use our everyday conceptions, since, after all, we have no option; but not fully believe them, at least not when we are doing philosophy (or science). Through this adjustment of attitude, although the contradiction between the scientific and the everyday *claims* would not be removed, our philo-sophical attitude toward the everyday claims would leave us with a set of *beliefs* that are consistent.

Thus we keep the full set of claims, the full content, contradictions and all, but adjust our attitude to avoid having to believe yet more impossible things before breakfast. We use more claims than we believe.

Science and religion: the usual suspects

What now about science and religion? There are a number of familiar points of apparent tension between the claims of science and the claims of religion – you can provide your own list. For example, there are various tensions between scientific accounts of the development of the universe and of life in it on the one hand, and the accounts of these matters in Genesis on the other. There are tensions between a scientific view of the world and the miracles and wonders described for example in the book of Exodus. There are tensions between the results of the secular historical study of the origins of the Bible and what that text says about its own origins. And there are apparent tensions between what science and religion seem to tell us about the status and indeed the existence of God. (Although the only religious text I refer to by name in this essay is the Bible, my hope is that my discussion applies more widely.)

Before I consider how tensions of these sorts might be managed, I issue two health warnings. Both are in effect warnings against identifying the tension problem with the much broader topic of the relations between science and religion. First, although I am focusing on the apparent incompatibility between various religious and scientific claims, I do not want to encourage the common and primitive practice of presenting a picture of religious life that would reduce it to religious doctrine. My intention is closer to the opposite: I want to make more room for a religious form of life in the discussions of the relation between science and religion, and I do not suppose for a minute that religion is reducible to religious claims: there is much more to religion than that.

The second health warning is that although I am here focusing on tensions between science and religion, I would not wish to give the impression that the histories of science and religion have been histories dominated by conflict. That is another surprisingly common view but it too is fundamentally mistaken. The constantly retailed story about Galileo and the Church notwithstanding, science and religion have often been seen as complementary. Indeed, a great deal of science has been driven by religious motivations and has performed essential religious functions.

Thus science has been taken to reveal the majesty of creation and the will of God, to illuminate religious doctrine, and to provide the technologies to support religious observance by, for example, providing for more accurate chronology. Conversely, it has often been held that religion is indispensable for science, for example because it underwrites the reliability of scientific methods.

These extensive co-operative relations show that the tension problem is only one part of the much broader issues of the relations between science and religion. But it is the part that concerns me in this essay. How are we going to manage these tensions between science and religion, arising from incompatible content? Recall that the general choice I wish to discuss is between changing content and changing attitude. There are a number of familiar ways of managing the tension by changing content, and in particular by diminishing content. Let me begin by putting three such views to one side, with unseemly haste. First, one could take the view that religious discourse is through and through figurative or metaphorical, so for example talk about God is really just an oblique way of referring to nature. That will eliminate much of the tension between science and religion; but I do not find this route attractive. The problem with the metaphor view is not with the idea that a religious text might contain metaphor. Some of the writing in the Bible certainly does appear to be metaphorical. For example, when God is described in Exodus as liberating the Jews from Egypt with a mighty hand and an outstretched arm, the text is not, I think, making an anatomical point. But nor is all of the text metaphorical, and in my view not enough of it is to solve the tension problem without extensive semantic violence.

Thus the story in Exodus is of a personal God who liberated the Jews from slavery, fed them in the wilderness and gave them the Torah. This material seems clearly written as a literal narrative, not as a metaphor. Of course we can choose to read any text as a pervasive metaphor, but in the case of the Bible this would be to go against the plain meaning, and it would in my view so diminish the value of that text and of the religious traditions it supports that we should try to find a less disruptive way of resolving the tension.

A second route I will not follow is the value view. Instead of saying that science is literal and religion metaphorical, you might say the following. There can be no real tension between science and religion because science is in the fact business and religion is in the value business. They are in such different lines of work that there can be no incompatibility between them. Fact claims and value claims can bear no logical relations (the maxim is that one cannot derive an 'ought' from an 'is'), so they cannot contradict each other, so they cannot generate the tension problem. But like the appeal to wholesale metaphor, the value view is unattractively diminishing, and for a parallel reason. Of course religious texts and traditions include value claims, but they make factual claims as well. To this one might add that the suggestion that science is a value-free zone is difficult to defend, and that the assumption that there is no logical contact possible between fact and value is dubitable. But my main objection to the value view is that it would force us to eliminate or ignore too much of the plain factual content of our religious texts. So the value solution is not for me.

Third, there is the selection view. On this view, science and religion both deliver factual claims and, taken together, these claims form a multiply inconsistent set. So we should weed out claims, until we have a consistent subset. The claims we remove should be those which we judge to have the weakest warrant, or anyway a weaker warrant than the claims they contradict. In some cases, this means the claim that goes is religious; in other cases it will be scientific: we have to decide on a case-by-case basis. This selection view is epistemically responsible, but in my view it would leave far too many holes in the religious text.

The metaphor, value and selection views all would deal with contradictions by diminishing content. The metaphor view does this by eliminating the literal meaning of the religious text, the value view by eliminating the factual content of the religious text, and the selection view by removing claims from both religion and from science.

The admirable motivation in all three cases is to avoid saddling ourselves with contradictory beliefs. If diminishing content were the only way to avoid contradictory beliefs, one of these three approaches might be our best option, anyway for those who are not willing to give up on religion altogether. But diminishing content is not the only way: it is also possible to maintain content and adjust our attitude towards it.

Antirealism

Philosophers of science have explored several ways to keep content while adjusting attitude. The content in question for them is the content of scientific theories, but some of their proposals may be adaptable to religious discourse. That is the possibility I wish to explore. Scientific realists take a stand on both the question of content and the question of belief. They maintain that theories are to be interpreted literally – given their full content – and that the best ones should be believed to be at least approximately true. Some antirealists agree with realists about content, but disagree about belief. This may provide us with ways to relieve the tension between science and religion. We may preserve content, what a scientific theory says, because that content serves various valuable purposes, yet at the same time we can forbear believing that content to be revelatory of a mind-independent reality. In so doing, we can manage contradictions without dropping content.

Descartes provided a striking example of how this adjustment of attitude towards science is possible, and specifically in the context of the relation between science and religion:

For there is no doubt that the world was created right from the start with all the perfection which it now has ... This is the doctrine of the Christian faith, and our natural reason convinces us that it was so ... Nevertheless, if we want to understand the nature of plants or of men, it is much better to consider how they can gradually grow from seeds than to consider how they were created by God at the very beginning of the world. Thus we may be able to think up certain very simple and easily known principles which can serve, as it were, as the seeds from which we can demonstrate that the stars, the earth and indeed everything we observe in this visible world could have sprung. For although we know for sure that they never did arise in this way, we shall be able to provide a much better explanation of their nature by this method than if we merely describe them as they now are or as we believe them to have been created.

Was Descartes sincere, or was he just protecting himself from religious persecution? My own view is that he was sincere and that his religious belief ran very deep. If you do not really believe in God, you do not make him the linchpin of your great philosophical system; but that is exactly what Descartes did. He was thus a realist about religion and an antirealist about certain parts of science, but he preserved the content of both realms. A scientific theory may be valuable even if we know it is false. Descartes took it that the theory of development from seeds must be false because it contradicted religious doctrine he knew to be true. Nevertheless, he maintained that the theory is valuable because it improves our understanding by providing a potential though not the actual explanation of how the world came about. That understanding requires that we take the scientific theory literally, but not that we believe it.

My own preference is the opposite of Descartes' – I want to consider how one might be a realist about science but an antirealist about religion – but like Descartes I want to be an antirealist who preserves literal content on both sides. And work on antirealism in the philosophy of science gives us a number of models for what such a position in religion might look like. There are two I would like to explore here, one associated with Thomas Kuhn, the other with Bas van Fraassen.

The 'many worlds' solution

I understand Kuhn's antirealism through Immanuel Kant, as Kuhn himself sometimes did. Kant held that the empirical world, the world that science investigates, is not even in its inanimate parts a world entirely independent of us.

Rather this 'phenomenal' world is a joint product of a 'noumenal' world – the things in themselves as they are entirely independent of us (but for that reason unknowable) – and the organizing activity of the human mind. According to Kant, the human contribution to the phenomenal world is very substantial, since it includes space, time and causation. It is only in virtue of the active contribution of the mind that we are able to experience or represent an external world at all, and we do this by creating a stage on which we can then view the appearances of the noumena, though not the noumena themselves.

Kuhn agrees with Kant that the world that scientific theories represent is not entirely independent of the scientists: it is a phenomenal world, a joint product of the things in themselves and the intellectual activities of the scientists. But there is an important difference. Kuhn is Kant on wheels. Whereas Kant thought that the human contribution that goes into the construction of the phenomenal world was generic and invariant, Kuhn maintained that the scientific contribution is quite specific and varies across the history of science. Scientific revolutions, on this view, are episodes where the human contribution to the world changes. One of the virtues of this interpretation of Kuhn as a dynamic Kantian is that it makes sense of his notorious claim that, after a scientific revolution, scientists work in a different world, a claim that otherwise seems either trivial or crazy. If 'different world' just means different *beliefs* about the world, then the claim is trivial; if it means different *noumena*, so that the world as it is quite independently of us changes, then the claim is crazy. But we can make sense of the claim that the *phenomenal* world changes, because after a scientific revolution the scientists' contribution to that world has changed. On this view, scientific theories are to be construed literally, but what they describe is a world that is partially the scientists' own construction.

The semantic reflection of Kuhn's doctrine of multiple worlds appears in his development of the idea that theories on either side of a scientific revolution are 'incommensurable'. In his earlier work, this was a blanket term for any feature that makes theory comparison complicated because scientists are not comparing like with like. Compare they must, but where there is incommensurability then intelligent and well-informed practitioners may disagree about the winner. The features that generate incommensurability extend from the relatively mundane fact that in a scientific revolution one is comparing achievement (the old theory) against promise (the new theory), all the way to the claim of different worlds that we have just considered. But in his later work, Kuhn came to focus on a different sense of the term: incommensurability as untranslatability. Theories that are incommensurable in this semantic sense do not just conflict: the conceptual resources of the one do not even allow full expres-

sion of the claims of the other. One reason for this semantic disassocia-
tion, according to Kuhn, is that the two theories divide the world up in
such different ways that they do not simply make conflicting claims about
the same things, but are talking about different things. This is the way in
which incommensurability ends up for Kuhn as the linguistic reflection of
the metaphysical plurality of phenomenal worlds. One world cannot be
characterized in the terms applied to the other.

Kuhn's multiple worlds and incommensurability have suggestive application to the relationship between science and religion. It might give us a way
of reconciling literal interpretation with incompatible content by taking
science and religion to be describing different phenomenal worlds in
incommensurable languages. These worlds would share their noumenal
component – the things in themselves are in common – but the human
contribution would differ. Thus at one level the Kuhnian account suggests
how science and religion, though incompatible, might in a sense be offering descriptions of a common world, the noumenal world. And at another
level, it suggests how the incompatible descriptions could both be correct,
since they describe different worlds, different phenomenal worlds. Each set
of descriptions, the scientific and the religious, are to be taken literally.
Those descriptions are in deep conflict: they do not simply make incompatible claims about the same things, since they are talking about fundamentally different things, and indeed the claims of the one cannot even be
fully expressed in the language of the other. Nevertheless, although those
sets of descriptions could not be jointly true of any one world, they might
each be a more or less correct characterization of different worlds, worlds
that are equally real and have noumena in common. Kuhn thus appears to
offer everything some of us could want. We acknowledge the deep differences and incompatibilities between science and religion, we understand
both discourses literally, and indeed we could even take both to be true of
their respective worlds. We can retain the conflicting content without
impossibly supposing that the world as it is in itself, independently of us, is
somehow self-contradictory.

Would this appropriation of Kuhn's account of science in order to give an
account of religion and its relationship to science do mortal violence to
Kuhn's ideas?

Certainly Kuhn would not endorse the wholesale application of his
account of science to religion, because he held that science is a distinctive
human activity and that his account helps to locate its distinctive feature.
But Kuhn does not find this in his claims about incommensurability and
multiple phenomenal worlds. Rather, according to him, what is distinctive
about science is the way it supports an empirical puzzle-solving tradition
during periods of normal science between scientific revolutions.

This sort of puzzle solving may not have a close counterpart in the case of religion, but nor do the notions of incommensurability and multiple worlds seem to depend on it. Indeed, although he does not himself seek to apply his account beyond science, Kuhn in effect acknowledges this broader applicability when, for example, he suggests that ordinary human languages (e.g. English and French) are incommensurable, on the grounds that the concepts they deploy carve up the world differently.

Another obvious difference between Kuhn's account as applied to science alone and the attempt to extend it to apply to both science and religion concerns competition. When Kuhn talks about incommensurable theories, he is talking about problematic choices, choices where there is 'no common measure' and where intelligent and well-informed investigators may disagree; but he is talking about cases where choices must be made. This is clearly different from the extension of Kuhn's ideas we are here exploring, since the point is not to analyse a forced choice between science and religion but rather to see how one could have them both, while yet admitting that they are in some ways incompatible. But here again Kuhn's willingness to apply his notion of incommensurability to different human languages suggests that the extension would be permissible. (Kuhn would, I think, also allow that certain non-competing scientific theories in different disciplines are incommensurable.) If this analysis were correct, one might expect there to be particular challenges in holding on simultaneously to both the scientific and religious worlds, but this is indeed what we find. Moreover, Kuhn makes an observation about incommensurability which suggests that the challenges, though real, need not be insuperable. He claims that although incommensurable theories or languages are untranslatable, this does not exclude bilingualism: you may be able to speak and understand both languages without being able to translate the claims of one into the claims of the other.

Kuhn thus offers us a suggestive resource for a distinctive account of the nature of religious discourse and its relation to science, of particular interest to those who wish to have their cake and eat it, with literal interpretation and acknowledgement of conflict, yet no forced choice. At the same time, I do have reservations about this resolution of the tension problem between science and religion.

One is a general ambivalence about the metaphysics of constructed worlds, whether in science or in religion. In what sense is a Kuhnian world really a world? As I have noted, 'different worlds' had better not reduce to 'different beliefs', lest we trivialize Kuhn's claims. Moreover, in the context of applying this view to the relationship between science and religion, such a reduction would undo my attempt to find a way to accept conflicting claims while avoiding conflicting beliefs. The promise that Kuhn's many worlds account offers is that, while my descriptions are incompatible, there is a sense in which my beliefs are not, because they are beliefs about different worlds. If 'different worlds' is just a hyperbolic expression for 'different beliefs', then we seem to be back to square one.

I can think of two philosophical models that might help us to articulate the nature of these phenomenal worlds. They only provide approximations to Kuhn's metaphysics, but they may be helpful nevertheless. The first is the model of a traditional philosophical view of secondary qualities such as colours. According to this view, colours are dispositions of the surfaces of objects to cause certain sensations in us. Thus colours are not simply sensations – they are properties of physical objects – but they are peculiarly anthropocentric properties, since they are dispositions defined in part in terms of our sensations. Colours are on this view phenomena, a joint product of the things in themselves (the surfaces of objects) and the nature of our mind. (Kant himself uses secondary qualities as a model for his view of the phenomena.) And if we imagine people who react to the same electro-magnetic radiation reflected off surfaces with systematically different sensations, as in classic philosophical thought experiments about 'spectrum inversion', we capture a sense in which those people live in different worlds.

The second model is a kind of nominalism about the noumena. On this view, in order to represent the world we must suppose it to consist of objects with various properties. But while the objects are out there independently of us, the properties are not: the world does not come predivided into kinds. So on this view the phenomenal world – which is the only world we can represent – includes properties, but these properties are our contribution, and indeed different people might divide up the world differently, might contribute different and incompatible properties. Here too we capture a sense in which the differences are not merely differences in belief but differences in the world, since unless we suppose them to be features of the phenomenal world, we would not be able to see our beliefs about the world as representing anything, which would be to say that they are not beliefs.

Both these models help to make sense of how some feature could be both of the world and put there by our cognitive activity. And I think this leaves us with an approach to science and religion well worth developing. But now I must confess that I am not myself entirely happy with the application of the Kuhnian metaphysics either to science, or to religion, for pretty much opposite reasons in the two cases. The Kuhnian approach gives too little cognitive credit to science and too much cognitive credit to religion for my taste. On the science side, as I have already confessed, I hold out the hope for a realist model, according to which properties and natural kinds are not put there by us but are features of the noumenal world that science may disclose.

Kuhn is unwilling to go this far. And if applied to religion, Kuhn's ideas seem to go too far. What is attractive about Kuhn's account of science is that he combines a kind of relativism with the insistence (even if this is not seen by all his readers) that science is empirically constrained. For Kuhn, the fact that scientists believe something does not make it so, even for 'their' world. Science is a game against nature, an attempt to meet the relentless constraints that observation and experiment impose. Indeed, on Kuhn's view nature always wins, because every normal science tradition is eventually overthrown by an overload of recalcitrant anomalies.

I do not see religion thus empirically constrained (though it may be constrained by our needs and desires). I see religious texts as human productions which, although obviously inspired by experience, have nothing like the close responsiveness to the nature of the natural world to which empirical science aspires.

This does not absolutely rule out seeing those texts as providing descriptions of Kuhnian worlds; for God might exist, have created the world in a certain way, and then informed us about that creation. At the same time, it might be that, our intellects being what they are, we are unable to take information about the noumena straight, so God descriptions are laden with a conceptual structure that both makes them comprehensible to us and generates a phenomenal world that is their subject. In other words, although the epistemology of religion might be non-empirical and thus radically different from the epistemology of science, what is required for a Kuhnian world is not that we know about it in a certain way, but that it includes the appropriate noumenal and conceptual components.

But I still cannot go this far. For me, religious texts are much more akin to imaginative writing than to scientific theories, different not only in their epistemology but in what they are about, and they do not in my view satisfy the noumenal constraints that a Kuhnian world requires. Novels do not create Kuhnian worlds; they create fictional worlds. Religious texts do purport to describe the actual world – they are not presented as fiction – but I maintain that the worlds they described are significantly closer to imagined worlds than to the worlds of science. At the same time, I hold fast to the view that religious texts may have the deepest value, and that this is best understood by finding a way of giving them a literal interpretation. So I turn now to another antirealist model from the philosophy of science, to see whether it suggests a religious analogue that may be, for me anyway, more congenial.

The immersion solution

This approach to retaining the literal content of both science and religion is inspired by a position in the philosophy of science known as constructive empiricism, a position developed and championed by Bas van Fraassen.[1]

Constructive empiricism has three core components: semantic, methodological and epistemic. The semantic component is that scientific theories are to be understood in the same way a scientific realist understands them. They are to be given a literal interpretation: they are not metaphors, and they are not shorthand for statements about observable states of affairs. If a theory seems to be talking about invisible subatomic particles, then it is talking about invisible subatomic particles. Moreover, these are descriptions of a possible noumenal world, of the things as they might be in themselves, not of a phenomenal world partially constituted by our concepts, as we have seen Kuhn to have it. So that is the first component: a literal semantics.

The second and methodological component of constructive empiricism is 'immersion'. To immerse oneself in a theory is to enter into the world of that theory and to work from within it. This is not to believe that the theory is true, but it is to enter imaginatively into its 'world'. In some ways this is like Eddington's familiar table. Even if as a physicist one does not believe that tables literally have the qualities of colour and solidity that common sense attributes to them, one may immerse oneself in the world of the everyday table: for everyday purposes we think about the table as if it were as common sense supposes it to be. Indeed, we cannot help but do this. The constructive empiricist makes the parallel suggestion for the scientific table. Here we do have a choice, but the suggestion is that even though we are not to believe everything physics tells us about the table, we are to do our science from within that model, almost as if we did believe in those invisible atoms. Indeed, one may wonder whether immersion is in the end distinct from belief. On behalf of van Fraassen's claim that it is, we might focus on incompatible models, such as Eddington's two tables. One may consistently immerse in both, but not consistently believe both. And incompatible models are common within science itself. Thus a fluid is sometimes modelled as a continuous liquid, sometimes as a collection of discrete particles, depending on which sorts of phenomena one is attempting to predict or explain.

Those are incompatible models, but the scientist may well use both, in some contexts immersing (as it were) in the one and in other cases in the other, though she does not believe both. Immersion is distinct from belief,

---

1 Bas van Fraassen, *The Scientific Image* (Oxford: The Clarendon Press, 1980), esp. ch. 2.

and this is important, because the third, epistemic component of constructive empiricism is the suggestion that scientists do not believe even their best theories. Scientists should only 'accept' them. To accept a theory, in van Fraassen's neologistic sense, is not to believe that the theory is true, but only that it is empirically adequate, that what the theory says about observable things is true. As for the balance of the content of the theory – all that talk about unobservable entities and processes – one is agnostic. So, in accepting a theory, one is believing only a part of it, and the suggestion is that acceptance is the strongest cognitive attitude one should take towards a scientific theory. There is neither warrant nor need to believe more than this. This brings out the contrast between the constructive empiricist and the realist, for while they share their literal semantics, the realist is willing to believe more, in some cases the entire content of the theory, even where that theory speaks of unobservable entities, properties and processes.

How much of a theory is one believing when one accepts it, in van Fraassen's sense? Along one dimension, a great deal, though still only a small part of the full content of a high-level theory. For to accept a theory is not only to believe the part of the theory that one has actually observed, but everything the theory says about what could in principle have been observed, whether it is ever actually observed or not.

Thus in accepting a theory about dinosaurs, one believes what it says about the skin colour of long dead dinosaurs, because skin colour is observable, though never observed by palaeontologists. At the same time, along another dimension the part of the theory one believes by accepting that theory is very limited, according to van Fraassen, because for him observable means naked-eye observable. A distant planet is observable, because although it may never be so observed, it would be visible to the naked eye if one were close enough. By contrast, a small amoeba is unobservable, because even though it may be 'seen' clearly through a powerful light microscope, it cannot be seen by our eyes without the instrumentation, however close we get to it.

What would it be to appropriate the ideas of constructive empiricism to religion? We may consider the three core ideas: literal interpretation, immersion and acceptance. First, literal interpretation. This would be to hold that the Bible means what the Bible says: it is not an entirely metaphorical document. Thus when the Bible says that God parted the Red Sea, what that means is that God parted the Red Sea.

Second is immersion. The idea here is that just as a scientist may immerse herself in the world of the theory, so we may immerse ourselves in a religious text. But here we might go even further than in the scientific case. We might understand religious immersion as entering the form of life of religious practice and religious thought. It involves a kind of participation and a kind of commitment to action. It also involves a kind of identification and solidarity with co-religionists.

What about acceptance? This is the most difficult of the components to bring across to religion, and it will require modification along the way. The governing idea behind acceptance is the idea of partial belief, in the sense of believing some but not all the consequences of a claim and remaining agnostic about the rest. But as the immersion component of constructive empiricism makes clear, this is a committed agnosticism: scientists are to deploy the theory as a whole, not just those parts of it they believe. In the scientific case, the part of the theory to be believed is that part that makes claims about observable states of affairs. Could we say that same thing in the case of religious texts? Like scientific theories, religious texts seem to make claims about both observable and unobservable states of affairs, for example about the nature of an invisible God and about the observable consequences of God's will and activity. So we might attempt to keep the notion of acceptance constant as we carry it over from science to religion. On this view, we are enjoined not to believe that the Bible is true, but only that what it says about observable states of affairs is true.

This may be a coherent position, but from my point of view it is both too liberal and too strict. It is too liberal, because it would require belief in the observable factual content of miracles the Bible describes – for example a belief that the Red Sea did part, a conspicuously observable state of affairs – though not the supernatural aetiology. But I myself cannot believe that the miracles in the Bible occurred, whatever their supposed causes and even if described in purely observable terms.

More importantly, this interpretation of acceptance would not solve the tension problem between science and religion, because I take it that the factual claims about some of the miracles contradict what our best science tells us about how the world has behaved. Thus acceptance of religion in this sense and belief or even just acceptance of science would still leave us with contradictory beliefs. That is why the observability criterion is too liberal for my purposes. It is also too strict, because it would remove from the believed part all the normative content of the Bible, since norms are not observable; yet some of these I do believe.

This suggests an alternative account of religious acceptance, which would be to mandate belief not in the observable content of the text, but rather in its normative content. But here too I think we would end up both with too much and too little. Too much, because I do not wish to endorse the entire normative content of the Bible; too little, because I want to take more, in terms of belief, from the Bible than its normative content. For example, I think that a religious text may be a powerful resource for working out what to believe about one's own nature and one's relations to other people, and these results seem to go well beyond the strictly normative content of the text.

To provide the epistemic flexibility I desire requires a third construal of acceptance, where the class of consequences to be believed is given an extrinsic characterization or, to avoid euphemism, where the characterization is more ad hoc.

The reason this is necessary is because, for the most part, I take it that the warrant for those aspects of our religious text and tradition that we believe must come primarily from outside the religious text. I say 'for the most part' and 'primarily', because I give the text itself independent epistemic weight in certain areas, for example where it enjoins certain forms of ritual behaviour and where it in effect characterizes certain group values. The source of that weight requires no divine role: in choosing to identify with a religious tradition, I choose to give that tradition this weight. But for most of the claims of my tradition, belief must be earned largely from outside the text itself, and this includes most of the moral claims. That is, I do not accept that in general something is made the right thing to do because the Bible says it is the right thing to do; nor do I accept that the Bible has a moral authority (whatever the source of values) that automatically trumps independent reflection and evaluation.

Accepting a religious text thus means believing some but not all of its claims; but which claims we believe is largely externally determined, by moral reflection, and in some cases by science. So the epistemology of religious acceptance as I am construing this notion is importantly different from the epistemology of scientific acceptance as the constructive empiricist construes it. For in the case of a scientific theory, while we are only to believe its observable claims, we are to believe those (in cases where we have not actually made the observation) because they follow from the theory, which has itself been empirically tested. Here the warrant for the observable consequences flows from the warrant for the empirical adequacy of the theory, which flows from observation and experiment. By contrast, in religious acceptance, as I have ended up construing it, the warrant comes mostly from other places. We are thus moving quite far from van Fraassen's notion of acceptance. In at least one respect, I would move even farther, since 'agnosticism' does not describe my own cognitive attitude towards the supernatural claims of the Bible. For it is not just that I don't believe them true, I believe them false. Where they contradict scientific theories I believe, I have no choice; but even if there are some supernatural claims compatible with that science, my epistemic attitude towards those claims will be determined by what I take to be their warrant or lack of it. The question then must be whether I have now have left constructive empiricism so far behind as to make the analogy worthless.

I think not. In part that is because I wish to emphasize the other two components of constructive empiricism, the insistence on literal construal and the advice to immerse oneself in the world of the text. But the notion of acceptance also helps me to articulate the religious attitude I wish to adopt. It captures the idea that one may define an epistemic attitude of partial belief, involving the belief in some but not all the content of a text. But as I have already indicated *en passant*, there is more to acceptance than this, as van Fraassen characterizes it, though the additional element is closely related to immersion. Acceptance is not just partial belief; it is also a kind of commitment to use the resources of the theory. In the scientific case, 'acceptance involves a commitment to confront any future phenomena by means of the conceptual resources of this theory'.

The religious case is not quite the same, but what I have in mind is that in accepting a religious text we not only believe parts of it; we also commit ourselves to using the text as a tool for thought, as a way of thinking about our world. The scientist accepts her theory and her techniques, and for van Fraassen that means she takes the stand of using the theory and the techniques as tools that help her to come to grips with the phenomena. Adapting constructive empiricism to religion yields a perspective from which religious people accept their tradition and their texts as tools for thinking through their lives, their projects and their attitudes. For those inside the tradition, the Bible is good to think with and to grapple with, and not just in the parts of it that are antecedently believed. On this view, acceptance and immersion are not passive activities, nor are they matters of all or nothing. In my view one sometimes has to struggle with one's religious text not just in order to understand it but in order to come to terms with its moral content. In some cases we may find this content morally unacceptable. As a progressive Jew, this will sometimes lead me to reject clear moral content present in my religious text, but here too I would continue to preserve its literal meaning. Nor is rejection to be taken lightly if we are to preserve the constructive attitude of immersion in the text, but in my view the difficult material is there to be struggled with, not to be bowdlerized or ignored.

The signal advantage of the immersion solution over the metaphor, value and selection solutions is that it is preserves the integrity and hence the useful power of the religious text. Recall that the metaphor view would have us construe all religious claims in conflict with belief-worthy science figuratively; the value view would have us construe the religious claims as without descriptive content; and the selection view would have us excise whatever conflicts with the science. If a religious form of life is of no interest to you, this may not matter. But for those of us who do wish so to engage, the trouble with those three views is that they allow science to mangle the text, and this would deprive it of much of its value. On the immersion view, by contrast, we have the text to use in its full, unexpurgated form, the form in which I believe it can do us the most good as a tool for thinking and for living.

Conclusion: religion without belief

This completes my sketch of what it might look like to adapt constructive empiricism to religion. We construe our religious text literally, we believe only parts of it, but we use all of it and we immerse ourselves in the world it describes. The point of exploring this approach is not to persuade those hostile to religious activity that they should repent, but to consider a way in which those who find themselves with a commitment both to a religion and to science might have it both ways. But while the immersion solution will clearly help relieve the tension of incompatible beliefs, are literalism, acceptance and immersion enough to do justice to religious commitment?

The immersion solution involves no distinctive religious faith and no belief in supernatural power. Indeed, isn't it tantamount to treating the Bible as a *novel*? After all, novels often invite literal interpretation, include some claims the reader believes, and may support a kind of immersion into a fictional world. Richard Braithwaite, whose work has influenced my development of the immersion solution, bit the bullet. He thought of religious texts as stories with morals, where 'it is not necessary . . . for the asserter of a religious assertion to believe in the truth of the story involved in the assertions'.

The immersion solution would have been enough for Braithwaite, but it is obviously not enough for everyone with religious commitments. Many religious people have difficulty seeing the point or value of religion without belief in God. If that is what you need, the immersion solution is not for you. But the immersion solution can provide a great deal, more than even the most enthusiastic book group.

The religious story has its life in the context of ritual observance and more generally as part of a religious form of life. It is a story in which the reader herself is also a participant, and it may provide extraordinary support for communal identification and moral reflection. Consider the natural worldly benefits that religious activities provide for the religiously committed, benefits that can be characterized independently of the question of a supernatural source. The immersion solution will not support the belief that their source is in fact supernatural, but it may support the benefits themselves. For some religious people, the satisfaction they derive from their religion would evaporate if they ceased to believe in the existence and influence of God. But for others, it is not belief that is doing the work, but rather intense and communal engagement with religious text and with religious practice. For those people, the immersion solution may be enough.

On the immersion solution to the tension problem, religious commitment and religious identification flow from the contents of the texts of one's religion literally construed. Some of the claims of religion may conflict with the claims of science. The immersion solution does not aim to remove that inconsistency, but by distinguishing acceptance from belief it finds a way to achieve consistency of belief without effacing incompatibility of content. On this approach, we preserve content by adjusting our attitude towards it. We have literalism without fundamentalism; inconsistency without irrationality. There is conflict between some of the claims we invoke, but not in what we believe. To some, this may smack of hypocrisy, but in the context of the relation between science and religion I myself think it is one route to personal and intellectual integrity, a route which tries to preserve as much as possible from both religion and science without ignoring the tensions between them.

2

What has Plotinus' One[1]
to do with God?

STEPHEN R. L. CLARK

Thesis: metaphysics

The first, historical, answer to the question my title poses ('What has Plotinus' One to do with God?') is obviously that theologians in all three major Abrahamic faiths shared Plotinus' conception, of a transcendent and incomprehensible simple, having no properties, and without any need of what worships it. Maximus the Confessor, writing *On Knowledge* 1/1: 'God is one, without beginning, incomprehensible, possessing in his totality the full power of being, fully excluding the notions of time and quality.'[2] God, it is axiomatic in all those faiths, is not a thing to be named or described, and 'belief in God' is not like a belief in extra-terrestrial intelligences, or fairies, or the Loch Ness Monster. What is called 'the One', or 'the Good', or 'the Centre', must be posited if there is to be any genuine explanation of the things that are – and such an explanation cannot itself be constituted by any one of the things there are. This is the point of Bertrand Russell's anecdote – or at any rate, I suspect it was his interlocutor's point. Russell was approached after a lecture, you may recall, by an elderly woman who assured him that he was quite wrong about the nature and origin of the world. It rests, she told him, on a turtle's back. And what, said Russell, does the turtle rest on? 'You can't catch me like that, Mr Russell. It's turtles all the way down.'

Such a scenario, of course, would be absurd. If it were really were 'turtles all the way down' (or one material cause before another), then the brute fact

1 Earlier versions of this essay were read to a meeting of the British Society for the History of Philosophy, at Keele, April 2000, a meeting of the British Society for the Philosophy of Religion in Oxford, September 2007, and the workshop at Westcott House in September 2008. See also *Understanding Faith: Religious Belief and its Place in Society* (Exeter: Imprint Academic, forthcoming).

2 Maximus Confessor, 'First Century on Knowledge' 1: *Maximus Confessor: Selected Writings*, tr. George C. Berthold (London: SPCK, 1985), p. 129.

of its being *turtles* rather than elephants or hippopotami would be inscrutable. Either there *is* no explanation – and anything at all could happen – or else the explanation lies outside all systems. The One does not *exist*, because it is the explanation of existence. Nor is it any particular sort of thing, identifiably different from other, co-existing things. These arguments, oddly enough, are now sometimes used to discredit theism, on the pretence that 'God' must name some especially large and very complex entity that might or might not *exist*. On the contrary, in the philosophical tradition in which Plotinus has been placed, it labels a principle that does not *exist*, and has no properties. It is not complex, and not contingent upon anything at all. Things that come to exist do so, in essence, because they are *required* to exist. What requires it is not a member of the class of all the things that have thus come to be, nor is it a particularly splendid example of any sort of thing. Philosophers may argue whether any of that makes sense (and especially whether an Explanation that no one can understand differs very much from No-Explanation-at-All[3]) but there is no point ignoring it in favour of dissecting the putative existence of a being which cannot possibly be what theistic thinkers point to. Neither the One nor God can be the same as Mega-Big, Galactic Engineers, nor yet the Gnostic demiurge Ialdobaoth. Theistic explanation of this sort is simply another sort of explanation, and the only game in town: without it, there *is* no explanation beyond the pretence of its being 'turtles all the way down'. On that account things just are the way they are, for no reason whatsoever, and without even any reason to suppose that they are the *same* from one instant or locality to another.

Recent efforts to explain or explain away the putative 'fine-tuning' of the cosmos, by suggesting that all possible variants of law and initial conditions occur 'somewhere' or 'somewhen' suffer the same fault: it really does not help to answer the question 'Why is there anything?' to say that there just is everything! It is especially unhelpful to pretend that such an answer is anything but outrageously metaphysical. The theistic alternative is to suppose that they are, in some way, called into being by . . . well, what?

Orthodox monotheists in all three of the great Abrahamic faiths – namely Judaism, Christianity and Islam – also share with Plotinus a cautious approach to images, an emphasis on personal responsibility and a disapproval of stellar determinism (a creed whose place is occupied in modern, respectable circles by *genetic* determinism). Where Plotinus speaks of gods,

---

3 'How [do] mystics, who maintain the absolute incomprehensibility of the Deity, differ from Sceptics or Atheists, who assert, that the first cause of all is unknown and unintelligible?': David Hume, *Dialogues Concerning Natural Religion (1779) Part 4* (Cleanthes speaks), in R. Wollheim (ed.), *Hume on Religion* (London: Fontana, 1963), p. 131.

Abrahamic believers more commonly speak of angels – and neither can be simply equated with the One or even with that derived divinity, the Word. What Plotinus says of the Intellect, that it gets its being from the One as it gazes back towards the One, is said, implicitly, of the Word of God. All three Abrahamic faiths acknowledge the significance of Torah, Koran or Logos, and all agree that it derives its being from God. Judaism and Islam are – at least at first sight – more easily reconciled with Plotinus than is orthodox Christianity, in that Torah and Koran alike are clearly subordinate realities, even if they are true expressions of what God requires of all. In Christendom, the Logos is as clearly God as the Father is. Though the heavenly Koran is uncreated, and 'enbibled',[4] Muslims would deny that God can have any companion or helper. That the heavenly Word should be actually *identical* (in some sense) both with God and with a particular, contingent entity, seems absurd or blasphemous, even though it could more readily be agreed that some contingent entity housed or represented that Word, very much as the dedicated philosopher might ascend to a moral equality with the World Soul, and a complete self-identification with Intellect. Plotinus does allow the abstract possibility of Zeus's taking human form (and looking like Pheidias' Zeus[5]), and of course any of us *may* rise to the level of 'a god', but even God the Intellect isn't the One's equal, and can't be *localized*. In one way Zeus (the Soul) already is embodied, multiply, but not in a body worthy of Soul, or fully representing the *whole* Soul. Even the World Soul, which has a worthy body, is not All the Soul There Is, let alone the Intellect or the One. Even the Intellect, containing all intelligible form, is not the One (for the One is *not* intelligible form).

Though Plotinus argues consistently for the claim that the whole universe is animated and united by the action of one Great Soul, which also provides the bodily forms by which other individual souls are attracted down from their original and eternal home, that Great Soul is no more than an individual soul itself – our sister, not our mother. That there is such a soul is required, in Plotinus' system, for the unity of the universe itself, for there actually *being* 'a universe'[6] rather than an aggregate of things. Soul itself is, as it were, the Zeus to the World Soul's Aphrodite – and any individual soul is also an Aphrodite.[7] So Plotinus is no more 'pantheistic' than any

4 Gai Eaton, *Islam and the Destiny of Man* (Cambridge: Islamic Texts Society, 1994), p. 80: 'for Christians the Word was made flesh, whereas for Muslims it took earthly shape in the form of a book, and the recitation of the Quran in the ritual prayer fulfils the same function as the eucharist in Christianity'.

5 *Ennead* V.8 [31].1. This was a standard trope, found also in Cicero *Orator* II.8-9. See A. H. Armstrong, *Plotinian and Christian Studies* (London: Variorum Reprints, 1979).

6 Cf. Stanley Jaki, *Is there a Universe?* (Liverpool: Liverpool University Press, 1994).

7 *Ennead* VI.9 [9].9, p. 28ff.

orthodox Abrahamist – Jew, Christian or Muslim. The World Soul is one soul, even if it is the greatest among many (and acts without any consciousness of its own action). Intellect contains all intellects, just as in that it contains all forms of being – the sum of everything that is, including our own eternal being. Nothing that we can see or comprehend is simply the same as the One.

In Hilary Armstrong's words, and to anticipate a little:

> Plotinus's divine mind is not just a mind knowing a lot of eternal objects. It is an organic living community of interpenetrating beings which are at once Forms and intelligences, all 'awake and alive', in which every part thinks and therefore is the whole; so that all are one mind and yet each retains its distinct individuality without which the whole would be impoverished. And this mind-world is the region where our own mind, illumined by the divine intellect, finds its true self and lives its own life, its proper home and the penultimate stage on its journey, from which it is taken up to union with the Good.[8]

That last phrase may mislead: there is no question of our ever becoming the One, though we may at last find ourselves, in some sense, 'in' that One, or alongside it, as it were 'in bed with it', simply because It is closer to us than anything. In turning toward the One, the intellect is filled with the intelligibles that are its being. That is, we cannot but appreciate the One through organized multiplicity, through being self-identified with Intellect.

To put it differently: we 'believe in God' (if the One is God) just as in that we manage to comprehend reality as a well-ordered whole, a thing of multiple beauty unified in love. 'A conviction that God does in some way order everything for the best seems to be an essential part of belief in him, if we mean by God what Christians have always meant.'[9] That 'best', of course, is not independent of what is meant by 'God': God or the One just is the criterion by which all things are to be judged – and Plotinus retained, as the Stoics did not, a notion that not everything that happened in the world was *right*. What makes it possible for us to do this, to learn to rejoice in being, and for there to be such a community is their, our, common focus: if we were focused 'downwards', towards stuff or towards private sensation, we would be at odds, and fail to see how things exist in beauty.

---

8 A. H. Armstrong and R. A. Markus, *Christian Faith and Greek Philosophy* (London: Darton, Longman & Todd, 1960), p. 27.
9 Ibid., p. 3.

Antithesis: theology

I shall return to those last remarks, and try to draw out more of their implications. But before doing so, we should consider some radical challenges, not so much to the *historical* claim that later theologians often owed a lot to Platonic thought and language, mediated through such authors as pseudo-Dionysius, Augustine or Ibn Arabi, but to the *theological* claim that this debt was proper. What about the God of Abraham, and *not* the God of the philosophers? Plotinus chose to allegorize even such brutal myths as Kronos's eating his own children, as if those stories contained, in riddling form, the true philosophy: maybe he meant this as a serious vindication of pagan religious practices (as some of his successors did), or maybe this was only an imaginative exercise. In either case, it is easy to suggest, *his* God is entirely different from the Creator-God of Abrahamic story. The world exists 'of necessity, and not as the result of any process of reasoning'.[10] Everything is, in some sense, 'in' God, or an immediate effect of God.

Maybe the God of the philosophers is unchanging, utterly transcendent, in need of nothing to complete it, and utterly unlike any ordinarily existing thing. But isn't this account, in which the Ultimate is presented as the outcome of a rational enquiry, a putative 'explanation' that actually *explains* nothing, itself a false image? The Real Origin, the fountain of creation, is not to be identified with any philosopher's cynosure – real just as long as it respects the philosopher's intellect. The very features of the God of Abraham that most shock respectable philosophers may be the ones that are truer to the tradition. The God of Abraham is *involved*, argumentative, demanding and recognizably 'human'. 'God appears and God is light to those poor souls that dwell in night, but does a *human* form display to those who dwell in realms of day'[11] – precisely because to be human is *not* to be a rational animal. We are most human, and closest in kind to the – admittedly unimaginable – Maker, when we are least constrained by any former system. To acknowledge and worship the God of the philosophers is to accept our total dependence on an immovable somewhat, to face up to reality, to know that God's ways are not ours. But the God that called Abraham out of Haran, Israel out of Egypt, and Jesus Christ from the dead, is simultaneously more than any intelligible fact, and also something, somehow, 'personal'.[12] There is

---

10 *Ennead* III.2 [47].3, 4–5. But note that this does not mean that the One is *compelled*. And even or especially the God of Abraham does not 'create' as a craftsman might. The differences need longer analysis.

11 William Blake, *Auguries of Innocence* (1803), lines 129–32: *Blake: Complete Writings*, ed. Geoffrey Keynes (London: Oxford University Press, 1966), p. 434.

12 See Robert W. Jenson, *The Triune Identity: God According to the Gospel* (Philadelphia: Fortress Press, 1982).

also a gulf between that God and his creation that is not to be bridged by talk of emanations or angelic in-betweens.

Correspondingly, the route to God cannot be simply 'philosophical', and God himself may be too vulgar for philosophers to stomach! Where Greek philosophers since Parmenides had thought that the proper name of God was simply 'ESTIN' ('It is'), the Hebrew tradition carried forward into Rabbinic Judaism, Christianity and Islam, is that his name is 'EHYE ASHER EHYE' – 'I will be who I will.' Ernst Bloch indeed identifies the Delphic slogan 'EI' ('Thou art') as symptomatic of the same Greek preference.

> EI means grammatically and metaphysically the same, namely Thou art, in the sense of the timelessly unchangeable existence of God. *Eh'je asher eh'je*, on the other hand, places even at the threshold of the Yahweh phenomenon a god of the end of days, with *futurum* as an attribute of Being.[13]

Bloch certainly exaggerates the contrast, since many Abrahamic theologians (including Philo, Clement, Origen and Augustine) have interpreted the Hebrew name, exactly, as affirming God's Present and Necessary Being – but perhaps that is the point: that the Hebrew tradition was contaminated by the Greek. God's *future* dominion, or the recreation of the world into the image of his glory, demands that we leave the past behind. All the old gods, the angels of the nations that the Emperor Julian wished us to follow (and hoped to use a post-Plotinian philosophy to allegorize and defend) are to be abandoned in the name of one fierce demand, to follow the Invisible God into an uncharted future, to risk everything 'for love'.

Because God is not given in any present rational system, and faith in him is not a tentative acceptance of the conclusion of a reasoned argument (except perhaps as the only option left once other 'materialist' or 'atheistical' systems of thought have self-destructed), we bind ourselves to his service through the ritual enactment of a mysterious future, when common goods are to be transformed. Philosophers are simply wrong to suppose that those closest to God's glory are 'the wise'. God has revealed himself, or at least his commands, to the foolish, and those commands are that we should allow ourselves to be remade through ritual – baptism, the laying on of hands, the Eucharist and regular concelebration; or else through regular prostrations, reading of the Koran in Arabic, and walking round the Ka'ba; or else through remembering Passover. Of course those rituals may them-

13 Ernst Bloch, *The Principle of Hope*, tr. N. Plaice, S. Plaice and P. Knight (Oxford: Blackwell, 1986), pp. 1235f.; Stephen R. L. Clark, *God's World and the Great Awakening* (Oxford: Clarendon Press, 1990), pp. 45–6.

selves be allegorized, but not therefore conducted *only* in our imaginations: 'the feast is a symbol of gladness of soul and of thankfulness to God, but we should not for that reason turn our backs on the general gatherings of the year's seasons'.[14] These rituals are reminders of the imagined, unknown future, and ways of being prepared – through their action on our bodies and our imaginations – to live within that future when it comes.

So the Plotinian system – itself a reinvigorated Platonism that perhaps owed something to Philo's effort to Hellenize the Hebrew scriptures – is to be regarded, from the Abrahamic point of view, as a vast error, which has contaminated theological understanding. By accepting that God, the One, is something that we could *reason* our way towards, and that we did not need the support of any historical and communal ritual, Plotinus made himself immune to the real lessons of Hebrew philosophy. From the Plotinian point of view, Christians – who claimed that they were to judge angels, and hoped to transcend this world's attractions by ritual devotion – were wholly in the wrong. How could they despise this best of all possible images of the Intelligible World? What business is it of theirs to judge the world at fault? How could they claim a special insight and revelation which did not depend on ethical purifications and rigorous thought? 'If God is not in the World, He is not in you.'[15] Conversely, when Plotinus declined to accompany Amelius upon his ritual occasions with the words that the gods should come to him, and not he to the gods, it seems, to any properly humble Abrahamist, that he was displaying a conscious arrogance, a mistaken trust in his own powers of understanding. His 'flight of the Alone to the Alone' (to use the common, quite misleading translation of *Ennead* VI.9 [9].11, 51) seems a denial of community, as well as a risky claim to know the way to that One, or to the Intellect.

Strangely, just as Plotinus found fault with those who criticized the workings of the world, so later theologians have found fault with those who seemed, like Plotinus, to distinguish Two Worlds. Dualism is currently unpopular in modern Christian circles, and both Jewish and Muslim thinkers also tend to identify a former Christian error as the dualistic assumption that *real* value lies aloft, and *real* selves are to be identified with souls. Modern Christian theologians prefer to point to the Resurrection of the Body as the vindication of bodily existence, and blame earlier and more etherial conceptions on 'the Platonic tradition'. What the God of Abraham promises is not, like Buddha, *release* from the circles of this world, but an age to come.

---

14 Philo, *De Migratione Abrahamis 92: Collected Works of Philo*, tr. F. H. Colson, G. H. Whitaker et al. (London: Loeb Classical Library, Heinemann, 1929–62), Vol. 4, p. 185.
15 *Ennead* II.9 [33].16, p. 26ff.

Finally, whereas the Greek – and the Plotinian – endeavour was to become 'like God', at least so far as we might think and speak 'with the mind of God',[16] it is axiomatic in Abrahamic circles that God is utterly *unlike* us, and far beyond any possibility of union. Once again, there are plenty of counter-examples – people even in the Islamic tradition who claimed to be so wholly filled with God as to find no gap between themselves and him. And it has been an axiom of the Christian churches at least since Athanasius that God became man so that men might become God. But the claim I am considering here is that this is a corruption, a consequence of listening too long and cosily to 'the philosophers'. The God of Abraham is one that summons us out from our complacencies, but without any promise that we shall ever *know* or be *united to* him. The closest we can come to him is to live in community with our fellows. William James' rejection of a 'speculative drinking up of God' in favour of a faithful obedience to his commands – which are, to love one another – is a conscious rejection of one strand in theism.[17] Lovers don't need to *understand* each other, but to love. 'And it is better for us to be drunk with a drunkenness like this than to be more respectably sober.'[18]

Synthesis: the Way

But anyone familiar with the *Enneads* of Plotinus must by now be restive, and I have already given several clues to a contrary interpretation. If it is true that there is a radical, transformative, apophatic, even anti-metaphysical and *practical* strand (that is, having to do with *praxis*: deliberate action) in the Abrahamic theisms, it is still more obvious that there is just such a strand in Plotinus. Indeed, there is a case for saying that there is actually no *other* strand in Plotinus, or at least that the sort of over-intellectual, solitary, abstract and depressive theology with which some critics seek to identify him (whereby the One is simultaneously wholly abstract and unconnected with anything we experience here, and somehow also to be known only through the ordered cosmos that is Its only effusion) is actually the theology that, explicitly, he expounds in order to reject. Everything I reported before about the strangeness of God, his *attractiveness,* his being beyond all finite and formal rules, and the importance of a communal and symbol-using life, can be confirmed in Plotinus' writings on the One.

---

16 'Intellect is our king. But we too are kings when we are in accord with it; we can be in accord with it in two ways, either by having something like its writing written in us like laws, or by being as if filled with it and able to see it and be aware of it as present' (*Ennead* V.3 [49].3, pp. 46ff.).
17 William James, *The Will to Believe* (New York: Longmans, Green, 1919), p. 141.
18 *Ennead* VI.7 [38].35.

Our grasp of Plotinus' personal character, of course, is mediated almost entirely through Porphyry, who comes across in his own writings as kindly, indefatigable, fairly humourless and subject to depression. Plotinus, on the other hand, writes with considerable humour of the human condition, encourages debate, and impresses even imperial officials. He was very much *less* solitary than many saints of the Abrahamic faiths, and often much more sceptical of imperial pretensions. 'Bad men rule by the feebleness of the ruled – and this is just.'[19] The power of those bad rulers rests upon the willingness of their subjects to be terrorized into obedience by threats no more realistic than are children's bogeys.[20] The solution is not overt rebellion, but simply to turn away, towards the One. He follows Aristotle in offering a positive argument for democracy: in an assembly the differing talents and experience of a multitude contribute more effectively to a sound decision than would any single, flawed individual.[21] – at least, we may suppose, an assembly whose souls and imaginations have been properly structured by the laws brought down from heaven by such as Minos.[22] There is even scope in the Plotinian system for resisting the standard rationalist distinction between the ritual and moral laws. All the laws are purificatory, and assist with the imaginative refocusing of attention, and our invocation of the gods. Plotinus does not wish to join in Amelius' ritualism – but it shouldn't be assumed that this is out of pride: rather that the gods – which is to say, a sudden awareness of beauty and the One, come by grace, and cannot be compelled, only invited. So also Plato distinguished magic and true religion 'in that magic makes every effort to persuade the gods, whereas the truly religious behaviour is to leave the gods a free choice, for they know better than we do what is good for us'.[23] Porphyry said that 'it seems that the gods often set him straight when he was going on a crooked course "sending down a solid shaft of light", which means that he wrote what he wrote under their inspection and supervision'.[24]

When Plotinus planned to found 'Platonopolis' it is easy to suppose that what he had in mind was, in effect, a university: an assembly – with supporting staff – of scholars dedicated to unravelling the truth, by various reasonable means. But perhaps we should take more seriously the thought

---

19 *Ennead* III.2 [47].8.
20 *Ennead* I.4 [46].8.
21 *Ennead* VI.5 [23].10; Aristotle, *Politics* 3.1281a 40ff.
22 *Ennead* VI.9 [9].7.
23 Fritz Graf, *Magic in the Ancient World* (Cambridge, MA: Harvard University Press, 1999), p. 27, after Plato, *Laws* 10. Emma C. Clarke, *Iamblichus' De Mysteriis* (London: Ashgate, 2001), pp. 23f., points out that Iamblichus, now remembered for preferring theurgic rituals to philosophy, also insisted that the initiative must lie with God.
24 *Life of Plotinus* 23.

that he had Plato's *Laws* in mind: a genuine city, all of whose citizens would share in the liturgical year. 'In the *Laws*', according to Catherine Pickstock's reading , 'it is the divine gift of the liturgical cycle with all the concomitant sustenance which the deities bring to these festivals, which distinguishes human beings from the wild animals which have no such gifts of order, rhythm or harmony'.[25] I am not so sure that Plotinus, any more than Porphyry, makes so radical a distinction between the 'human' and the 'non-human' – one might as well, as Plato said, divide the world into 'cranes' and 'non-cranes'.[26] But the main point, that such liturgies embody and reinforce the themes which souls should rehearse at all times, seems a fair one. That, after all, is what the Egyptian priests – perhaps – intended: by using paintings and statues to convey their messages they allowed the gods an entry into the human soul.[27] The imaginative exercises that Plotinus himself devises are, as Greg Shaw among many others has observed,[28] *theurgic* in intent: that is, they are meant to allow the gods an entry, to help remake our souls. Sara Rappe likewise: 'Decoding these texts involves seeing them as something like meditation manuals rather than mere texts. The non-discursive aspects of the text – the symbols, ritual formulae, myths, and images – are the locus of this pedagogy. Their purpose is to help the reader to learn how to contemplate, to awaken the eye of wisdom.'[29]

Progress is not made exclusively by intellectual, argumentative means – indeed, such arguments depend upon the real existence of an intellectual grasp of 'immutable justice and beauty',[30] for which we can have no *argument* if we cannot already see it. He himself celebrated the birthdays of Plato and Socrates 'with sacrifice and philosophical discussion'.[31] He finds nothing odd in appealing to oracles about honouring the dead – or as themselves the heroic dead.[32] Even the star-gods, though they do not determine what we shall do, may serve as examples, and we may request their aid.[33] And the mysteries are constantly invoked as meaning what Plotinus himself has come to see, with Plato's help, as true.[34]

---

25 *Laws* 653d ff. according to Catherine Pickstock, *After Writing: On the Liturgical Consummation of Philosophy* (Oxford: Blackwell, 1998), p. 40; p. 42 further cites *Laws* 803d, 644d ff. on *paideia*.

26 Plato, *Statesman* 263d.

27 *Ennead* V.8 [31].6, IV.3 [27].11; see *Asclepius* 37.

28 Gregory Shaw, 'Eros and Arithmos: Pythagorean Theurgy in Iamblichus and Plotinus', *Ancient Philosophy* 19, 1999, pp. 121–43.

29 Sara Rappe, *Reading Neoplatonism* (Cambridge: Cambridge University Press, 2000), p. 3.

30 *Ennead* V.1 [10].11.

31 *Life* 2.

32 *Ennead* IV.7 [2].15.

33 *Ennead* IV.4 [28].30.

34 *Ennead* I.6 [1].6, VI.9 [9].11.

The rediscovery, the uncovering, of beauty in our own souls will be cued by our perception of the beauty of bodies and of noble characters. But that 'turn within' is not an abandonment of community. On the contrary, as my earlier quotation from Hilary Armstrong suggested, the world of intellect, the age of gold, is what is attained when we no longer squabble to keep ourselves 'our own'. Conversely, our fall into the world of sensory experience can be characterized as a risky turning away from interdependence. 'As if they were tired of being together, they each go to their own.'[35] Whether Plotinus supposed that this was 'literally' true is not, for the moment, important. The descent of the soul is as metaphorical and mythological an event as the equivalent 'sort of error' – the desire to stand away from the One – which produces Intellect itself.[36] There was no actual moment when Intellect came to be, and none when Soul stepped a little away from Intellect and began to fill the empirical world with life. What matters to Plotinus is the present structure of existence, and the possible ways of living.

The world of intelligible form, of beauty, which is the real world behind and within our separate perceptions of it, exists within and depends upon the Formless: strangely, by Greek standards, there is a certain similarity in the language used of the One and what is used of Matter! Both are without form, and both, in a way, have the potential to be everything. The One holds beauty before itself as a veil.[37] Matter itself, the very principle of evil, can never itself be seen beneath the beautiful chains in which it is bound.[38] The beauties of the intelligible world and of the sensible are not *different*. What makes the difference, to us, is the way that we attend to them. Looking 'downward' we experience disconnected sensa which entice us into consuming and controlling what we foolishly imagine is outside the soul, but beauties remain even then as challenges to our independence. Looking 'downward', we imagine a world of discrete, disconnected atoms, spread out across an infinite expanse that cannot be brought to unity. Here I find myself largely in agreement with Douglas Hadley's online paper[39] which argues that the intelligible and sensible world aren't different worlds: there is in the end only *one* reality, and our problem is that we're looking at things in the wrong way. Plotinus' exhortation should be understood as a

---

35 *Ennead* IV.8 [6].4; see V.1 [10].1.

36 *Ennead* III.8 [30].8 ; see VI.9 [9].5, V.8 [31].13.

37 *Ennead* I.6.9.

38 *Ennead* I.8.15.

39 http://www.bu.edu/wcp/Papers/Meta/MetaHadl.htm (accessed 7 January 2007): Douglas Hadley, 'A Variation on the Dog and His Bone: The Unity of the World in Plotinian Philosophy (*Ennead* VI.4–5 [22–3])', given at the Twentieth World Congress of Philosophy in Boston, Massachusetts, 10–15 August 1998.

reorientation, a reordering within the world here and now, not a rejection of one reality in favour of some other.

> That One, therefore, since it has no otherness is always present, and we are present to it when we have no otherness; and the One does not desire us, so as to be around us, but we desire it, so that we are around it. And we are always around it but do not always look to it; it is like a choral dance: in the order of its singing the choir keeps round its conductor but may sometimes turn away, so that he is out of their sight, but when it turns back to him it sings beautifully and is truly with him; so we too are always around him – and if we were not, we should be totally dissolved and no longer exist – but not always turned to him; but when we do look to him, then we are at our goal and at rest and do not sing out of tune as we truly dance our god-inspired dance around him.[40]

'Clearly, then,' Hadley goes on to say,

> for Plotinus we dwell presently in the presence of divinity (all of reality) *but are turned away from it*. We are facing the wrong direction, thus experience the same sort of trouble faced by an orchestra or choir which is not paying attention to the conductor. In order to gain sound knowledge and truer life – greater order, rest, stability – the questing soul needs to re-orient, thereby seeing what was always there but which was not seen previously: 'But if you went away, it was not from it – for it is present – and you did not even go away then, but were present and turned the opposite way.'[41]

The phenomenal world, or worlds, that we encounter are no more than echoes or phantoms of the *real* world which we can occasionally recognize through intellect. This is not an esoteric or mystical insight, but a simple observation. All I ordinarily *see* are coloured surfaces, having only a contingent relationship, not even a 'resemblance', to the things I believe (and you believe) there are. Indeed, all that I *see*, and imagine is 'over there', is actually in me, and I could not even see the sun if my soul had no internal light, if it could not generate that illumination for itself. Most of us make do with the merely notional conviction that there are real people, real creatures, unremembered histories and unknown islands quite distinct from the

---

40 *Ennead* VI.9.8.34–45; see also VI.9.7–8. Note that Plotinus makes reference here to 'otherness' and 'body'. It is undeniable that in his perspective troubles arise the more one is wrongly involved with 'body'; he does in fact reserve the strongest derision for matter as well. Still, body as such is not evil, but our concern for body is. For discussion, see *Ennead* I.8.4–5; II.1.4, 9.8, 3.12, 17; III.4.1; IV.8.6.

41 *Ennead* VI.5 [23].12.28–9; see also VI.5 [23].7.15–17, 9–15.

shape they take in our usual, sensual imagination. But sometimes we do wake up, to *realize* this – and fall asleep again. The moment of discovering that our child, our spouse, our colleague, even our dog or our computer, is a separate existent, with her own perspective – a perspective within which we ourselves may play a smaller part than we had casually assumed – will always be a shock. And one that we habitually forget as soon as possible: 'It is as if people who slept through their life thought the things in their dreams were reliable and obvious, but, if someone woke them up, disbelieved in what they saw with their eyes open and went to sleep again'.[42] Can we manage somehow to create those wakenings?

> Our country from which we came is There, our Father is There. How shall we travel to it, where is our way of escape? We cannot get there on foot; for our feet only carry us everywhere in this world, from one country to another. You must not get ready a carriage, either, or a boat. Let all these things go, and do not look. Shut your eyes, and change to and wake another way of seeing, which everyone has but few use.[43]

That 'other way of seeing' may turn out to be surprisingly commonplace: simply follow the instructions! Shut your eyes, and notice where you are! Notice the reality that sustains you even in your least agreeable moments. The realization that I am Here is the beginning of understanding, a revelation that – in other traditions – is induced by silly questions (as it might be, 'What is the sound of one hand clapping?').[44] Becoming present to oneself is also becoming aware that there is a real world, as it were 'behind' or 'within' phenomena. What is it that is 'behind the scenes'? We are.

> When we look outside that on which we depend we do not know that we are one, like faces which are many on the outside but have one head inside. But if someone is able to turn around, either by himself or having the good luck to have his hair pulled by Athena herself, he will see God and himself and the all ... He will stop marking himself off from all being and will come to all the All without going out anywhere.[45]

42 *Ennead* V.5 [32].11.

43 *Ennead* I.6 [1].8, 22ff.

44 I owe the insight to J. Nigro Sansonese, *The Body of Myth* (Rochester, VT: Inner Traditions International, 1994), a book well worth reading despite its later descent into dubious etymologies. What *is* the sound of one hand clapping? Well, listen! Where are you at the moment? Here!

45 *Ennead* VI.5 [23].7, 9f. The reference is to an episode in Homer's *Iliad* (I.197f.) in which Athena (the goddess of good sense) recalls Achilles from a murderous rage (in the recent film the rôle is given to Briseis).

This is more than a bare, neutral recognition: it is revelation. Intellect is in one sense merely cognitive – but it has another mode: a divinely inspired drunkenness, a surge of the wave of Intellect.[46] This is, explicitly, an erotic moment, not simply a 'rational' one. The end is that of a lover at rest in the beloved,[47] precisely because it is in such moments that we are most aware of where we are. We are, in brief, being urged to recognize in our most intimate occasions just the form of life which it is possible to practise and live by. Let us love more than symmetry and order: better a live face – even an *ugly* face – than a dead statue.[48] Let us recover beauty (which is to say, let us be reminded of our own life) – and be so swept up into that devotion as to forget ourselves, our independence, and be united in contemplation of – well, of what exactly?

What is the One? The answer seems to be – 'the productive power of all things'.[49] Plotinus shows how intellect is carried out of itself, how we depend on myths and theurgic meditations and the passion of love, to fall in love at last with Love himself. The One is unique, indeed – but very far from solitary. The One is everywhere – but not because it fills a pre-existent space. Rather, every place and every entity exists in love. The One *is* Love, and therefore a Trinity in Unity: it is 'lovable and love and love of himself (*erasmion kai eros ho autos kai autou eros*)'.[50] 'Many people', said Armstrong years ago, 'are looking for an unorganized and unorganizable Good as the only true object of worship, the source of value and the goal of desire, whose light shines everywhere in this ever-changing world as we contemplate it with our ever-changing minds.'[51] That Good promises a future which is always other than our present, an infinite realm of possibility that will be forever filled to overflowing with the forms of beauty,[52] 'boiling with life'. The God of Plotinus, quite as much as the God of Abraham, is the God of an infinite future.

I am here partly endorsing Armstrong's suggestion that Plotinus' account of the One actually marks the *end* of two-world thinking – 'the Good does

---

46 *Ennead* VI.7 [38].35, 24–7; 6, 17–18.

47 *Ennead* VI.9 [9].4; for further discussion of Plotinus' use of erotic metaphor see Zeke Mazur, 'Having Sex with the One', in Panayiota Vassilopoulou and Stephen R. L. Clark, eds, *Other Ways of Seeing: Late Antique Epistemology* (Basingstoke: PalgraveMacmillan, forthcoming).

48 *Ennead* VI.7 [38].22.

49 *Ennead* III.8 [30].10; see Eric D. Perl, 'The Power of All Things', *ACPQ* 71, 1997, pp. 301–13.

50 *Ennead* VI.8 [39].15. This is the better analogue of the Christian Trinity: Father, Son and Holy Spirit. The usual comparison with One, Intellect and Soul is misjudged – but that is another and longer story.

51 A. H. Armstrong, 'The Escape of the One', *Studia Patristica* 13, 1975, pp. 77–89 (*Plotinian and Christian Studies*, op. cit., ch. XXIII), p. 88.

52 *Ennead* VI.7 [38].15.

not give us a share in his own ideas: he has not got any. He creates ideas in us to supply our needs at the time . . . The Eternal Mind seems to become something very like our minds seeking God, and the Eternal World our world seen from the inside.'[53]

Where I think Armstrong is mistaken is in his disregard of the myths that Plotinus chose to allegorize. He comments a little later, for example – *a propos* of Plotinus' recognition of the star-gods – that 'it would be difficult for us, imaginatively as well as intellectually, to recognize and venerate the goddess Selene in the dreary, dusty receptacle for excessively expensive junk with which we have all become so boringly familiar of late years'.[54] On the contrary, we have cause to be grateful, in a way, to just that goddess. Looking only at the material, we may suppose that the moon, Selene, is indeed no more than rubble. But consider instead what it is to look back from the moon. Consider the images of earth seen from the moon which have decorated websites and student bedrooms for the last many years. That vision of our little segment of the wider world, the blue and silver bubble against a darkened sky, has helped to remind us – at the deepest imaginative level – that we do indeed inhabit a single, beautiful world, and that our political and social divisions must fade before that insight. Looking in turn towards the moon herself, what we should see is the love that binds, the universal sympathy that makes causality possible. What Plotinus called magic we now recognize as universal law – but our words make no clearer than Plotinus' what explains that law, that magic. Those who can think of the moon – or the earth itself – as no more than rubble may indeed feel themselves to be in that imagined hell which Armstrong evoked in his – somewhat exaggerated – account of third-century sensibility:

> It was a period in which the sense of individual isolation in a vast and ter-rifying universe was perhaps more intensely felt than even immediately after the breakdown of the city-state into the Hellenistic world. For in the Roman Empire, under Babylonian influence, the view of the ruling power of the universe as a cruel, inaccessible Fate, embodied in the stars, worship of which was useless, had come to its full development. The indi-vidual exposed to the crushing power of this Fate, and the citizen also of

---

53 Armstrong, 'Escape', pp. 84, 85; see also Michael Wagner, 'Plotinus's World': *Dionysius* 6, 1982, pp. 13–42.

54 'The Apprehension of Divinity in the Self and Cosmos in Plotinus', in R. Baines Harris (ed.), *The Significance of NeoPlatonism*, Studies in Neoplatonism, Vol. 1 (Norfolk, VA: Old Dominion University, 1976), pp. 187–98), reprinted in *Plotinian and Christian Studies*, op. cit., ch. XVIII, p. 192.

an earthly state which seemed almost as vast, cruel and indifferent as the universe, felt to the full the agony of his isolation and limitation.[55]

The hell-world is one that we ourselves create, by looking on things as meaningless collections or expanses of stuff, by grabbing things for ourselves, by ignoring the larger world. That is why Matter as such is Evil – not because bodies are evil, but because when we see bodies (that is, entities) as so much stuff, we despise them, and head further down into depression. Plotinus asks us to internalize the myths and metaphors of traditional Greek religion with a view to reconstructing, reorienting our imaginations: they aren't just literary allusions.

And what, finally, does Plotinus' One have to do with God, with the God of Abraham or the God of Jesus? I suggest that by grappling with Plotinus we can in fact get a little closer to a renewed understanding of the myths, rituals and saintly exemplars with which we decorate that movement of the spirit that is true, Abrahamic religion. As long as we suppose that either the One, or God, is a merely abstract principle, or alternatively that it names an incomprehensible despot, we shall *misunderstand* both. The God of Abraham may indeed be different from the God of the Philosophers – but so, on a plausible reading, is Plotinus' One. We encounter the One – in little – on those occasions when we recognize the valuable being of another, when that unnamed and unique other *requires* our full devotion, when we are carried onward 'by the swell of intellect' to rest within the beloved. What matters is that we should not dissipate or corrupt that vision, that divine drunkenness, but seek to live from it, without greed or fear, in worship of what we cannot name or grasp. 'Believing in the One', on a first approximation, is setting ourselves to seeing things clearly and to seeing them whole, and feeling disdain for none. It is as true for Plotinus as for the Christian Church that being lies in communion,[56] that we are invited to join 'the dance of immortal love'.[57]

The details of the doctrine that encapsulates that vision are open to reasoned discussion, and to the lifelong exploration of the spiritual exercises that he and others have suggested. It may even be that the scandal of particularity, which divides Christendom from its Abrahamic fellows, is something that can be accommodated in the Plotinian view. And questions about the reality, and meaning, of doctrines of immortality shared – and

55 A. H. Armstrong, 'Plotinus and India', *Classical Quarterly* 30, 1936, pp. 22–8; reprinted in *Plotinian and Christian Studies* (London: Variorum Reprints, 1979), ch. I, p. 28.
56 *Pace* S. Mark Heim, 'The Depth of the Riches: Trinity and Religious Ends', in *Modern Theology* 17, 2001, pp. 21–55. Heim's account of Trinitarian theology is otherwise an excellent one.
57 Porphyry, *Life of Plotinus* 23.36f., after 22.54ff.

disputed – by Plotinus and the Abrahamic faiths, also require some thought. I end by simply affirming that the Plotinian theorems still seem to me to be, at least, the sort of images that we should welcome: not merely propositions, but pictorial invocations of the God.

Believing in God is putting our trust in a certain way of seeing, and seeking to live out of that insight. 'It does no good at all to say "Look to God", unless one also teaches how one is to look':[58] Plotinus made every effort to teach us.

---

58 *Ennead* II.9 [33].15, 33.

3

Thinking, Attending, Praying

NICHOLAS LASH

On watching one's language

In the autumn of 1968, shortly after moving to Cambridge, I took part in a seminar in which one of the other participants was the Australian Jesuit theologian, Gerald O'Collins. I have often quoted a remark which he made on that occasion. A theologian, he said, is someone who 'watches their language in the presence of God'. To which admirable definition I have sometimes added the gloss: a philosopher is someone who watches their language.

But, of course, philosophers who are also religious believers will know that they do *all* the things they do in the presence of God, including watching their language. Does this mean that such people, when they engage in philosophical practices, are not in fact doing philosophy at all, but, whether they wish it or not, are doing theology?

That would be a curious conclusion, and one way of avoiding it might be to change the subject from what one might call the 'style' of intellectual practices to their subject-matter. A rather better way, I want to suggest, would be to sustain alertness to misleading hypostatization and never to forget that, as Bernard Lonergan said to my uncle, Sebastian Moore, at their first meeting, 'Concepts have dates.'

Before attending to these issues, and staying for a moment with the question that I have just raised, it would, I think, be odd to call Wittgenstein a theologian, even if a good case can be made for saying that 'he constructed his later philosophy very much on the basis of bits and pieces of what it is easy to regard as central to Catholicism'.[1] More generally, Fergus Kerr, who makes this case persuasively, says that 'whatever else needs to be said, Wittgenstein's work, early and late, reaches back to the ancient practice of

---

1 Fergus Kerr, '*Work on Oneself*': *Wittgenstein's Philosophical Psychology* (Arlington, VA: The Institute for the Psychological Sciences Press, 2008), p. 46.

philosophy as a "way of life" – as "spiritual exercises"'.[2] And the correct
rejoinder, I suggest, to the objection that Wittgenstein is hardly a typical
philosopher, would be: who is?

Avoiding 'faith' and 'reason'

Anyone who knew Donald MacKinnon at all well will remember having heard
him thunderously denouncing the illusion that 'to every substantive there is a
corresponding substance'. Talking about 'faith' and 'reason', and about the
relationships between them, easily coaxes us into supposing that they are the
names of different *things*. There is a whiff of this in the reference, in an otherwise excellent commentary on Pope John Paul II's encyclical *Fides et Ratio*, to
'the encounter between Christian faith and the human mind'.[3] Where else
does Christian faith exist, for goodness' sake, except within the human mind?
Where, then, was this faith before such an encounter took place?

On the Feast of the Epiphany, 1839, Newman preached a sermon before
the University of Oxford entitled 'Faith and Reason, Contrasted as Habits
of Mind'.[4] Habits of mind, ways of behaving as human beings.[5] Habits of
mind, moreover, which, although they may be, and frequently are, contrasted, may also be considered, as I shall seek to do later in this essay, in
respect of certain similiarities.

In an essay entitled 'The Diversity of Philosophy and the Unity of its Vocation: Some Philosophical Reflections on *Fides et Ratio*', John Haldane picks
out, as the first of three 'obligations for contemporary philosophy', according to the encyclical, the need 'to recover the sapiential dimension of the discipline'.[6] He is, I believe, correct in seeing this as among the most important
and original features of the encyclical, not least in its implication that any
philosophy which concentrates exclusively on technical rigour, to the neglect
of any interest in being not only well argued but also contributing to human
wisdom, is seriously impoverished. Yet even here we need to be attentive to

2 Ibid., p. 45.
3 James McEvoy, 'Commentary', in Laurence Paul Hemming and Susan Frank Parsons (eds),
Restoring Faith in Reason (London: SCM Press, 2002), pp. 175–98; 191.
4 John Henry Newman, *Sermons, Chiefly on the Theory of Religious Belief* (London: Rivington,
1843), pp. 167–93.
5 Janet Martin Soskice sees the 'distinctive contribution' of the encyclical *Fides et Ratio* as con-
sisting in the fact that 'whereas so much English-language philosophy of religion takes the
issue of *faith and reason* to be *au fond* epistemological, the Pope sees it as . . . to do with our
concept of the human person' ('*Fides et Ratio*: The Post-modern Pope', *Restoring Faith in
Reason*, pp. 292–6; 292.
6 John Haldane, 'The Diversity of Philosophy and the Unity of its Vocation: Some Philosophical Reflections on *Fides et Ratio*', in *Faithful Reason: Essays Catholic and Philosophical*
(London: Routledge, 2006), pp. 31–42; 33.

the history of the terms we use, and of their referents. There is indeed, these days, a 'discipline' of philosophy, in the sense that there are departments with a subject of that name in most universities. However, the distinctions that we draw today between 'philosophy' and 'science' were only worked out in the nineteenth century. When the University of Cambridge, in the 1840s, established Honours examinations in moral philosophy, political economy, modern history and law, it did so under the general description of the Moral Sciences. (And to this day the Cambridge 'Philosophical Society', established in 1819, admits only natural scientists to its membership.)

It is, I believe, a significant weakness of *Fides et Ratio* that John Paul II tended to work with an historically inadequate sense of the range of intellectual practices that 'philosophy' has named. Thus the assertion that 'Saint Albert the Great and Saint Thomas . . . were the first learned men to admit the necessary autonomy that philosophy and the sciences needed, so that each should depend upon arguments belonging to their own sphere' is, I believe, anachronistic, as is the claim that the Fifth Lateran Council's confirmation, in 1517, of the decision that 'before the study of the theological *curriculum* begins, a period of time must be allotted to the special study of philosophy', had 'its roots in the experience of the Middle Ages', when the Council was, surely, simply stipulating that students for the priesthood, before they entered into the study of theology, should have received a good general education.[7]

There is no one thing called 'faith', and no one thing called 'reason', and the 'habits of mind', or mental practices, which these two terms connote are vastly more varied than is usually acknowledged by those who insist that they are not only different but fundamentally antagonistic. It would be interesting to see what results one got if one asked a group of people unversed in academic philosophy to discuss the differences and similarities between 'faith' and 'reason', and another group to discuss the differences and similarities between 'believing' and 'reasoning'. The second group might, more quickly than the first, reach the conclusion that there is not much reasoning one can do without believing something.

In recommending, for the reasons indicated, that we do better to speak, not of the relations between 'faith' and 'reason', but rather of the relations between 'believing' and 'reasoning', it is not at all my intention to suggest that we should, as it were, sidle away from the stern demands of faith, as understood in traditional Christianity, into what might seem the safe and shallow waters of 'believing' – this, that, or the other. On the contrary, I would wholeheartedly endorse the traditional insistence on the *fidelity* that

---

7 *Fides et Ratio*, 45, 62. See Lash, '*Visio Unica et Ordinata Scientiae?*', *Restoring Faith in Reason*, pp. 225–36; 233.

faith requires, '*usque ad effusionem sanguinis*', even to the shedding of blood, in martyrdom. Yet 'faith', thus understood, remains one of three forms of credence, or believing, classically distinguished by Augustine.[8]

Loch Ness theology

When invited to comment, nearly 20 years ago, on the first draft of that uneven compendium, *The Catechism of the Catholic Church*, I remember being alarmed to see that the opening section was entitled 'Man in Search of God'. This is what I call Loch Ness theology: a story, a construct of modern rationalist impertinence, of plucky little *homo sapiens* striding out into the great unknown, anxiously seeking for some evidence that, somewhere out there in all this darkness, deity may be discerned. Those inclined to set out on this search would be advised, before doing so, to consider Donald MacKinnon's remark that 'man is brought face to face with God, not through his effort, but through his failure'.[9]

When Hegel remarked that 'God does not offer himself for observation',[10] he was not denying that we may come to some knowledge, some glimmer of understanding, of the mystery of God, but insisting that God is not, as it were, available to be picked up with conceptual tweezers, inspected, dissected, evaluated. The Creator does not lie in wait for his creation. As I have remarked elsewhere, there is always good work to be done on the question of God, work as intellectually rigorous and demanding as in any other field of study, and yet there is a sense in which if such work is not done, at least metaphorically, on one's knees, then it will miss the mark.[11] It may find something, but it will not be God that it finds.

If we are creatures, then we are, as creatures, absolutely dependent, in every fibre of our being, on God's creative utterance. God speaks a Word, one Word, the Word God is, the Word that finds expression in all the things there are and (on a Christian understanding of these things) finds fullest focus, flesh, in Jesus Christ. Christians, like Jews, and Muslims, are people who have learned that all the world, and everything we are and have, is utterance, is gift, expression of God's love.

'The supreme insight of the distinctively Christian doctrine of God', said Donald MacKinnon, is the recognition of 'the primacy of the divine initia-

---

8 For a brief account of the sense of 'believe' in its credal use: 'I believe in one God', and of Augustine's distinctions between '*credere Deo*', '*credere Deum*', and '*credere IN Deum*', see Nicholas Lash, *Believing Three Ways in One God* (London: SCM Press, 1992), pp. 17–22.

9 D. M. MacKinnon, *God the Living and the True* (London: Dacre Press, 1940), p. 76.

10 G. W. F. Hegel, *Lectures on the Philosophy of Religion, 1: Introduction and Concept of Religion*, ed. Peter C. Hodgson (Berkeley: University of California Press, 1984), p. 258.

11 See Nicholas Lash, *Theology for Pilgrims* (London: Darton, Longman & Todd, 2008), pp. 27–8.

tive'.[12] An insistence echoed by a pupil of his: 'The language of revelation is used to express the sense of an initiative that does not lie with us and to challenge the myth of the self-constitution of consciousness'.[13] Earlier in the same essay, warning that theology 'is perennially liable to be seduced by the prospect of bypassing the question of how it learns its own language', he lamented the extent to which so much theology, 'liberal' and 'conservative' alike, 'still operates with a model of truth as something separable *in our minds* from the dialectical process of its historical reflection and appropriation'.[14]

Loch Ness theology supposes that the initiative does, indeed, lie with us, imagines that it might make sense for us to search for God, supposes us to have to hand appropriate criteria for identifying God, should we succeed in finding him. A less misleading image of our human journey would be to say that human beings are set, not on a voyage of discovery of their own invention, but on a process of lifelong learning to which they have been called. Human beings are pupils, called to listen, to attend, to learn. The textbooks used to distinguish 'general' or 'natural' revelation, God's utterance in all the things there are, an utterance only audible, however, 'as a question, not an answer',[15] from 'special' revelation, that 'clarification' of the question of God[16] that is the history of Judaism, Christianity and, perhaps, Islam (I say 'perhaps' because it seems to me that one of the challenges confronting Christians with increasing urgency is to work out the sense in which they are able to acknowledge the revelatory status of the Qur'an. Where official Catholic teaching is concerned, it is worth reporting the second Vatican Council's acknowledgement that the Church 'looks with esteem' upon Muslims because 'they adore one God, living and enduring, merciful and all-powerful, Maker of heaven and earth, and *Speaker to men*'[17]).

On this account, all human beings are pupils, but Jews, Christians and Muslims believe that they have something more to say about what is meant and entailed by being, all our life, at school.

---

12 MacKinnon, *God the Living and the True*, p. 81. Distinctively Christian, but not exclusively so, for the same is true at least of Judaism and Islam.

13 Rowan Williams, 'Trinity and Revelation', *Modern Theology*, Vol. 2, No. 3, April 1986, pp. 197–212; 200.

14 Ibid., pp. 197–8 (my stress).

15 Karl Rahner and Herbert Vorgrimler, 'Revelation', in Cornelius Ernst (ed.), tr. Richard Strachan, *Concise Theological Dictionary* (London: Burns and Oates, 1965), p. 410.

16 I have in mind another remark of Rahner's: 'The answer given in revelation clarifies the question a man asks' ('The Foundation of Belief', in *Theological Investigations* XVI, tr. David Morland (London: Darton, Longman & Todd, 1979)), pp. 3–23; 9.

17 Declaration *Nostra Aetate*, art. 3.

Academies of attentiveness

Once upon a time, 'religion' named a virtue, a virtue similar to justice. To act justly is to give other people their due; to be religious is a matter of giving God God's due. In an Aristotelian ethical framework, of course, acting virtuously is a matter of steering a path between opposing vices. In the matter of religion, these opposing vices are the failure to give God God's due either, on the one hand, by treating him as a thing: as some entity or idea which we might pick over, comprehend, master or manipulate; or, on the other hand, by treating some thing as God: by setting our hearts on, bowing down before, ourselves, our country, money, sex, or 'reason' (idolatry is endlessly diverse).

In the fifteenth century, 'religion' began to name communities of men and women whose lives were specially dedicated to the exercise of this virtue. The communities they called 'religions' we would call religious orders. Marsilio Ficino's *De Christiana Religione*, in 1474, marks a shift towards presenting 'religion' as a universal impulse implanted in the human heart. Religion is thus interiorized and abstracted from particular contexts of ecclesial practice. One more step, taken during the sixteenth and seventeenth centuries, removed religion entirely from its status as a virtue. It now became a set of privately entertained beliefs without direct public or political relevance or impact. It was now entirely a private matter for the individual 'soul' (not the *'anima'* of traditional Christianity, but the newly invented Cartesian 'consciousness'), for the body – the public self – had been handed over to the State.[18] It is hardly surprising that, three centuries later, religion has come to be widely regarded as simply a private pastime in which people may indulge if they happen to have a taste for it.[19] Nor is it surprising that, since the term nevertheless still carries ancient overtones of public life and conduct, of established norms and practices, many people prefer to describe the games they play in the private playgrounds of Cartesian consciousness not as religion but as 'spirituality'.

One outcome of this history of what 'religion' might mean is that Christianity – an ineluctably public fact with distinctive memories, practices and institutions – has become, with bewildering rapidity, widely unintelligible

---

18 See William T. Cavanaugh, '"A Fire Strong Enough to Consume the House": the Wars of Religion and the Rise of the State', *Modern Theology*, October 1995, pp. 397–420; a fine essay which draws on Wilfrid Cantwell Smith, *The Meaning and the End of Religion* (New York: Macmillan, 1962) and John Figgis, *From Gerson to Grotius, 1414–1625* (New York: Harper, 1960).

19 The philosopher A. C. Grayling sees joining a religion as analogous to joining the Scouts: see Grayling, 'The Rise of Miliband Brings 'at Last the Prospect of an Atheist Prime Minister', The *Guardian*, 21 August 2008, p. 29.

in our culture. In this situation, if Christians[20] wish not only to be better understood by others, but appropriately to understand *themselves*, then they would be well advised to seek some other descriptive framework for being a Christian than that of belonging to a 'religion'.

I have long argued that Christianity does have an appropriate descriptive category to hand in the resources of its own tradition. The central argument of the Teape Lectures which I gave in India in 1994 was to the effect that 'the modern dissociation of memory from argument, of narrative from reason, made us forget how deeply all understanding and imagination is shaped by memory, coloured by circumstance, constituted by tradition. With this forgetfulness we lost sight of the extent to which the ancient traditions of devotion and reflection, of worship and enquiry, have seen themselves as *schools*', schools whose pedagogy 'has the twofold purpose – however differently conceived and executed in the different traditions – of weaning us from our idolatry and purifying our desire'.[21]

The proposal is hardly revolutionary. To be a Christian, I suggested earlier, is to be a pupil. That is what the word 'disciple' means, as does the Greek term in the New Testament which it translates: μαθητης, the pupil of a rabbi. And, if we are pupils, then presumably we are members of some kind of school.

Taking a short-cut through the historical and philosophical undergrowth, I shall assume that 'gods' are whatever people worship, have their hearts set on, and that the word is neither the name common to all members of a class of things called 'gods', nor, by the cunning acquisition of an initial capital, the proper name of the holy mystery on which the world depends. The word 'god' names, not this or that class or individual, but whatever it is that someone worships.

The project of learning to worship, to give one's whole heart, to hand one's whole life over, to absolutely cherish, yet without worshipping any person, nation, fact, idea or thing (especially not oneself) may be incoherent or irrational, but it certainly is not stoicism!

It is, however, coherent and entirely rational if it is a matter of acknowledging, with all one's heart as well as with one's head, that we and all things are, in the last analysis, not brute facts but creatures, gifts lovingly and absolutely given; gifts for which we are enabled to give thanks in praise. The question of God is, in the last analysis, the question of which kind of thing things are, and this is not the kind of question which can be sorted out in

20 And members of cognate traditions: Jews, Muslims and others. See my Teape Lectures, the first three chapters of *The Beginning and the End of 'Religion'* (Cambridge: Cambridge University Press, 1996). I would ask the reader to keep this in mind as, for clarity's sake, I illustrate my broader argument through Christianity.

21 Lash, *The Beginning and the End of 'Religion'*, p. 21.

theory before we attempt enacting a response, living as if one account of what things are is true, the other false.

I called the other side of the pedagogy of the Christian school 'the purification of desire'. We talk about learning to think straight. I wish we had an expression for learning to love straight, learning to desire straight. The classical name for what I am talking about is, of course, 'detachment', but I suspect that, to modern ears, that sounds suspiciously like disinterestedness or, even worse, like standing aloof, not getting involved. But, by detachment, the tradition meant being weaned off *in*appropriate attachments, loves which consume and enslave, rather than cherishing and liberating the beloved. Lust and idolatry are closely related.

Idolatry and misplaced desire are forms of folly. The antithesis of folly is wisdom. Christianity, in other words, is supposed to be a school of wisdom, an education into truth. 'When the Spirit of truth comes,' says Jesus in the fourth Gospel, 'he will guide you into all truth.'[22] Commenting on that verse, Augustine remarked: 'That cannot be loved which is altogether unknown. But when what is *known*, in however small a measure, is also loved, by the self-same *love* one is led on to a better and fuller *knowledge*.'[23] That is how wisdom grows; as a deepening grasp of reality by heart as well as head.

According to Aquinas, wisdom is the art of sound judgement. But we judge, and thereby display our wisdom or our foolishness, in different ways. On the one hand, there is the almost intuitive sureness of touch of the person who has their head screwed on and their heart in the right place. This is the wisdom of the virtuous that is the Spirit's gift. It has nothing to do with erudition or the lack of it; it is calibrated on a different axis. On the other hand, there are judgements that are the fruit of reasoning and reflection. There is, therefore, a wisdom that is the fruit of study. Wisdom in the second sense is dependent on wisdom in the first, inasmuch as all our strenuous labour in libraries and laboratories catches some glimmer of the eternal wisdom whose self-gift, in Word and Spirit, gives us the possibility of wise or 'faith-ful' thinking in the first place.

Wisdom and detachment go hand in hand, for wisdom is the fruit of passionate disinterestedness: its sole concern is for the real, the true. That is why learning to be wise entails learning to be attentive. It may seem preposterous for someone as loquacious as myself to say so, but it follows that learning to be wise, learning to watch one's language in the presence of

---

22 John 16.13.

23 Augustine, 'Lectures or Tractates on the Gospel according to St John', tr. John Gibb and James Innes, Tractate 96.4, *A Select Library of the Nicene and Post-Nicene Fathers of the Christian Church*, ed. Philip Schaff, vol. 7, St Augustin: Homilies on the Gospel of John, Homilies on the First Epistle of John, Soliloquies (Edinburgh: T. & T. Clark, 1888), p. 373.

God, is a matter of learning not to *chatter*, learning to be still. Hence my heading for this section: Christianity is, or is supposed to be, 'a kind of school of silence, an academy of attentiveness'.[24] I was, I think, fortunate in first learning about prayer as a boy in the school at Downside and later, for some months, as a novice in the monastery there. There is, in the admirable sanity of the Benedictine tradition, nothing in the least *esoteric* about contemplation. Perhaps it is the influence of that tradition which persuades me of the importance of considering the relations between the familiar activities of praying and thinking.

To be attentive is to stay awake, and this, in all the pain and darkness of the world, is exceedingly difficult to do. The paradigm of the attentiveness we need remains Gethsemane. In the garden, Jesus remained attentive to the Father's silence – while the disciples, unfortunately, slept.

'Contemplata aliis tradere'

At one point in the *Summa*, Aquinas, considering what we would probably nowadays call Christ's 'life-style', asks whether, instead of dealing as he did with other people, it would not have been better for him to have led a solitary life, the life of a hermit perhaps, because surely the contemplative life is, as Aquinas himself had argued earlier, the most perfect form of Christian living: '*perfectissima vita*'. This is true enough in the abstract, he replies, but, in practice, even more perfect is the active life of those who, through preaching and teaching, hand on to others the fruits of contemplation: '*vita activa, secundum quam aliquis praedicando et docendo contemplata aliis tradit*'.[25] Hence the Dominican motto: '*Contemplata aliis tradere*', which we might perhaps paraphrase as: 'Handing on to others the fruits of our attentiveness'.

I mention this because it seems to me that it is an admirable motto, not only for Dominicans, not only for theologians generally, but for all those engaged in every kind of teaching and research. It is as good a motto for the physicist or molecular biologist as it is for the philosopher or theologian.

Some years ago the issue of 'realism versus anti-realism' was much debated among philosophers of science. Not so much, I think, among the scientists. When comparing the 'habits of mind' of theologians with those of natural scientists, their most striking common feature, it seems to me, is what I earlier called a passionate disinterestedness in enquiry after truth not of our construction.

---

24 Nicholas Lash, *Holiness, Speech and Silence: Reflections on the Question of God* (Aldershot: Ashgate, 2004), p. 93.
25 *Summa Theologiae* IIIa, 40, 1, ad 2.

We can, I think, go one step further. I said earlier that believing in God entails the recognition that everything there is is, in the last analysis, gift. The Danish historian of astronomy, Olaf Pedersen (a very dear friend who was my son's godfather), in an essay on 'Christian Belief and the Fascination of Science', once quoted the Austrian physicist, Wolfgang Pauli, as saying: 'The subject-matter gives a lot away'.[26] It would, of course, be easy to dismiss this use of the metaphor of 'donation' because, although we still speak of 'data', the metaphor has gone quite dead, and no one asks, these days, who gives these gifts. Nevertheless, Pedersen picked up Pauli's expression because he wished to argue that, in practice, the labour of the scientist, no less than of the theologian, often goes well beyond the rigorous disinterestedness required in every serious search for truth, to something more like wonder, awe, a kind of reverence.

When, a few years ago, I was asked to read a paper to the Danish Science–Theology Forum at the University of Aarhus, where Pedersen had taught for many years, it was that essay of his which suggested the title of my paper: 'Attending in Wonder to the World: The Common Responsibility of Christian Theology and the Natural Sciences'.[27]

'Docta ignorantia': addressing the dark

Having suggested that the scientific and theological 'habits of mind' have neglected affinities, fundamental differences between them nevertheless remain, the most basic of which arises from our nescience of God's nature.

Thomas Aquinas could be quite succinct. The first two questions of the *Summa* discuss the enterprise of 'holy teaching', in which he is engaged, and whether it is appropriate to say of God that he 'exists'. In any enquiry, however, in order to acquire knowledge of something, we need to consider not only *whether* it exists, but *how* it does and *what* it is: not only '*an sit?*', but '*quomodo sit?*' and '*quid sit?*'. But, he goes on, we can't know what God is, but only what he isn't: '*de Deo scire non possumus quid sit sed quid non sit*'.[28]

Simple as that. No ifs and buts. He then gets down to considering the ways in which God does not exist, a discussion which occupies 150 pages of close argument. Our nescience of God's nature is not a matter of straightforward ignorance: if it were, the *Summa* might have been a great deal

---

26 Olaf Pedersen, 'Christian Belief and the Fascination of Science', in Robert J. Russell, William R. Stoeger SJ and George V. Coyne SJ (eds), *Physics, Philosophy and Theology: A Common Quest for Understanding* (Vatican Observatory, Vatican City, 1988), pp. 125–40; 133.
27 The paper was included in Nils Henrik Gregersen, Kees van Kooten Niekirk and Knud Ochsner (eds), *Science and Theology: Twin Sisters?* (Aarhus: University of Aarhus, 2002), pp. 1–24.
28 Prologue to *Summa Theologiae* I, qq. 3–11.

shorter! Nor does it arise from lack of *information*: in such schools as Christianity, Judaism and Islam, there is much that we may learn of God. Ours is an 'educated ignorance': a '*docta ignorantia*'. If, nevertheless, neither the greatest theologian nor the wisest saint knows God's nature, their insuperable unknowing is due to the inability of language and imagination hewn from the wood of the world to comprehend the world's creator. (To the extent, although it would take too long to elaborate the suggestion, that I think it well worth considering whether the very notion of God's 'nature' is not misleadingly anthropomorphic, because it seems to imply that God is a thing of some kind, a divine kind; but kinds and categories are the framework of the world.)

People sometimes talk of 'negative theology' as if there were two kinds of theology: one which consisted in saying things about God, and another which consisted in denying them! Newman was nearer the mark: 'We can only speak of Him, whom we reason about but have not seen, in the terms of our experience . . . We can only set right one error of expression by another. By this method of antagonism we steady our minds, not so as to reach their object, but to point them in the right direction; as in an algebraical process we might add and subtract in series, approximating, little by little, to a positive result.'[29]

Just two more points. The first is that one reason why it does not seem adequate to describe our acknowledged nescience of God's nature as 'agnosticism' is that we are enabled, indeed required, to respond to God in prayer. In praying we *address* the dark, sometimes to the point of crying to the silence which surrounds us as the voice of God. 'Fear', said Nadezhda Mandelstam, 'is a gleam of hope, the will to live.'[30] Here, as elsewhere, the paradigm of our experience remains the Garden of Gethsemane.

Finally, even if there is little we can say straightforwardly of God, there are things which we can say quite straightforwardly about the world as God's creation. Of these, the most important is that, in all the darkness of the world, everything there is, is being given, and given with unfeasible fidelity, the expression of 'l'amor che move il sole e l'altre stelle'.[31]

29 John Henry Newman, *The Theological Papers of John Henry Newman on Faith and Certainty*, Hugo M. de Achaval and J. Derek Holmes (eds) (Oxford: Clarendon Press, 1976), p. 102.

30 Nadezhda Mandelstam, *Hope Against Hope: A Memoir*, tr. Max Hayward (London: CollinsHarvill, 1989), p. 42.

31 Dante Alighieri, *Paradiso*, Canto 33, 145.

4

Mystery, World and Religion

DAVID E. COOPER

In the first part of this essay, I want briefly to describe the path that led me to think that reality as it 'anyway' is, independently of human perspective, is mysterious. Here 'mysterious' is to be understood in a strong way: mystery is what cannot, even in principle, be conceptualized or literally articulated. It is not, to borrow Kant's useful term, 'discursable'. Any world which is discursable is a 'human world' – one that is the way it is only in relation to human perspective. In the final part of the essay, I ask how the idea of mystery, so reached and understood, relates to the notion of God and, more widely, to religion. The question of this relationship can only be addressed, however, after another relationship has been discussed – one between mystery and the human world. Discussion of this relationship is the business of the middle section of the essay.

A path to mystery

Many people – those we call 'mystics', but not just those – have come to a sense of the mystery of reality through special experiences which they have had or claim to have had. My own life has not, I hope, been entirely devoid of Tintern Abbey moments – ones of a kind which, if people are forced to speak of them, have them calling on a poetic vocabulary of 'mysterious presence', of something 'deep' that 'rolls through all things', and so on. Though, in my own case, it has tended to be littler and more humble things than great ruined abbeys which have had me groping for the appropriate terms – things like the frog-plopping, bird-cheeping and bamboo-rustling that have been the occasions for Zen poets to communicate their sense of the mystery of things. But it is not these experiences or moments which have fashioned my path to mystery. This has been a more intellectual, a more philosophical path. Though – who knows? – maybe this philosophizing would have struck me as too dry, too abstract, and would have failed to go deep with me, except in conjunction with experiences that I am tempted to construe as intimations of mystery.

I do not want the story of this philosophical path to become a self-indulgent and interminable *Bildungsroman*, so I'll begin it in 1990, when I had already reached an age well beyond the range of any *Bildungsroman* I have ever read. In that year, I published a book called *Existentialism: A Reconstruction*.[1] A proper *Bildungsroman* would, no doubt, record that writing this book marked a return to a boyhood fascination with Sartre and Nietzsche that was, for many years, extinguished by my philosophical education at Oxford. A glance at the cover blurb of the book reminds me that it was intended to provide a 'sympathetic account of a movement of thought, reconstructed from the best writings of Heidegger, Sartre, Merleau-Ponty and others'. And certainly there was much in these writings with which I had, and still have, sympathy.

To begin with, existentialism starts with a good issue, one that, arguably, drives the whole enterprise of philosophy. Philosophy, wrote Novalis, is a kind of 'homesickness'. In effect, this is an endorsement of Hegel's vision of philosophy as spirit's struggle to overcome the alienation that is consequent on spirit's opposing itself, as the realm of freedom, to a natural realm that is 'out-and-out other' to spirit. Twentieth-century existentialists may not have used quite that vocabulary, but for them, too, the central issue was how human beings – crucially distinguished from all other beings by their freedom – could, without lapsing into inauthenticity or 'bad faith', recover from a sense of estrangement from the world. Impressive, too, in my judgement, is the crucial move made by existential phenomenologists to resolve this issue. Sartre sums up this move when he writes that human beings are those 'by whom it happens that *there is* a world'[2] – when, that is, he proposes that any world we can discursively encounter is a human world, one that is how it is only in relation to 'the human contribution', as William James called it. Nothing – to switch to a more Heideggerian idiom – would 'show up' or 'light up' for us except in relation to our aims, desires and perspectives. The world, as Heidegger understands it, is comparable to a language – a giant 'referential totality' in which each thing has significance only as part of a whole, a whole whose significance in turn depends on being 'for-the-sake-of' *Dasein*.[3]

I was and still am sympathetic, therefore, to the concomitant demonstration – by Husserl, Heidegger and Merleau-Ponty – that the claim of modern

1 Oxford: Blackwell, 1990, 2nd revised edn, 1999.

2 *Being and Nothingness: An Essay on Phenomenological Ontology*, tr. H. Barnes (London: Methuen, 1957), p. 552.

3 *Being and Time*, tr. J. Macquarrie and E. Robinson (Oxford: Blackwell, 1978), §18.

science, today's front-runner in the competition to provide an 'absolute' account of the world, is bogus. The scientific account of the world owes too much to an all-too-human 'ground-plan', and to the privileging (driven by discernibly practical, technological interests) of a certain style of explanation (causal, roughly), to be viewed as offering an objective, absolute account of the world and as having succeeded, therefore, in weeding out the human contribution.

During the decade after 1990, I did not lose my existentialist sympathies, but – eclectically influenced by, among others, Zhuangzi, Hugo von Hofmannsthal, Gabriel Marcel, (post-*Kehre*) Heidegger, and Thomas Nagel – I became increasingly antipathetic to a much-trumpeted aspect of existentialism, at least of the Sartrean variety. His position struck me more and more as an impossibly raw and hubristic style of humanism. What I have in mind here is the claim, or boast, that human commitments, values and perspectives neither permit nor require any warrant beyond themselves – for there is no 'beyond' for them to answer to. In Sartre's words, 'There is no legislator' but man, so that 'life is a game' whose 'principles man himself ordains'. It is not, of course, just card-carrying existentialists who have made such boasts: indeed, they became almost *de rigueur* among followers of several late-twentieth-century philosophical fashions. Richard Rorty, for instance, proclaimed that our beliefs and values can only be 'obedient to our own conventions', while the novelist Alain Robbe-Grillet announced that, by 'modern men' like himself, who take the 'emptiness' of everything on the chin, 'the absence of meaning' beyond what we project onto the world is not felt as any kind of 'lack' or 'distress'.[4]

This raw humanism is hubristic since it attributes to human beings a capacity they do not have – that of genuinely living with the thought that nothing they commit themselves to, none of the values and beliefs they embrace, can be answerable to anything beyond this commitment and embrace. Those who make claim to possession of such a capacity are guilty of 'bullshit', in the sense made familiar by Harry Frankfurt. They cannot really believe what they saying – not at any rate when they are outside of their studies and engaged in the thick of things. For, when immersed in the stream of life, we are required to make decisions, take directions and pursue objectives that it is impossible for us to regard as having no further authority than their being the ones we happen to have made, taken and pursued. If that were the only authority, then it could not have mattered to us if the decisions, directions and objectives had been different. And that is

4 For these and other similar utterances, see my *The Measure of Things: Humanism, Humility and Mystery* (Oxford: Clarendon Press, 2002), chs 9–10. This book elaborates the path to mystery I am briefly rehearsing in this essay.

tantamount to saying that nothing we do matters more or less than anything else. This is the thought that Kierkegaard understandably labels 'despair', and rightly argues that we may pay lip-service to, but cannot authentically internalize. For, unless the thought were successfully suppressed, it must lead to the unbearable sense that nothing one does can be worth any more than anything else one might have done instead.

I will not, here, rehearse the arguments and testimonies that convinced me of the unliveability of a humanism that is not, as it were, compensated by the thought that there is a 'beyond the human', something which could serve to give measure to our lives. Instead I want to focus on the apparent impasse to which the sympathies and antipathies I have just sketched lead. For it is the attempt to escape from this impasse that very quickly brings us to the idea of mystery.

The apparent impasse results when one rejects, as I have just done, both the absolutist contention that there is a discursable way the world anyway is, independently of human perspective, and the raw humanist claim that there is nothing beyond the human world, beyond what humanity 'legislates'. Now, it should be clear from this way of putting things that absolutism and raw, hubristic humanism are contraries rather than contradictories. They cannot both be true, but each may be false. And they will indeed both be false if the following thought is right: there is a way the world anyway and independently is, but this way is not discursable. Absolutists, according to this thought, are right to insist that reality is independent of the human contribution, but wrong to suppose that this reality can be articulated. Humanists, correspondingly, are right to maintain that any discursable world is a human one, but wrong to equate reality with this world.

How should we label the thought or doctrine that thus resolves the threatened impasse, by showing that there is an alternative to the other contenders? We might call it a radically amended absolutism that dispenses with the usual absolutist assumption that reality is describable. (Certainly this is an assumption built into the currently favoured form of absolutism – scientific realism.) Or it could be called a sort of humanism – not, of course, the raw, hubristic humanism abandoned earlier, but a compensated and humbler humanism. Better still, let's just call it a doctrine of mystery – with mystery understood as what cannot, even in principle, be literally articulated and described. Mystery cannot even be experienced if the notion of experience is invested – as by Kant, Wilfrid Sellars and others – with the requirement that experience involves the application of concepts. I am not sure that this investment is a reasonable one, and therefore I am not sure that Tintern Abbey moments should be debarred from counting as, strictly speaking, *experiences*. But I do not want to become embroiled in this sort of issue about the criteria for experience. For it should be clear that my path to mystery was not an essentially experiential one. It may be, as I allowed earlier, that in the absence of what I take to be personal experiences of 'mysterious presence', the line of thinking that led me to a doctrine of mystery as the only way of resolving a philosophical impasse would have had less appeal for me; would not, as Buddhists put it, really have 'penetrated'. But that's another, and in the present context, irrelevant, autobiographical matter.

Mystery and the human world

My path led to a doctrine of mystery that has a strategic role. A sense of mystery is to compensate for the recognition that the only discursable world is a human world, and is to provide measure for the leading of our lives, something for these to answer to. Because of this, one cannot be content simply to announce that there is the mysterious and then stay *stumm*. For while there must not, of course, be any eff-ing of the ineffable, it is essential – if a sense of mystery is to play its role – that one is offered intimations of, and an attunement to, the mysterious which enables the faith that lives led in certain ways do answer to, are consonant with, the way of things.

There are many, many rhetorics and poetries of mystery which have sought to intimate and attune to the mysterious. Daoism, Neo-Platonism, Advaita Vedanta, Mahayana Buddhism, medieval Christian and Islamic mysticism, German Transcendental Idealism, Bergsonian vitalism, Process philosophy, later Heideggerean meditations – each of these deploys a vocabulary that gestures towards a sense or vision of the mysterious.

And some, I want to say, do it better than others. Some are better at affording the intimations which enable the faith that a life may be consonant with reality. There are, then, various desiderata that must be satisfied by any rhetoric or poetry of mystery – some of which we shall encounter in the final part of this essay when discussing mystery's relationship to religion. The desideratum on which I now concentrate – which is also of direct relevance to that discussion – concerns the relationship between mystery and the human world. It is to the effect that a disjunctive, dualistic picture of this relationship should be rejected. The mysterious should not be imagined as some thing or realm that causally produces the human world, or as itself a kind of world (of Forms, say) that is the 'original' or 'model' of the human world, or – more generally – as anything that might have existed in splendid isolation, that might have been even if there had never been any humans and any human world. We might call this unacceptable way of imagining the relationship the 'two-levels' approach.

Now, some of the philosophical positions listed in the previous paragraph do seem to employ a disjunctive, two-levels picture – Advaita Vedanta and Transcendental Idealism, for example (on certain interpretations, at any rate, of Shankara and Kant). Here the hypothesis is of the mysterious – *brahman* or things in themselves – as giving rise to the human world of *maya* or appearances through impacting on human minds. It is through the interaction or contact between the two – the mysterious and the human – that the human world is generated. And, indeed, when the relationship of the mysterious and the human world is imagined in disjunctive, dualistic fashion, it is difficult to see what other way of thinking about the origin of the human world is possible.

But the disjunctive picture should be rejected for two reasons. To begin with, the account of the origin of the human world that it entails, or at least encourages, is incoherent. To be sure, rather different versions of the two-levels account of the arising of a human world are possible. On one version, the human mind has an *a priori* structure through which, as if through a pasta-making machine, anything must pass in order to be shaped into objects of experience. The world can only be experienced in limited ways, since nothing to which the mind's innate stock of categories is inapplicable is a possible object of experience. On rather more muscular, Promethean versions of the two-levels approach, the picture is instead that of a human world that is 'constructed' or 'projected' by human beings in and through their purposive, interest-driven practices. Cookery metaphors are popular among champions of this version. For William James, 'We carve out everything . . . to suit our human purposes', while for Roland Barthes we cut up reality into bite-sized objects, using our language as a utensil and in accordance with our needs and tastes, in the way a chef transforms raw potato into *pommes frites*.[5]

Whatever the version, however, the picture is surely incoherent. For notice that, in the two-levels approach, a striking exception is being made to the general claim that the nature, shape and furniture of the human world depend on human beings – on general *a priori* structures of mind, on 'constructive' carving, or whatever. This exception, of course, is human existence itself. In such pictures, we humans are, as it were, already there, up and running, in order to then act as the filters, carvers or chefs responsible for the world assuming the contours that it does. We are already there as the beings by which the world is conditioned. But this surely makes no sense. As the Buddha long ago recognized, we are no less conditioned than the things in the world with which we engage. (This is surely the real force and substance of the Buddha's doctrine of 'not-self'.) Hence, the thought that

---

5 See *The Measure of Things* for these and similar remarks, especially pp. 96 and 103.

we were already in place, with our structures of minds, needs and tastes, prior to the emergence of a world with which to engage, must be wrong. We are creatures, to switch to a different idiom, whose being is that of 'being-in-the-world': ours is the existence of creatures whose being – whose practices, structures of thought, and forms of life – is not even notionally separable from the world in which we are. It is for this reason that the world, though dependent on the human, cannot, as Heidegger puts it, be 'our handiwork', or as Merleau-Ponty prefers, 'an object such that I have in my possession the law of its making'.[6] The human world is not something that we, standing before it, can make, with our hands or with anything else. For apart from the way we 'always already' find ourselves in the world, there is no We to make anything.

Even if the disjunctive picture were coherent, there would remain a strong reason of a more practical kind for rejecting it. The idea of mystery, recall, is intended to play a strategic role, by providing compensation for acceptance of the human world doctrine, by providing measure and answerability. Now it is hard to see how it can succeed in this role on the two-levels approach. That, in the various versions of this approach, the human world gets described as appearance, *maya*, illusion, projection, and the like indicates the downgrading of the human world that is characteristic of the approach. When contrasted with the thing in itself, *brahman*, or absolute reality, the human world seems, inevitably, to come in a poor second. Schopenhauer remarked that, were there no thing in itself under-lying the world of appearances, this world would 'pass us by like an empty dream'.[7] Fortunately, there is the thing in itself, so the human world is saved from being an *empty* dream – but, it nevertheless remains, as Schopenhauer's Advaitin mentors had stressed centuries earlier, like a dream.

Now an idea of mystery that is paired with the notion of a human world which is like a dream, or a human projection onto a screen, is not one to compensate or give measure. For if raw, hubristic humanism – according to which there is only the human world – is unliveable, a humanism that is qualified by a two-levels, disjunctive picture of mystery is hardly less so. The human world, on this picture, is without solidity, without a real presence, for it is a shadow, dream or veil: and this would be a world that people who recognized it as such would not so much live in and with as pass through. Their focus would be, not on how to live in this world – not on the measure of their commitments and purposes – but on getting through it to, so to speak, the other side or the higher level. Their consciousness of the human world would be the 'unhappy' one that Hegel associates especially with

6 *Phenomenology of Perception*, tr. C. Smith (London: Routledge & Kegan Paul, 1962), p. xi.
7 *The World as Will and Representation*, tr. E. Payne (New York: Dover, 1969), Vol. I, p. 99.

medieval Christianity, but which is surely also an ingredient in any meta-physics that contrasts an unknowable, but entirely real level of being with the lame runner-up that is the human world we experience. Nietzsche was nearly right, therefore, when he insisted, in *Twilight of the Idols* (IV.6), that if human beings are to affirm life in the world – if they are to care enough about this life to seek measure for it – then the contrast between this world of appearances and a 'true world' is one we must be rid of. Only 'nearly' right, because Nietzsche intended in this remark to impugn the very idea of a mysterious reality as just one more 'true world' fiction. But we might see the strength of his point as residing in a rejection, not of mystery as such, but of the disjunctive opposition between mystery and the human world required by the two-levels approach.

Nietzsche was well aware of the difficulty of exorcising the disjunctive, oppositional picture and put his finger on one important source of the difficulty – grammar. ('We are not free of God because we still believe in grammar', to recall another remark from *Twilight of the Idols* (III.5).) In describing my path to mystery, I used expressions such as 'beyond the human world', 'something that provides measure', and a 'reality' that is not to be equated with the human world – all of which encourage a picture of the mysterious as disjoined from the human world. Still, while this vocab-ulary is heuristically useful when initially trying to convey a line of thought, it is not strictly necessary. With care, circumlocution, cumbersome syntax and some neology, it is possible to devise a rhetoric of mystery whose grammar is less liable to encourage a dualistic, two-levels approach. And such rhetorics are to be found in, for example, the texts of classical Daoism, of Zen, and of Heidegger. One may, for example, speak of the human world as a 'presencing' or 'epiphanizing' of mystery – ugly enough, to be sure, but less liable to conjure up a dualistic image. Or perhaps one should speak with the Zen monk, Dōgen – of the cypress tree, the reflection of the moon in the water, of everything in fact that we encounter in this human world, as 'realizing' the 'mysterious power'.

Far from impugning or downgrading the ordinary world, such ways of speaking surely elevate it. This world is not simply a human world, unthinkable in isolation from us, but at the same time a realization of, a coming forth of, something to which we can strive to answer and measure up. Whatever the final choice of a rhetoric or poetry, it is crucial that the sense of mystery it evokes or attunes to should be focused on the ordinary world, not directed towards some realm that stands apart from and in-different to the ordinary. Otherwise a sense of mystery cannot play the compensating role that it was destined for.

Mystery, God and religion

A few months after the appearance of *The Measure of Things* – the book in which I first articulated the thoughts about mystery I have been summarizing in this essay – I was invited to lunch by a distinguished colleague at Durham University, the theologian Andrew Louth, a leading authority on Orthodox Christianity. There is, we know, no such thing as a free lunch, and my contribution to the meal was to explain to Andrew why, in my book, I had been unwilling to identify the mysterious with God – and why I had not treated acceptance of mystery as a form of religious belief.

You might think, on the basis of my remarks in the previous section of this essay, that you know what I said to Andrew. I would have pointed out, wouldn't I, that by identifying the God of the great monotheistic religions with what is mysterious, I would have defied several of the desiderata that I stipulated for an account of mystery to satisfy. This God, as popularly conceived, is quite distinct from the world he created – a being that might have been without creating a world at all. So the desideratum of eschewing a disjunctive picture of the relation of world to mystery would have been violated. Again, as popularly imagined, this God is invested with many properties that people claim to know that he possesses – wisdom, for example, or love for his creatures. So, the desideratum of not effing the ineffable looks to be violated as well. Precisely because this God is discursable then, according to the thesis of my book, he belongs to the human world. He is, and he is what he is, only in relation to human perspective. As such, he cannot provide that independent measure for our conceptions of the world – for our beliefs and values – that only the genuinely mysterious can do. If people are answerable to what is 'beyond' the human, this cannot be answerability to something all-too-human, something invested by human beings with their own perspectives on what is true and good. This, I take it, is akin to the point that Marx, Nietzsche and Freud were making when they argued, in effect, that we find in God only what we have put there in the first place.

But while, perhaps over the soup, I may have made such remarks to Andrew Louth, I must have known that they would cut little ice with him – or with some of the Orthodox and also post-modernist theologians (such as Jean-Luc Marion) about whom Andrew writes. For theirs, of course, is not a 'popular' or 'ordinary' conception of God. Here are some remarks from Andrew's introduction to a book by the contemporary Greek Orthodox theologian, Christos Yannaras, which give an indication of the conception of God to which Andrew, like Yannaras, is drawn. Following Heidegger, Yannaras rejects the 'onto-theology of the West', that is 'the reduction of God to a being, even if the highest'. He develops this Heideggerian point through invoking the writings of Dionysios the Areopagite, for whom 'God is not the first cause or highest being or highest value', for God 'utterly transcends the world he created' and is 'not "one of the things that are"'. Apophantic theology, as Yannaras sees it, is 'an acknowledgement of the experience of the God beyond any human conceptual grasp . . . In terms of being that we can know and measure and argue about, God is not being'. The real implication of Heidegger's attack on the God of onto-theology is 'the unknowability of the God beyond being'.[8] Here, clearly enough, God is not the being spoken about on Sundays in the parish church or in the mosque on Fridays. Here is a God who sounds altogether more . . . well, more mysterious.

I do not recall in any detail what I said to Andrew about my reluctance to identify even this more recondite God with the mystery addressed in my book. But here, I think, is what I should have said. To begin with, it seems to me that it remains difficult, even when it is this more recondite God of apophantic theology that is invoked, simultaneously to satisfy my various desiderata for an account of mystery. First, there is, I find, a disturbing tendency among 'negative' theologians to announce the total unknowability and ineffability of God, and then say really rather a lot about him. In my book (p. 284), I took an example from a commentary on Rumi, where the author – having insisted that the Sūfis' God can 'never be the theme of thought and discussion' – proceeds to tell us that their God is, among other things, active, omniscient, the creator of the world, the source of all love, the God of the Koran, and so on. By the end of her description, the Sūfis' God has become as much a 'theme of thought and discussion', and just as effable, as the God of Sunday services or Friday prayers. Second, there is the tendency – apparent in the Yannaras text, for example – to understand the unknowability of God, and the reason for his not being 'one of the things that are', in terms of his utter transcendence of the world, of his being totally 'other' to the world and its component beings. And this – if God were to be equated with mystery – would become an expression of precisely the kind of disjunctive vision of the relationship between world and mystery rejected in the previous section.

The two tendencies just noted – to eff the allegedly ineffable God and to render him utterly transcendent of the world – both have the effect, in their different ways, of disqualifying God from providing the type of measure that mystery is intended to do. Descriptions like that of the Sūfis' God cited in the preceding paragraph are depictions, surely, of a God that is far too human – too much a denizen of the human world – to provide measure for

---

8 *On the Absence and Unknowability of God: Heidegger and the Areopagite*, tr. H. Ventis (London: T & T. Clark, 2005), pp. 8–9.

our conception of that world, too much a 'projection', as it were, of what we anyway hold dear and important to serve as any kind of warrant for our holding them so. But if, instead, in a laudable attempt to remain faithful to the declaration of God's ineffability, this is taken to entail God's utter transcendence of – his out-and-out otherness to – the world, then we are back with the problems, discussed in an earlier section, of a disjunctive, two-levels account of world and mystery. What would a God matter to us who is so disjoined from our world? W. G. Sebald writes of Sir Thomas Browne that, precisely because he saw the 'unfathomable mystery' as located in another world 'far beyond' our everyday 'shadow' of a world, he looked upon 'earthly existence . . . with the eye of an outsider'.[9] Browne's position is entirely understandable, for to view the human world in the manner of an outsider, rather than as one engaged in it and seeking measure for this engagement, was, I argued, precisely what to expect when world and mystery are, as in Browne's vision, disjoined.

There is a further reason for the difficulty I have in identifying the sense of mystery argued for in my book with recognition of the existence – albeit not as a 'thing' or 'being' – of the recondite God of apophantic theology. I just do not understand the urge to introduce the word 'God' here in order to name such a mystery. I do not, therefore, understand the insistence by Karl Rahner, among others, that this name is essential for bringing us 'face to face with reality'. The only explanation of the urge that I am able to envisage is that what 'God' is introduced to name is held to be the appropriate 'object' of attitudes and practices – love, fear and worship, say – that belong to, or intelligibly derive from, a traditional stance towards God as a person. But then I am unable to see how such attitudes to what is mysterious, as this is conceived in my account, could be appropriate. We would need to know more about mystery, for these attitudes to be appropriate, than, if I am right, we could possibly do. And if we did acquire this knowledge, then it would no longer be mystery that gets named. It is, in my judgement, a merit of the attunement to mystery that several rhetorics of mystery attempt to provide that they do not encourage emotions and comportments that have their origin and proper place in the context of relationships with persons. Such labels for what is mysterious as 'the Dao', 'emptiness', or 'the appropriating event' belong to rhetorics or poetries that attune to a sense of presence that is not hospitable to love, fear or worship.

Does it follow from my reluctance to identify mystery with the God of even the most sophisticated modern theologians – all of them scornful of 'onto-theology' – that there is nothing 'religious' in my path to mystery?

---

9 W. G. Sebald, *The Rings of Saturn* (London: Vintage, 2002), pp. 18–19.

Well, there is nothing religious, I think, in the path itself and its philosophical destination: for the path, we saw earlier, was an intellectual one culminating in a certain doctrine – that what is 'beyond' the discursable human world is radically mysterious. I am inclined to agree with Michael McGhee that the religious is never to be equated with belief that this or that is the case. Indeed, religion does not require religious *belief* at all.[10] But a possibility also urged by McGhee remains open – that the religious is discernible in a person's stance to what is believed, in his or her 'perspective', in his or her life. So if there is a religious aspect to my position, it is to be discerned not in the argument for, or the bare doctrine of, mystery but in a subsequent attunement and comportment.

To qualify as religious, could it be enough, as McGhee suggests in his contribution to this volume, that this attunement and comportment is suffused by a 'vision of a possibility of liberation that at the same time and integrally looks back at human suffering and its causes'? Maybe – but there is something I would want to add to this Buddhistic conception of the religious that itself owes to Buddhism. What needs adding is *saddhā*   – often translated as 'faith', but better rendered perhaps as 'confidence' or 'trust'. For an attunement and comportment towards the mysterious to invite the name 'religious', it must incorporate confidence in . . . , thereby providing that element of bonding or binding that is at the root of the term 'religion'. But confidence in what, and of what kind? Not the confidence of blind faith, and not unfounded certainty as to the existence of some being. In effect, it must be the sort of confidence of which the Buddhist texts speak: an intelligent, reflective confidence in the wisdom of a great thinker and in the path he follows and teaches. Earlier, I stressed that it is essential – if a sense of mystery is to play its role – that one is offered intimations of, and an attunement to, the mysterious which enables the faith that lives that are led in certain ways do answer to, are consonant with, the way of things. This essential role is only possible where there is trust and confidence, not mere hope, that our lives may be consonant with the way of things. It is true, of course, that, as the Buddha himself emphasized, each of us is finally alone when it comes to judging or experiencing the authenticity of intimations and attunements, and hence to appraising the consonance of our lives. But it is equally true that we need to start somewhere – with quiet, unassertive confidence in the wisdom, integrity and receptivity to mystery of figures, like the Buddha, who then compose a rhetoric or poetry that helps the rest of us to share their experience. I am comfortable with the description of this gentle, reflective confidence, and the direction it gives to a life, as a religious comportment.

---

10 See his 'Seeke True Religion. Oh Where?' in J. Cottingham (ed.), *The Meaning of Theism* (Oxford: Blackwell, 2007), and his chapter in the present volume.

5

Searching for God?

DAPHNE HAMPSON

In his famed inaugural lecture of 1929 'What is Metaphysics?', Martin Heidegger proposes that the answer to the question as to what is *meta phusis*, beyond nature, is 'Nichts', nothing.[1] It was a turning point in Heidegger's career. From then on he begins to work out the implications of this conclusion. If the answer to the question of the 'beyond' is nothing, then our focus must be on this world.[2] Heidegger's was in some way a very 'Lutheran' stance. And indeed Heidegger was a renowned Lutheran scholar who knew Luther's work intimately and had adsorbed him deeply. The structure of Lutheran faith is that one lives by an *extrinsic* righteousness; thus 'from' God (rather than 'towards' God, understanding life as a *via*, as the Catholic Augustinian tradition had taken for granted). Secure with God, the Christian is turned towards the world, free to let the world be the domain of humans, for it is not a path to God.[3] In Heidegger's case we live 'from' death and, given that finality, are thrown into the attempt to fully live. But Heidegger was by upbringing Catholic, a tradition which has often seen the world as transparent of God. One might well say that, following upon his inaugural lecture, Heidegger attempts to discern what one may call another dimension to reality in the everyday. In and through the world he finds a premonition of being. It is a displacement of the Christian Platonic tradition, a spirituality of the here and now.

---

1 Given in *Wegmarken*, GS, Band 9 (Frankfurt am Main: Vittorio Klostermann, 1976). (ET in D. Krell, ed., *Martin Heidegger: Basic Writings* (London: Routledge, 1994).)

2 Cf. James Robinson, commenting on Walter Schulz, 'Über den philosophiegeschichtlichen Ort Martin Heideggers', *Philosophische Rundschau*, I (1953–4): 'The nothing that emerged when metaphysics sought to ground Dasein in something outside itself ceases to emerge as nothing, and instead being dawns . . . Once the Promethean direction of metaphysics is renounced, the positive emerges.' 'The German Discussion of the Later Heidegger', in J. Robinson, ed., *The Later Heidegger and Theology* (New York: Harper & Row, 1963; reprinted by Greenwood Press, Inc., 1979), pp. 12–13.

3 For the differing structures of the two traditions see my *Christian Contradictions: The Structures of Lutheran and Catholic Thought* (Cambridge: Cambridge University Press, 2001).

Heidegger's move did not arise from nowhere. Notably Nietzsche, in oft-quoted lines: 'How the "Real World" at last became a Myth: History of an Error', foretold the 'end' of the history of metaphysics which stretched from the ancient world into the present.[4] By the 'real world' is of course meant the Platonic forms, the idea that reality lies 'beyond', of which this world is but a pale copy. Nietzsche's point is that when the 'real' world is no more, the 'apparent' world in which we live is no longer the 'apparent' but the only world; all that we have is here, now. This for him is a matter for rejoicing: Nietzsche breathes a sigh of relief. But Nietzsche too has ancestry. Hegel is surely the crucial figure here. For Hegel grasped reality as unfolding and historical: *Geist* is actualized in history. Thus for him too there is no need, no place, for that which is unchanging, other, outside: a reality which calls ours into question as somehow inferior and imperfect.[5] This conclusion marked the end of an era, the solution to a problem: the eighteenth century had been wracked by the disjunction between the timeless God and the man Jesus.

The development caused a crisis for Christianity, most starkly felt and strikingly tackled by the Dane Søren Kierkegaard. Kierkegaard was an admirer of Lessing, who in the eighteenth century had posed the problem in unforgettable terms.[6] In accord with the whole philosophical development from the ancient world down through Leibniz, Lessing understood God as eternal, changeless. How then could one ever move from the historical Jesus (if he was the incarnation of God) to this unchanging God? Lessing confronted a 'ditch' he could not cross.[7] Kierkegaard does not attempt to cross the ditch. He, too, thinks of God as absolute. Christianity thus represents a paradox for thought, for the Christian holds that this man (so evidently a man) is God.[8] The question could not have arisen a century earlier in quite this form, for Christendom had lost hold of the full humanity of Christ, tending to merge the two natures to form a human god. But with the whole 'quest of the historical Jesus' and the new sense, with the Enlightenment and Romanticism, of what it meant to be 'human', it was bound to emerge.

Kierkegaard had further taken cognisance of the work of Feuerbach who, following upon Hegel, had declared the God beyond a human projection.

---

4 *Twilight of the Idols* (1889).
5 Hegel's great work which first expresses this is of course his *Phenomenology of Spirit* (1806).
6 See the humorous and appreciative debate with Lessing 'Something About Lessing', *Concluding Unscientific Postscript to Philosophical Fragments* (1846).
7 'On the Proof of the Spirit and of Power' in *Lessing's Theological Writings: Selections in Translation; With an Introductory Essay by Henry Chadwick* (London: Adam & Charles Black, 1956).
8 The best statement of this is *Philosophical Fragments* (1844); its implications are considered in the *Postscript* to that book (see note 6 above).

The only possible way out for Kierkegaard was to hold, in faith, to the proposition that God had broken through to humankind in Jesus Christ. Kierkegaard the Lutheran never seeks to discern God through the world; nor, Lutheran and post-Kantian that he is, does he think it possible to move from the world to God. Thenceforth Continental thinking on religion will be divided. There will be those who, following Kierkegaard, are prepared to hold to there having been a unique revelation of God in Christ. The Barthian revolution of the twentieth century was largely predicated on such a move. And there will be those for whom, following Feuerbach and Niet-zsche (furthermore the Jews Marx and Freud), the world beyond is a human conjecture. This latter conclusion carried with it, in a final fling of an Enlightenment which had now disposed of God, the admonition that humanity should come into its own.

I have indicated that the break-up of Platonism in its Christian incarna-tion was in some ways a Lutheran affair, and it will be worthwhile momen-tarily to turn to Luther. A precondition for the 'Copernican revolution' which was Luther's theology was the rejection of the philosophical context of the ancient Greek world. Of course Luther had a 'transcendent' God; how could it have been otherwise? But it was not the transcendence of neo-Platonism which had been absorbed by the Catholic tradition. Luther holds neither to the Aristotelian postulation of God as Being to whom we bear likeness, nor the neo-Platonist sense of one towards whom we should strive, stripping ourselves of our material encumbrance and desires.[9] By profes-sion an exegete of the Hebrew scriptures, 'transcendence' was for Luther that of the Hebrew God, the Other in our midst.[10] Luther is deeply suspi-cious of mysticism, of 'climbing up into God'.[11] The movement is always *from* God *to* us, in the unexpected revelation that God accepts us as we are as sinners. Luther rejoices in the body.[12] Our lives hid with Christ in God, we are as never before thrown into the world. This double sense of self is fundamental to Lutheran faith: it is what is meant by being *simul justus et*

9 On the philosophical move behind Luther's theology see Wilfried Joest, *Ontologie der Person bei Luther* (Göttingen: Vandenhoeck & Ruprecht, 1967), unfortunately untranslated. For the early date of Luther's break note his 'Disputation Against Scholastic Theology', 4 September 1517.

10 Note Luther's divergence from the Swiss theologians here. Confronted with the proposi-tion that Christ must have a local presence and, subsequently to the Ascension, this is at the right hand of God, Luther responds incredulously that Christ is 'not in heaven like a stork perched in its nest'. WA 26.422.27 (1528).

11 On Luther's anti-mysticism cf. Anders Nygren (tr.), *Agape and Eros* (New York: Harper & Row, 1969), pp. 703–5, 733–5 and my consideration *Christian Contradictions*, pp. 18–20.

12 Jürgen Moltmann's *Theology and Joy* (London: SCM Press, 1973) is good on this.

peccator, at once justified and sinner. In the 1920s the Lutheran theologian Rudolf Bultmann, whose seminar Heidegger attended at the University of Marburg, will translate the Lutheran 'simul' to mean that we live 'from' the future, substituting the word 'future' for God, to which it is equivalent.[13]

Now we have set Heidegger in context. The former Catholic seminarian, well aware of Lutheran theology, will re-pristinate this world. As a young man Heidegger had been impressed by the work of the early nineteenth-century liberal Protestant theologian and thinker, Friedrich Schleiermacher. Coming from a Reformed (not Lutheran) background, Schleiermacher was a renowned Plato scholar, who spoke of seeing 'All in God and God in all'.[14] In his *Speeches on Religion* (1799), addressed to its 'cultured despisers' (his friends), he cajoles them into discovering a reality before their very eyes. The young Heidegger was furthermore impressed by Rudolf Otto's 1917 work *Das Heilige* (translated *The Idea of the Holy*), an attempt at a phenomenology of human religious awareness. Otto had provided the classic introduction to the reissue of Schleiermacher's *Speeches*. Following his master Husserl, Heidegger would be a phenomenologist, but unlike Husserl he turned not to human consciousness but outward to the world. As his thought develops he understands *Dasein*, the human person, to be in integral relation with and open to that which is beyond himself which is *Sein*.

Thus, responding to Jean Beaufret (and behind him the atheist Jean-Paul Sartre), who had enquired of Heidegger as to how the word 'humanism' was to be understood, Heidegger (in 1947) turns the tables on his French interlocutors.

> Consider Being, what is Being? It is itself. To experience and articulate this is what future thought has to learn. 'Being': that is not God and not foundational to the world. Being is further from and at the same time closer to humans than every thing which exists. Being is that which is next (the word in biblical German for 'the neighbour').[15]

Heidegger differentiates *Sein* from a transcendent 'God' and, equally, denies that *Sein* is foundational. Heidegger was rightly to refuse the question as to whether he was atheist or theist: he had moved sideways.

---

13 Bultmann makes this equation at the conclusion to his 1955 Gifford Lectures, *History and Eschatology: The Presence of Eternity* (New York: Harper & Row, 1957), p. 154.
14 J. Oman (tr.), *On Religion* (New York: Harper Torchbook, 1958), p. 36. Calvin of course has a sense for the discernment of God through the world, and described it in the *Institutes* Book I as a 'theatre for displaying the glory of God'.
15 'Brief über den Humanismus', *Wegmarken*, GS, Band 9, my translation (ed. and tr. in Krell, *Basic Writings*).

Why this historical-cum-theological-cum-philosophical prologue to what I wish to say? Because I am concerned that philosophy of religion as practised in the Anglo-Saxon tradition has run into the sand. I do not think it profitable to continue to search for God in the 'beyond', if indeed that is where we should ever have looked.[16] To say this is obviously a tall order if one is thinking in terms of the Abrahamic religions. But then I judge that, on both epistemological and moral grounds, we need to abandon the Abrahamic myths (as I have extensively discussed in my published work).[17] If one has, as have I, a marked spirituality, the subsequent question presents itself as to how then we should conceive of God. Together with Heidegger, I am convinced that we should see the world as the scene of our activity and the place of our discernment of what I refer to as a 'dimension' to reality which is God. Thus knowledge of God is grounded in awareness. We are not about 'reasoning to' (as though one could prove or disprove the 'existence' of God) but rather a 'discernment of' that which is the case. Such a move is not devoid of epistemological claim. But it is not an epistemology which seeks an ontology, conjecturing a separate being, an entity which we name God. It is this contention and its consequences which I shall pursue in this essay.

It is first necessary to consider why it is not possible for Christianity – or the other Abrahamic religions, but I shall concentrate on Christianity as that is my context as a Western, post-Christian, person – to come to terms with modernity. What has always seemed to me decisive is that Christianity is predicated upon the postulation that there has occurred a particularity. That is to say Christians believe (though I shall need to qualify this) that there has been an interruption of the causal nexus of nature and of history. A definition of what it is to be Christian might well be that it is to believe that, in the phenomenon surrounding Jesus of Nazareth, there is present a uniqueness. Christians hold that there was a (unique) incarnation of God; or that Christ and he alone rose from the dead; or that the scriptures which tell of him are a class apart from other religious literature; or (in the case of Catholicism) that the tradition and institution which stemmed from God's incarnation is a source of truth. Of course the other Abrahamic religions also hold to uniqueness; believing that a particular history reflects God's dealings with humankind, or in the absolute nature of scripture given through a prophet who was God's mouthpiece.

The problem is that in the modern world it is difficult to give credence to such particularity. In the Enlightenment it came to be recognized that

---

16 It is interesting that the characteristic English response to the Enlightenment is deism, in which God becomes even more superfluous and remote.

17 See in particular my *After Christianity* (London: SCM Press, 1996/2002).

history, or nature, is one inter-related whole. Further, that from the series of causal relations within the world one cannot extrapolate to a prime mover.[18] The events of which we know, or the examples of nature we find, are always one of a kind. Thus (to take an example from history), whether or not he did this, that Caesar crossed the Rubicon is wholly conceivable, belonging as it does to a category, crossing rivers; to do which furthermore, acting within the causal nexus, one's horse places one foot in front of the other. By contrast, a resurrection must represent discontinuity. Such an 'event' belongs to no category; further, it is impossible in terms of what we know, not only biologically but in being discontinuous with all else. Again (to take an example from nature) if we see a green beetle it is axiomatic to us that its parents were also green beetles (and, since Darwin, we know nature to be slowly evolving). Christian orthodoxy is subtle here: it is not that this man Jesus was one of a category, a human God; rather is his full humanity proclaimed. Nevertheless there is particularity in that he and he alone is said to have a second and divine nature. It is this postulation of uniqueness which distinguishes Christianity from the epistemology of the modern world. Christians may ever have pronounced their stand a scandal; as St Paul said, 'we proclaim Christ crucified, to the Jews a scandal [Greek *skandalon*]' (1 Corinthians 1.23). But in Paul's case the scandal consisted in the fact that one who was crucified (the ultimate humiliation) is Lord; it is not a scandal in the sense of the 'scandal of particularity' (significantly, the term arose in the eighteenth century), that the causal nexus of history and nature is held to have been broken.

To my mind therefore the most provocative Christian apologist of the modern world is Rudolf Bultmann. For Bultmann faces foursquare, as a fundamental axiom, that nature and history are a causal nexus not allowing of exceptions, of interventions. He proceeds, however, to postulate two 'realms' (one senses as a neo-Kantian), *Historie* and *Geschichte* (the common German word for history but also, significantly, simply 'story'). Now the event of the cross is a normal historical event, part of the causal nexus; whereas, Bultmann proposes, the 'resurrection', unthinkable in terms of what we know, lies in the realm of *Geschichte*. Thus does he find a way to speak of the uniqueness necessary to a Christian position, saying that the gospel is the proclamation of the resurrection of *this particular man* who died, tying together the two 'events' as closely as possible without there being a causal relationship;[19] or, as Karl Barth would have said, 'as a tangent

---

18 The great philosophical statement of this is Kant's 'First' *Critique* (1781).
19 'New Testament and Mythology' (1941), in H. W. Bartsch (tr.), *Kerygma and Myth* (New York: Harper & Row, 1961).

touches a circle, that is, without touching it'.[20] But what could *Geschichte* be? In Bultmann's hands it appears to be the realm of 'meaning'; a postulation of another reality, living in terms of which our lives are cast in a different light (*simul justus et peccator* we may well say). The question which arises – and was immediately apparent to Bultmann's left-wing disciples – is, why admit of 'resurrection'? Should one not also in this case de-mythologize (the German term simply connotes translate-out-of mythology) 'resurrection' as being the ancient world's way of expressing what today we should state otherwise?

I hesitated above to define Christians as those who credit that there has been an interruption of the causal nexus. In particular through dialogue with my friend Janet Soskice, a Catholic philosophical theologian, it has become apparent to me that there is a way of conceiving of reality, such that the Christian claim does not appear interruptive quite as I have surmised. Soskice – if I can attempt to express where she stands – holds (intelligently so) that God is 'other' not in the sense that so much Western thought has seemed to infer as outside space and time, a kind of being; but rather entirely Other, God as Creator holding all in his hands and instrumentally present in every action; such that it is not at all incredible that he should 'intervene' in the incarnation in Christ. It could well be said that Luther holds to just such a position in his 1525 *The Bondage of the Will*, and I gather it would also be close to Thomas Aquinas and an older Catholic tradition. This suggests that the way in which the problem strikes one like me arises post the Enlightenment. Nevertheless I can but remain with the modern world. Commencing from what might be called 'below', from our knowledge of *this* world, I must hold that history and nature are a causal nexus which cannot allow of the particularity which Christians propose. When I respond to Janet that 'our earth belongs to a solar system, which lies part-way out in one arm of a galaxy called the Milky Way, and galaxies form clusters – and you mean to say that God visited planet earth?' my comment may strike Janet as wide of the mark, but I am not simply being facetious.[21]

So much for epistemological considerations. There are furthermore compelling moral arguments as to why we should abandon Christianity (indeed all 'Abrahamic' religions). Consider the notion of God as some kind of transcendent entity. (My initial argument here applies less to Soskice's position, though when I turn to the import of the Christian myth equally to hers.) As soon as such an entity is postulated and is, moreover, understood

20 *The Epistle to the Romans* (1918/1922), tr. E. Hoskyns (Oxford: Oxford University Press, 1968), p. 30.
21 This debate finds its reflection in D. Hampson (ed.), *Swallowing a Fishbone? Feminist Theologians Debate Christianity* (London: SPCK, 1996), pp. 22, 113–14.

through gendered metaphors, as it has been in the Abrahamic traditions, we have a hierarchical relationship pertaining between God and humanity; further, a gendered hierarchy. Since the rise of the Abrahamic religions the West has known nothing else. If God is good and almighty, humanity by contrast is sinful and puerile. JHWH is always called by male terms (the male sometimes embodying the female, as though man could take all to himself); the people of Israel conceived of as female in relation to him. It may well be that men place themselves in this 'feminine' position in relation to God – the Church is the bride of Christ – but this simply underscores the respective connotations given to 'male' and 'female'. Men (or maleness) always occupy the subject position in relation to women (or femininity). Woman becomes the 'other'. The Abrahamic religions are a form of fascism, if the definition of fascism be an ideology that casts a part of humanity as normative, such that those who do not belong to their number become 'the other'. From the Creation story to men elevating one of their number to the godhead, this myth has underlain Western culture, with extraordinary consequences for the other half of humanity.

Yet it is incontrovertible that, believing in this myth, men and women have found meaning in their lives and fostered a deep spirituality. What, thus, it becomes incumbent upon us to do is to distinguish the myth, patently untrue and morally indefensible, from that which it has carried and articulated. As Kant would have said, the historical or revealed religion has acted as a 'vehicle'.[22] The fact that Christianity is, in this peculiar sense, 'historical' sets it apart from the rest of human thought and knowledge, whether the arts or sciences. In all other disciplines humans draw on the past insofar as it remains valid or apposite, casting it aside as new knowledge or different moral axioms dawn. By contrast, in the case of Christianity (and the other Abrahamic religions), a point in past history is intrinsic to the religion, this on account of the fact that there is believed to have been a revelation. Transcendence, revelation and particularity mutually imply one another. A juncture in the past becomes the benchmark for truth. It is this which makes the Abrahamic religions sexist; there is, of necessity, constant reference to that past. Even in the case of a non-fundamentalist stance, the human imagination is shaped at a subconscious level by the history and literature of a past in which male is normative. That such texts are held sacred only makes them the more potent: the medium is the message.

Why it should be that one half of humanity has formed our systems of thought – most notably our religions – would appear impenetrable. But that this is the case is incontrovertible; as Jacques Lacan pronounced, the

---

22 *Religion within the Limits of Reason Alone* (1793), tr. T. M. Greene and H. H. Hudson (New York: Harper Torchbooks, 1960), pp. 97, 98.

symbolic is male. The book of Genesis captures it thus: Adam names – and in Hebrew to name is to express the essence of something – all that God brings to him, including the woman and her reality. There being little empirical constraint on the religious imagination, religion becomes a screen on which the (male) subconscious is writ large; both reflecting and in turn legitimating the mores and social structure of patriarchal society. In recent years feminists have argued that it is the male need to escape and, on the other hand, desire for woman which is sublimated in masculinist religion.[23] Certainly it would seem that, cross-culturally, what object relations theorists refer to as 'splitting' is endemic to the male construct of 'woman' in his religion. On the one hand pure and unattainable, the object of desire, whether as mother or virgin (or both); on the other hand she represents that which would lead him astray, with which he fears entanglement, both temptress and slut. (In Hinduism both are united in the one overwhelming figure of Kali.) What is singularly lacking in the Abrahamic religions is any representation of woman the equal of man, an agent in her own right. Reality is not represented as bi-polar between a male and female principle. (Nor does it help when yin is defined as insubstantial, soft, wet and feminine, while yang is solid, focused, dry and masculine: *plus ça change, plus c'est la meme chose.*) Such systems of thought must pervert the moral imperative of human equality that we have so recently gained. Yet such religions are still taught in our schools – and not as a form of fascism but alongside ethics!

What we are up against is of course that the vehicle which is the historical religion is so integrally related with people's sense of God as to be inseparable. Though this is not entirely the case: there are today many within the Christian Church who do not credit the fundamentals of Christian faith other than as myth; many more who, having rejected institutional religion, count themselves spiritual persons. One would think religions to be a complex amalgam of many strands: ethical injunctions, the ordering of human life projected as ultimate reality, and a mythological creation which functions to assuage anxiety and express a celebration of life. But furthermore, central in particular to Christianity, both at its genesis and in the continuing tradition, has been religious experience: one would think that it has been fundamental to the postulation of the existence of God. If it is the case that human beings cannot think apart from 'language' (in the widest sense of the word, to include symbols and the whole concretion of colour, taste and form), it follows that we shall not easily re-shape our conception of that which is 'God'. We may well not require a myth quite in the sense of religion as we have known it. But we shall need some form of articulation

---

23 See in particular the work of Luce Irigaray.

if we are to grasp what it is that we mean by 'God'. It is no less a task with which I believe theology is faced today. I shall devote the remainder of this essay to some consideration of this agenda.

I do myself hold, beyond reasonable doubt, that there is a domain of empirical or quasi-empirical evidence – which people have then hypostasized (made into a definite entity), 'God'. I shall here briefly consider the nature of the evidence. We are asked in these essays to be personal, so I make mention of the moment when I concluded that I must cease to be a historian and turn to theology. I was walking back to the station in Wiesbaden where I had spoken with Martin Niemöller, the man who had been the leading figure in the Confessing Church in the Third Reich. The case against him dismissed (astonishingly) by the court which had tried him in 1937, Niemöller was despatched to prison as Hitler's first 'personal prisoner'. In 1945 the Americans who liberated the concentration camp in which he was then housed were amazed to find – Martin Niemöller. I asked him to what he attributed his survival? Niemöller's response was unequivocal: all over the world people were praying for him. I realized that I did indeed credit this as causal. But secular history has no net with which to catch this: I must move to theology. (What has interested me, since becoming a theologian, is how few in the profession appear to credit that power which we have called God.)

I turn to a consideration of religious experience.[24] Exactly as we should expect if 'God' is the name we give to a dimension of reality and God is thus a constant, related in the same way to all times and places (there is no particularity), we find that the same phenomena were in evidence in the ancient world as are today. Such an understanding of God does not of course preclude the possibility that human recognition of that which is God is more prevalent in some times or cultures than in others. People learn to possess an openness to such an eventuality from one another. (Schleiermacher, rightly, commences his Christian dogmatics of 1820/21, *The Christian Faith*, by speaking of that community, which in his case is the fellowship of the Church, from which people gain the sense of what it is to be Christian, or we may say experience God.) Take the example of spiritual healing, evidently known in the first century, for long largely lost by Christendom, and coming to the fore again in late-nineteenth-century Boston. Today there are associations of spiritual healers in England and in Scotland. Further, we should note that people with healing gifts hold an eclectic variety of views, including to my knowledge Buddhist and atheist. This well suggests that the life-philosophy to which people hold is but a vehicle.

---

24 In Britain a compilation of evidence was undertaken by the (formerly Oxford) Religious Experience Research Centre. Cf. its founder Sir Alister Hardy's *The Spiritual Nature of Man* (Oxford: The Clarendon Press, 1979).

It is hardly a matter for surprise that people cast their experience in terms of the lens through which their community sees the world. However, as theologians considering how we should articulate that which is God, we should exercise the negative criterion that we do not allow that which is clearly incompatible with the current state of scientific advance. That is to say, we must de-mythologize. We need not doubt that one Jesus of Nazareth had healing powers about him: the evidence is overwhelmingly that that was the case.[25] It does not follow that what occurred was exactly as has come down to us; for example, it would be hard to credit that the dead were raised. People may be healed from mental illness; we should not today say that they were possessed by 'devils', which then entered a herd of pigs, causing them to plunge into the sea. Again, people remembered Jesus as possessing clairvoyance and reported him as seeing Nathanael under a tree or knowing where a donkey was tied up, though these examples may not have occurred exactly as stated. Clairvoyance is something frequently experienced by spiritually attuned persons today. On the other hand we know that, given its specific gravity, people cannot walk on water. Nor can it be changed into wine, for wine has carbon atoms and water does not. (But then this may be a 'symbolic' miracle in John's Gospel.)

To be a spiritual person is not, however, simply to witness healing or clairvoyance, but rather is it to ground these experiences in a certain way of being in the world. Those who evidently possess a spirituality have about them certain qualities: truthfulness, powers of observation, and generosity of spirit. They seem translucent of God (if these are the terms in which we would express ourselves). It is an interesting question as to whether, fundamental to living a spiritual as opposed to simply an ethical life, is the faith that in the last resort good reaches deeper than evil; that there is light which the darkness cannot quench. Humans would appear to possess an intrinsic desire and sense for wholeness or completeness. Of course, that this corresponds to what is, may be delusion. It seems naïve to postulate a *summum bonum* in which virtue should be rewarded with happiness. (Kant himself apparently came to regret such a statement as liable to undermine his injunction that, irrespective of consequences, we should obey the moral law.)[26] Again, it may well be that our end is dust and ashes. But one may hazard a guess that, at least in some fleeting moments, many of us are moved to conclude that the whole is good and to give thanks.

---

25 There is, interestingly, no report of his healing broken bones; something also unknown today.
26 See the discussion of Kant's change of stance in the *Opus Postumum* in T. M. Greene, 'The Historical Context and Religious Significance of Kant's *Religion*', pp. lxv–lxvii.

The way in which we conceptualize that which is 'God' should surely correlate with our experience. Clearly we cannot think God some kind of being whom we should implore to use his agency. We should be faced with the most horrendous theodicy questions, well encapsulated by Celie's comment in Alice Walker's *The Colour Purple*: why he 'just sit up there being deef [deaf]?'.[27] Rather is it that God is a dimension of reality to which we can be open, bring into play, or allow to work through us. Blocking God, it is human beings who perform horrendous evil. Whether we should in any sense consider God to possess agency independent of ours is an interesting question. It would represent a misunderstanding to think that talk of God as a 'dimension' of reality has as consequence that, were we to grasp for example how clairvoyance or spiritual healing work, this would be the end of God. We should simply comprehend more fully that which hitherto we named 'God'. Presumably we should marvel at it. Indeed, the evidence points to a conceptualization of 'God' as being intimately, even integrally, related with what we are. It is understandable that in distress people are moved to address God as 'Thou'; it does not follow that this represents God. We may well have a 'sense of presence' of what is more than we are, of love itself. But again this does not entail that God is actually an anthropomorphic being.

Part of the conceptual framework that we should refine if we are to consider how God can best be conceived and, more particularly, how that which is God relates to what we are, is the question as to the nature of the self. Implicit in what I have said, is that the understanding of God which we have had is modelled on the (masculinist) understanding of the self. Thus God is self-sufficient, all-powerful, and separate: clearly a nightmare of a conjecture! Furthermore the relation between God and humanity is held to be both appositional and oppositional, a master/slave dynamic in which each is understood by contrast with the other. If, however, we conceive of both the self and of human relationality quite otherwise, we may in turn conceptualize differently both that which is God and the nature of the relationship between that dimension of reality which is God and we ourselves. The claim here is that the paradigm intrinsic to this other way of thinking would appear better to explain the evidence, on account of which we have concluded that there is a dimension to reality which we name 'God'. Like Schleiermacher, I believe we should commence from human experience; though, unlike him, I wish to draw on data which is quasi-empirical, and thus in some sense exterior to or at least more than we ourselves.

One figure whose thinking majors on the relation of the human reality to that which lies immediately beyond the human – and whose work may

---

27 London: The Women's Press, 1983, p. 164.

therefore be pertinent for our endeavour – is Heidegger. Interestingly Heidegger employs vocabulary which blurs the distinction as to whether it is with us or that which lies beyond us that agency lies. Thus his *Ereignis* has in German the connotation 'happening', the common meaning of the word (which sounds 'external'), or, as *Er-eignen*, that which we appropriate or make our own. Again he employs the term *unter-schied*, which ordinarily (without hyphen) means 'difference' to emphasize relationality between two which differ. Quite apart from vocabulary (always so central to his meaning as he plays with the German language), Heidegger has a profound sense of receptivity; for example in his adoption of the word *Gelassenheit*, taken from Meister Eckhart, meaning an active passivity. It does not of course follow from the fact that elements of Heidegger's thought are suggestive that we should not also be critical. We may well wish to see the self as gathered, 'centred'; and indeed thereby also 'open'. Heidegger could have done with a little more *Eigentlichlichkeit* (owning of oneself, translated 'authenticity') in the circumstances of the Third Reich. Again one cannot help remarking on his lack of attention to the inter-subjectivity which should characterize the relationship between persons.

A further source for our consideration should be a trend of thought widely discussed in feminist theory over the last 25 years. (It is a real problem in academic scholarship that it does not apparently occur to otherwise widely read men that they have overlooked, often even not heard of, feminist writers whose work has been widely influential; a reflection of the normativity accorded to the male world to which I have drawn attention.) Feminist psychoanalytic object relations theory, and the social psychology which draws on it, notably in the hands respectively of Nancy Chodorow and Carol Gilligan, has suggested on grounds of considerable evidence that women tend to have 'flexible' ego-boundaries; men, by contrast, commonly have 'hard' ego-boundaries and competitive relations with others.[28] If we hold the self to have 'porous' ego boundaries, open to that which lies immediately beyond self, this may enable us the better to conceive of how it is that we are open to that dimension of reality which is God. Again, it has been notable (considering how few women are philosophers) that the understanding of attentiveness, quite fundamental to the religious disposition of which I have been speaking, has in large part been developed by women thinkers (among others Simone Weil, Iris Murdoch and Martha Nussbaum).

Picking up an orange at a dinner table that he might explain how misguided are 'Arts' people in their understanding of the 'Big Bang', a theoretical

---

28 Nancy Chodorow, *The Reproduction of Mothering* (Berkeley: University of California Press, 1978); Carol Gilligan, *In a Different Voice* (Cambridge, MA: Harvard University Press, 1982).

physicist commented in my presence that first you must set co-ordinates, only then can one 'measure' from what one has chosen. The talk of God as 'outside' the world or 'before' time, the people of Israel the apple of his eye, is simply anachronistic today, stemming from an age when the world was thought but 6,000 years old, the earth at the centre of the universe and Jerusalem at the centre of the earth. No more appropriate is talk of God as King, Lord, Judge and Father, the patriarchs of an ancient nomadic society. We should be less timid in re-thinking our religious paradigms. Human liberty and progress have been associated not with religious but secular ages: Ancient Greece, the Renaissance, the Enlightenment and the twentieth century. Placing ourselves at the centre of our world, we should exercise that autonomy which Kant considered the hallmark of human maturity.[29] Then alone shall we take into our own hands such urgent matters as the population explosion which, devastating our planet and crippling our resources, engenders conflict. Furthermore, given an understanding of God such as I am advocating, we can better engage with those who equate God with a superfluous object for which, together with fairies and Father Christmas, there is no evidence. The God of our fathers is the lynchpin of structures of thought and of a society fast disappearing. On both epistemological and moral grounds it is incumbent upon us to speak otherwise of that love and power which we may truly name 'God'.

---

29 Kant, 'What is Enlightenment?' (1784) in Lewis White Beck (ed. and tr.), *Kant: On History* (New York: Macmillan, 1985).

6

Love and Reason

JANET MARTIN SOSKICE

I

I can remember being an atheist, or perhaps an agnostic, for in those days I did not think much about God one way or another. I knew at that time there were Christians – and I suppose adherents to other faiths whose adherence I judged 'ethnic' and thus not applicable in my own instance. As for Christians, I assumed they came in two sorts – those who went along for a sense of belonging or from a sense of nostalgia, rather like attending a bridge club or square dancing; and evangelicals, who were clearly under-educated and over-excited. I can remember, from my lofty, 21-year-old height of wisdom, thinking that it must be soothing to be one of the latter, all of whose problems in life could be seen to be answered. In my assumed clarity about religion I, in fact, knew nothing about it at all, and in my own case it was only dramatic conversion which turned me round and put my feet on a slower, steadier, more modest path into a truth whose depths are fathomless. Can I even say to those who, it seems to me, stand where I once stood (the cultured despisers of religion, as Schleiermacher might have said) what I now feel I know, and don't know, about God? It would be hard. Because it is not just that faith gives new answers to old questions – it gives new questions, a new world where even the most educated come as babes, born again.

In my own case, and as I have discussed elsewhere, faith came from a dramatic religious experience.[1] It was not theatrically dramatic – I was not rescued from a shipwreck by passing dolphins, or saved from falling to my death off a cliff-face by a gracefully placed liana; nevertheless it was dramatic to me. I was in the shower, on an ordinary day, and found myself to be surrounded by a presence of love, a love so real and so personal that I could not doubt it. I had not, as far as I know, been looking for God or

---

1 See Rupert Shortt, *God's Advocates* (London: Darton, Longman & Todd, 2005), pp. 24–42.

thinking of God, or enjoyed a particularly good or an especially bad day – although at a later date my friends gently, one by one, took me aside to say that, although they did not in any way wish to appear to discredit my experience, I had at the time of this momentous shower been either thus or so, happy or depressed . . . their various explanations were conflicting.

As for me, I could not doubt the reality of that loving presence, and still cannot. I now know that one-off 'religious experiences' of this sort are rather frowned upon by the best theologians, among whom Thomas Aquinas, the confessors of Teresa of Avila and Professor Nicholas Lash, as susceptible to mood and delusion, and if I have my life to live over I will try to have a higher class of conversion experience – but this is what happened to me. I was turned around. Converted. Not that I had been the sort of person who kicked old ladies and found myself now helping them across the street. I was much the same person, but facing in a new direction. Above all, I felt myself to have been addressed, not with any words or for any particular reason and certainly not from any merit – it was in that sense gratuitous – but by One to whom I could speak. For this reason I am particularly drawn to theologians and philosophers who interest themselves in address, in the God who calls and the God who speaks.

It is the sense of address that Paul Ricoeur, writing of what he did not find in the books of the philosophers, marked out as distinctive of his own Protestant faith – this sense of finding oneself to be addressed, in the words of scripture, by the Word of God.

Ricoeur's portrayal of his religious life is as that of a listener and as a listener to texts. After years of seeking to keep the religious and the philosophical apart (religious faith being so despised in the French academy of his youth), it was only in later years that he began to seek a 'twofold reference' and to ask 'What would it mean for a philosopher to be a listener?' What would it be *for the philosopher to listen to Christian preaching*? In an essay entitled 'Naming God' which addresses this theme, Ricoeur writes that this *listening* involves two kinds of letting go – the dismissal of two kinds of hubris. First we must 'let go (*se depouiller*) of every form of onto-theological knowledge. Even – and especially when – the word God is involved. In this regard, the amalgamation of Being and God is the most subtle seduction'.[2]

But this alone is not sufficient. Indeed, Kantian philosophy achieves this by philosophical means by moving knowledge from the side of the object to be known to the side of the knowing subject. This is no advance.

---

2 'Naming God', in Ricoeur, *Figuring the Sacred*, ed. Mark Wallace, tr. David Pellauer (Minneapolis: Fortress Press, 1995), p. 223.

For if a first hubris is knocked down, that of metaphysical knowledge, a second one replaces it, that of knowledge that is no longer metaphysical but transcendental. This knowledge makes the 'I think' the principle of everything that is valid . . . The idea of a subject that posits itself thus becomes the unfounded foundation, or better, the foundation that founds itself, in relation to which every rule of validity is derived. In this way, the subject becomes the supreme 'presupposition'.[3]

This is the fantasy of self-founding, when the subject becomes the supreme 'presupposition'. But to 'confess that one is a listener', Paul Ricoeur writes, 'is from the very beginning to break with the project dear to many, and even perhaps all, philosophers: to begin discourse without any presuppositions'.[4] Those who listen to Christian preaching stand in 'the order of presupposition' – they have entered that famous 'circle of believing in order to understand and understanding in order to believe'. By the end of his essay it appears that philosophy, too, and despite its ambitions to neutrality rarely if ever escapes presuppositions, one of which, for modernity, is that of the self-founding subject. By contrast, the listener to preaching willingly stands in the *order of presuppositions* but:

the presupposition is no longer self-founding, the beginning of the self from and by the self, but rather the assumption of an antecedent meaning that has always preceded me. *Listening excludes founding oneself.* The movement toward listening requires, therefore, a second letting go, the abandoning of a more subtle and more tenacious pretension than that of onto-theological knowledge. It requires giving up (*dessaisissement*) the human self in its will to mastery, sufficiency, and autonomy. The Gospel saying 'whoever would save his life will lose it', applies to this giving up.[5]

II

In principio erat verbum et Verbum erat apud Deum et Deus erat Verbum.
(John 1)

In the second edition of the famous New Testament in Greek (1519), Erasmus startled his readership by suggesting that a better Latin translation than *Verbum* (Word) for the Greek original of this famous opening to John's Gospel might be *In principio erat sermo* – in the beginning was

3 Loc. cit.
4 Ibid., p. 217.
5 Ibid., p. 224,

speech or conversation. To support his position, Erasmus noted that Cyprian (in the third century CE) used *sermo* whenever citing this verse and that Tertullian, writing slightly earlier, remarks that *sermo* is the customary reading. Augustine, in the late fourth–fifth century, is aware of both translations.[6]

But why prefer *sermo* to *verbum* as a translation of the Greek, *logos*? Erasmus provides several reasons: *sermo* has a softer and more mellifluous sound; *sermo* is a masculine noun and thus a better match for the masculine Christ (the '*sermo*' made flesh) than the neutral *verbum*. But over and above all these, *sermo*, he thinks, catches the sense of dialogue – or address, 'In the beginning was – the address'.[7] It is this that the Word made flesh does – creates, calls, addresses.

The early Christian theologians mentioned above almost certainly understood that John 1 was written deliberately to echo the first books of Genesis, and that in those books God creates through speaking. God calls creation into being and names its elements, God creates human beings, male and female, who are speaking beings. God in Genesis goes on to call Abram out of the land of Ur to become Abraham, the father of a new people. God calls to Moses from the burning bush requesting that he lead the Israelites out of their Egyptian bondage. In this sense the early books of the Old Testament are vocation narratives, for they are about calls, callings and thus finding oneself to be addressed.

Already in the *Book of Wisdom*, a Jewish text that has come down to us through the Greek of the Septuagint, we find God's Word (*logos*) identified with God's powerful agency. Philo of Alexandria, a Greek-speaking Jew of the first century CE, regularly designates God in his creative power as the *Logos*. Is this a Hellenistic slippage away from pure Semitic ideas? It seems not, and one of our best clues is indeed the translation into the Latin of the first chapter of John. In this, as we have seen, the word *Logos* of John's prologue is rendered *verbum* or *sermo* but not, as would be more natural in philosophical Greek, *ratio*. It is a reasonable guess that *verbum* is preferred to the more obvious *ratio* by Jerome and others because it retains the Hebrew link to speech and speaking.

Philo's identification of the *Word of God* as the agent of creation is not entirely clear. Did Philo intend a subordinate power, or was this a way of speaking of the power of God, Godself? Philo, who is famously inconsistent, suggests both. However, it is clear that he wants to connect the creating God with the God who gives order. In his exposition of the first seven days of

6 Simon Goldhill, *Who Needs Greek?: Contests in the Cultural History of Hellenism* (Cambridge: Cambridge University Press), pp. 25–6.
7 Ibid., p. 26.

creation in *On the Creation of the Cosmos According to Moses*, Philo makes clear his belief that Moses, who he by faithful tradition believes to be the author of the books of the Pentateuch, is not writing literally but rather using the device of the *ordering* of the first days of creation as an introduction to books that will substantially be concerned with the giving of the Law, order for God's reasoning creatures, given by divine address.

What is it to know oneself to be addressed? By what? By whom? Augustine frames his *Confessions* as a search for a God whose existence he never doubts but whose reality and presence elude him. He tells us that in his early years, fired by his reading of Cicero, he sought everywhere for Wisdom (or for God, he identifies the two). He interrogated various theories of the divine nature and even attempted a Plotinian spiritual ascent, none of which satisfied him until his famously elusive 'conversion' in the garden in Milan.

Some theologians have detected in Augustine's writings a confident grasp of his own subjectivity, whether in Cartesian or post-Kantian mode, which is then paralleled by a confident grasp of the nature of God. By this argument the subject, finding no certainties in the world, becomes by introspection directly certain of itself. Certainty of God then becomes the correlate of direct certainty of the self.[8] This sounds too tinny and smooth to be Augustine. It is true that in the *Confessions* he discovers God to be 'more inward than my most inward part and higher than the highest element within me' (*Confessions* III.vi.11) but this, in light of his continued insistence on God's incomprehensibility to us, is scarcely to resolve a mystery. Far from certainty of God being the direct correlative of certainty of the self, Augustine says more than once, and even in his late writings, that from the experience that we do not even know ourselves we can gather how incomprehensible God is.[9] According to Augustine we do not understand ourselves – and this not only when we are far from God but even as we are drawn near. Augustine, entering into fullness of faith in the Milan garden, does not come to know what God *is*, not at any rate in the sense of knowing the Divine essence. He comes to know rather that *he is known by God*. He comes to believe that the God of Abraham, Isaac and Jacob has addressed him and that he can speak to God. And that is what he does in the *Confessions*, composed as a prayer addressed to God. This is possible, Augustine believes, not from any philosophical or spiritual athleticism on his part, but as the effect of grace. Before, he knew no humility. He wanted to storm the citadel of the divine by intellect or action, to gain God by his own works.

---

8 For an argument of this nature see Jürgen Moltmann, *Trinity and the Kingdom of God* (London: SCM Press, 1982), p. 14.

9 Augustine, *On the Trinity*, XV.VII.13.

But in the garden, epistemological obsession is quietened before what is given, before the 'I AM'.

How then does this fit with philosophy? Does Augustine cease to be a philosopher on becoming a Christian? Not at all, rather he begins to be a Christian philosopher. When he comes to believe that God has always seen him, always known him, has always been with him, even when he wandered far away, he comes to understand more fully what divine omniscience, omnipresence, immutability and eternity are. They are not the features of a deity who is far away but of one who is 'more inward than my most inward part', and at the same time creator of all that is.

It is not surprising that Augustine comes back time and time again to Exodus 3, where God speaks to Moses from the burning bush. Here, it seems, is God at his most metaphysical, giving his name to Moses as 'I AM WHO I AM'. Augustine understands this to mean that God is Being Itself and understands this in terms of a thesis that is altogether Christian (and Jewish) – *creatio ex nihilo*. God is the source of all that is, including space and time. God creates all that is and, moreover, does so freely, out of no compulsion (thus discounting any theory by which creation emerges inevitably, like rays from the sun). God creates as Gift, and out of Love.

This teaching, only fully embraced by both Christian teachers and Rabbis from about the third century CE onwards, is emergent much earlier and, for instance, clearly detectable in Philo. Although Philo is not entirely consistent on the matter, the fundamental convictions which inform *creatio ex nihilo* are present in his writings: God has created the world out of non-being, moulding formless matter. God, Philo believes, has created time itself.[10] But precisely because he is moving in the Greek milieu he needs to distinguish his Jewish position from the philosophical consensus of this day. He rejects outright Aristotle's idea that the universe is eternal, an idea which he sees as incompatible with providence. The cosmos is totally dependent on God, and God is in no sense dependent on the cosmos.[11]

Now this is the critical point for the doctrine of God and also, as Philo clearly realizes, for religious language – for since God the Creator cannot

---

10 See *Leg. All* III 10; *Fuga* 46; *Mos.* II 267. For a fuller version of this argument see Soskice, 'Athens and Jerusalem, Alexandria and Edessa: Is there a Metaphysics of Scripture?', *International Journal of Systematic Theology*, Vol. 8, No. 2, April 2006, pp. 149–62.

11 'He is full of Himself and sufficient for Himself. It was so before the creation of the world, and is equally so after the creation of all that is' (*de Mutatione Nominum*, 26–7). As to *creatio ex nihilo*, Philo appears not to be much interested or consistent. It seems likely he lacks the doctrine in a strict sense, tending more to an idea of God moulding some primal matter in the manner of Plato's *Timaeus*. On the other hand, it is clear that this matter has no reality over and against or apart from God.

strictly *be like* any created being then we *cannot class* God or insert God into any category appropriate to our created kind.

God is thus, for Philo, in the strict sense unknowable and unnameable by us, yet despite this we cannot cease to praise God and should not cease to search after the essence of God, 'For nothing is better than to search for the true God, even if the discovery of Him eludes human capacity, since the very wish to learn, if earnestly entertained, produces untold joys and pleasures.'[12]

Whenever these epistemological problems arise, Philo turns to the example of Moses, 'sacred guide, most beloved by God'. For did not Moses himself cry out and ask God, 'Reveal Thyself to me'.[13] The request was of course refused, but Philo's paraphrasing in *The Special Laws* of the divine reply to Moses is worth noting,

> Thy zeal I approve as praiseworthy, but the request cannot fitly be granted to any that are brought into being by creation. I freely bestow what is in accordance with the recipient; for not all that I can give with ease is within man's power to take, and therefore to him that is worthy of My grace I extend all the boons which he is capable of receiving. But the apprehension of Me is something more than human nature, yea even the whole heaven and universe will be able to contain.[14]

Philo will also return, again and again, to Exodus 3 – God's address to Moses from the burning bush – and especially to God's reply to Moses' request for a name. Since no name can represent God's nature, no name is correct. This Philo takes to be the purport of God's reply to Moses, 'I Am He that IS'. God alone, Philo tells us, 'by His very nature' cannot be seen, and God alone cannot, in this sense, be named. 'My nature is to be, not to be spoken.' It is worth pointing out, especially since it is usually assumed that it is the work of metaphysical medieval Christians, that the Jewish Philo takes God's reply to Moses to mean that God is Being Itself, and the source of all being. Hellenistic Jews were already doing metaphysics. Yet Philo then makes a remark which is entirely Jewish and entirely alien to any pagan philosophical notions of God as 'the One'. Glossing the mysterious name Philo says:

> ... 'I am He that IS' (Exodus 3.14), which is equivalent to 'My nature is to be, not to be spoken.' Yet that the human race should not totally lack a

12 *The Special Laws*, I.36.
13 *The Special Laws*, I.41.
14 *The Special Laws*, I.43–4.

title to give to the supreme goodness He allows them to use *by licence of language*, as though it were His proper name, the title of Lord God of the three natural orders, teaching, perfection, practice, which are symbolized in the records as Abraham, Isaac and Jacob.[15]

God is unnameable but '*by licence of language*' gives Moses a name so that the human race should not be bereft. Scripture is both nettle and dock-leaf. A God who creates heaven and earth cannot properly be named in earthly words; however, that same God has given names by which God may be named for '. . . those who are born into mortality must needs have some substitute for the divine name'. Why? 'So that they may approach if not the fact at least the name of supreme excellence *and be brought into relation with it*'.[16]

In spite of, or perhaps *because* of, God's utter transcendence (a transcendence that goes further than in Aristotle), Philo's God is still a God of grace, 'a personal being with which man has a reciprocal relation'.[17]

Philo has noticed, as will Augustine, Aquinas and many others who follow, that while it may be that, at the burning bush, God gives a name which 'is no name', *nonetheless God gives a name!* We can name God, Philo believes, because God has given us names by which we may call upon him. God is above all named, not in terms of essence, by who God is for us – ' the God of Abraham, and of Isaac and of Jacob', the God who called Israel out of Egypt, who spoke from the burning bush. The ultimacy of God is matched by God's kindness and love, his intimacy.

And this is what Augustine comes to know in the garden in Milan. God remains eternal, immutable One, but One who has addressed him (something the god of the philosophers could never do) and whom he can now address.

When I read the current critics of religion, Richard Dawkins and others, I take them to be saying that religious belief in general, maybe monotheism as we know it, holds a tidy and consoling picture of a God, a 'sky fairy' quite easy to understand, who affords a rosy glow to life's daily complaints and failures.[18] I find something quite different in scripture and tradition – a God beyond all my conceiving: 'Whatever way we have of thinking of him is a way of failing to understand him as he really is', says Aquinas in the *Summa Theologiae* (*S.T. 13, 11*); but, it must be added, a God whose love is beyond

15 *de Mutatione Nominum*, II.12–13, my italics.
16 *de Mutatione Nominum* 13, my italics.
17 David Runia, *Exegesis and Philosophy: Studies of Philo of Alexandria* (Aldershot: Variorum, 1990), p. 12.
18 I owe 'sky fairy' to George Pitcher.

my conceiving, whose kindness is beyond my conceiving, whose power is beyond my conceiving and who has chosen to address us in his Word – the Word of creation and, for me as a Christian, the Word of Redemption, the two being one and the same.

I can speak to God not because I know what God 'is' but because I believe that God knows who I am, and because I have been addressed – not just in that primitive religious experience but in the words of scripture, through the teachings of the tradition, through the preaching of the gospel and the sacraments of the Church.

Writing from the heartland of the Syriac-speaking Church in the mid-fourth century, St Ephrem develops his theology in Semitic categories. His theology is delivered in teaching songs, or madrasha, and one madrasha is in the form of dialogue between Reason and Love on whether God can be named.[19] What interests me is the sides they respectively take. Following Locke, Hume and others, we naturally suppose that Reason (metaphysics) would come forth with a number of positive titles for God (all-powerful, all-present, and so on) while Love would wish to keep the mystery intact. In fact St Ephrem's madrasha proposes the reverse – Reason says it is blasphemy to try to name God who must transcend all our categories of naming. Love responds, and in so doing wins the argument, by saying that Praise is the response made possible *and* necessary by the divine self-disclosure. 'Blest are You (God), who finally grant the victorious crown to purest Love.'

The dynamic is the same as in Philo: given the holiness and otherness of the One who has made all that is, Reason recommends silence, but God's own gift, through the creation in which we observe God's traces and through Scripture, licenses praise.

---

19 Robert Murray SJ, 'St Ephrem's Dialogue of Reason and Love', *Sobornost*, 2 (1980).

7

Beyond My God, with God's Blessing

FRANCIS X. CLOONEY, SJ

I

For some 35 years now I have studied Hindu religious traditions with care and attention. In my research and writing I have positioned myself as an Indologist or scholar of Hinduism, but more importantly as a Christian theologian seeking to deepen my and our Christian understanding of our faith. Indological and cultural concerns aside, my main hope has been to take these traditions seriously, even to the point that my study would have a long-term effect on my own Christian intellectual and spiritual identity. My goal has been to know God (insofar as theology can), understand the world in relation to God, and our human destiny in light of God's intentions – all in light of Hindu wisdom, and while still a Catholic. I have also found that this determination to learn more of God through Hindu traditions has not caused or demanded any permanent dilution of my commitment to the truth of the Christian tradition, God revealed in Jesus Christ and in the Spirit. Hinduism, honestly explored, has much to do with Catholic identity; I have always thought of my study of Hinduism as a Christian mission imposed upon me, to carry out better the inter-religious learning that is necessary and popular today.

But what I have just written is not enough, since it would be dishonest to make the learning process appear to be a safe borrowing from another religion. If engagement with that other is to occur in a way that is neither superficial nor merely a predictable enterprise, I must once in a while step beyond my commitment to ways of thinking, speaking and acting that are intimate to my, our, Christian way of thinking about and encountering God. The proliferation of Hindu images and words about God creates possibilities for insight, available only if we turn to these sites for learning with utmost seriousness, as if each alone matters at this moment. This is learning at the edge – but I have also come to see this letting go as a real, though extreme Christian practice, intimate to my Christian faith. This entry upon another tradition is undertaken for the sake of learning of God in a new way; it is, I believe, a deeply necessary Christian act, of the kind that one can discern to be God's will for us at particular points in our lives.

II

I have found some inspiration for this spiritual adventure and spiritual risk in the history of the Jesuit order to which I have belonged for over 40 years. From its origins the Society of Jesus has been a religious community with a sense of mission – being sent out, away from the established and non-contested centres of Catholic faith, to the places, in Europe but then more famously elsewhere in the world, to preach the gospel where it had not been preached. It is common for Jesuits to see Francis Xavier, one of the first Jesuits and the first to travel to the East, as representing a quintessential Jesuit prospect, that of leaving behind Christendom and the settled life of a Christian context, to go where the Church and its culture are not at all present, to live, work and die there, without expectation of return. The earliest Jesuits gave no hint that they were seeking God in the East or beyond Christendom; they already had found God, God had encountered them in the Church. But they fulfilled their mission as Christians, and thus their relationship with Christ, only by going far away from the familiar linguistic and cultural religious places in which they had grown up. They dressed and ate differently, spoke and wrote new languages, and lived by different cultural customs. They changed more than they knew, and saw in Francis Xavier a model and permission for what happened.

More than 60 years later, Roberto de Nobili (1579–1656) came to India with new ideas, and worked as a missionary and scholar – scholar because missionary – in deep south India. He is remembered in part because of his radical adaptation, his decision to dress like a Hindu holy man, to keep the same strict diet and purity rules, 'becoming as Indian as possible' for the sake of his mission. In his *Report on Indian Customs*, he defends maximal cultural adaptation as simply in keeping with the traditions of the earliest Church. Near the end of the treatise, he gives some inspirational examples, promoting particularly the idea that St Paul was so free and dedicated to his apostolic mission that he could put on or take off his religious and social markings, as needed:

> Surely [Paul] was a man enamored with the love of abjection and desti-tution from human pomp, and he gloried in the fact that he was unknown to fame, financially insecure, and without resources for the sake of saving souls, living so poorly that he denied himself the service of pious women, whom the other apostles made use of quite legitimately.

Yet he did not desist at other times, when it was necessary to extol the dignity of his family and birthplace and to disclose the noble qualities with which he was more richly endowed than others.

de Nobili also points to the example of Francis Xavier:

Neither did our holy Father Francis Xavier hesitate to copy the same usage when he saw that the glory of God demanded it. Thus, in Japan he removed his customary humble dress and assumed robes of silk and various ornaments. Indeed, the religious of our Order who followed in his footsteps on the China Mission and are engaged in the task of winning over souls for Christ our Lord always appear in public dressed in silken garments, wearing a long beard, their fingernails and hair well trimmed, and holding a fan of honor in their hand.[1]

de Nobili is defending inculturation, adapting oneself to local styles, accepting but not settling for the tradition of radical poverty and the stripping of self for the gospel's sake. Apostolic need highlights the necessity and wisdom of stripping off accustomed garb in order to dress oneself in accord with strange new customs, so that communication might occur. It did not diminish Christian commitment to put on and take off its external signs; rather, as Paul and Xavier and others saw it, the greater glory of God sometimes demands this freedom from real but lesser goods for the sake of the greater.

Our challenge is different, certainly, and external adaptation is not enough, if inter-religious learning is to be meaningful. But a useful analogy between exterior and interior adaptation can be drawn, even if the early Jesuits would never have imagined our challenge to foster a necessary openness that also entails some distance from the forms and words of Christian commitment. Today, accommodation in appearance and social location do not go far enough, even though such matters remain important. Rather, a still more interior stripping is necessary, a letting go of God as named and known in order to learn from another tradition, for the greater glory of God: this is a risk of heart and mind given over to a new religious possibility, a risk and self-giving analogous to the efforts of the early missionaries. Understood as a mission, this deep engagement in another religious tradition is not in denial of Christian commitments, or a concession to a secular age; rather, it is a moment of detachment for the sake of encounter with the

---

1 *Report on Indian Customs* 9.1.4, pp. 169–70 in *Preaching Wisdom to the Wise: Three Treatises by Roberto de Nobili, SJ, Missionary, Scholar, and Saint in 17th Century India.* (Re)translated by Anand Amaladass, SJ, and Francis X. Clooney, SJ (Chennai: Satya Nilayam Publications, 2005).

religious wisdom of Hindu India (or, of course, with other traditions we might choose to encounter).

If I have been willing to believe that Hindu traditions can communicate the truth of God to me, this becomes a new Christian mission that stretches more radically the noble ideal of detaching the Christian message from particular cultural contexts. It is a matter of taking them to heart while at the same moment believing that God *wants* this extreme learning to occur. The choice I thus make to learn seriously outside the Christian context remains, I believe, well within the frame of Christian faith, having no meaning after or apart from that faith. But it really does mean to learn religiously, in faith, beyond the boundaries of my faith.

III

It may be that a Hindu saint offers the most vivid guidance here. Ramakrishna (1836–86) was a nineteenth-century Hindu mystic in Bengal, an ecstatic devotee of the goddess Kali. Though a simple priest in the temple near Calcutta and not a public figure, his life and experience form the inspiration for the Ramakrishna Mission and Vedanta Society that continues to flourish today. Since he was not a writer, we know of him through early secondary sources, most importantly Mahendranath Gupta's *Gospel of Ramakrishna* and Swami Saradananda's *Sri Ramakrishna and His Divine Play*.

Although Ramakrishna was deeply devoted to Kali, he pursued various forms of practice connected with other spiritual paths – such as Vaisnava devotionalism, and non-dualist Vedanta – as if to expand his spiritual capacities and experiences. His early biographer Swami Saradananda tells us that at one crucial point Ramakrishna was learning the way of non-dualist Vedanta practice under the guidance of a renunciant known as Tota Puri. But he kept falling short of the end of this practice, unable to reach the anticipated goal; his devotion to Kali, the divine person utterly central to his life, stood in the way of his appropriating a non-dualist unity in which any relationship to the goddess would have to be put aside, transcended. To complete the path proposed to him, he would have to forgo his *relationship* with Kali:

> But despite all my attempts, during meditation I could not cross the realm of name and form and bring my mind to the unconditioned state. I had no difficulty in withdrawing my mind from all objects except one: the all-too-familiar form of the Blissful Mother, radiant with Pure Consciousness, that appeared before me as a living reality and prevented me from passing beyond the realm of name and form . . .

Tota Puri gave him a sliver of glass, and told him to press its point against his forehead, for the sake of better concentration. Ramakrishna's recollection of the experience suggests that for him the glass symbolized the sharp edge of true discrimination, by which he could cut through even his devotion to Kali, letting go of his interior image of her, as if putting aside his devotion to her:

> I sat down to meditate again, firmly determined. As soon as the form of the Divine Mother appeared in my mind, I used my discrimination as a sword of knowledge and with it mentally cut that form in two. Then all distinctions disappeared from my mind, and it swiftly soared beyond the realm of name and form. I lost myself in samadhi.[2]

Later in the *Divine Play*, Saradananda returns to this event, and reports that this 'rending' of the Mother had its full meaning only in light of Ramakrishna's enduring love for her:

> As soon as I [Ramakrishna] gathered my mind and made it one-pointed, the Mother immediately appeared before me. I then had no inclination to push beyond that form. As many times as I tried to make the mind empty by driving everything away, so many times did that form appear. After long deliberation I at last strengthened my mind, envisioned knowledge to be a sword, and mentally cut that form in two. Then the mind became completely empty, and it speedily reached the nirvikalpa state [beyond all concepts and words].[3]

The resultant emptiness is painful and distressing, precisely as a 'removal' of the Goddess by and from someone deeply attached to her:

> He knew that the Divine Mother was his heart's only desire, and he spent his time meditating on Her form and serving her day and night. So when he somehow removed that form from his mind, what else could his mind hold on to? His mind became completely objectless and free from thought waves and finally reached the nirvikalpa state. O reader, if you cannot understand this phenomenon, please at least try to imagine it. Then you may understand the extent to which Sri Ramakrishna made the

---

2 *Sri Ramakrishna and His Divine Play*, 312, as translated by Swami Chetanananda (St Louis: Vedanta Society, 2003). In Swami Nikhilananda's older translation, it was entitled *The Great Master*.
3 Ibid., 419.

Divine Mother his own and how he loved Her with 'one hundred twenty-five percent' of his mind.[4]

The scene concludes with Ramakrishna reporting that his intense meditative emptiness came to an end when the Mother spoke to him, commanding him to return from the non-dualist state to a quasi-ordinary existence. She had protected him during his ecstasy, keeping him alive when the body might otherwise have ceased to function, since 'much of the Mother's work was yet to be done through this body, and many people would benefit if it were preserved'. According to this account, it was she who wanted him to reach her in a state that let go even of their very distinctness – and yet too it was also her will that he return to a more ordinary state, for her sake and the sake of the world (419–20).

To fulfil his encompassing vision of her as the universal Mother, Ramakrishna had thus to let go of her and move beyond her before returning to her yet again more intensely, at her bidding. To make possible this dynamic of going away – to the other religious practice – and back, he needed her permission – and received it.

Even if we had more accounts and historical data by which to get entirely clear who Ramakrishna was and how he was thinking about his Mother and his experiments in non-dualism, it would still be impossible for someone today to replicate Ramakrishna's situation. But even so, we can learn from his instinct that he needed the goddess's permission for his journey to find her beyond any way he had known her thus far. Believing and loving 'one hundred twenty-five percent' put him in the situation of a wilder, unexpected devotion that drew him closer to her and left her behind.

Refusing to limit expectations simply on faith or rational grounds, I have hoped to enter as if fully into the religious and intellectual world of Hinduism, beyond the images and expectations of my Christian faith – with a cultivated sense that God would allow me to let go of the knowledge of God I already had. Can I not likewise cut through my images of God even today, and see this as God's will?

Like Ramakrishna who was ambivalent about the prospect of a radical non-dualist experience but moved forward with the conviction that his Mother was calling him to advance, I (or any Christian) in this position may suffer the difficulty of taking another religious tradition (too) seriously, experiencing the cost of following through on what we learn in a vividly different, other tradition. This is a costly affair, letting go of my basic, most familiar and appropriate way of praying as a Christian, so as to embrace for a time a Hindu way of knowing God, in a spiritual vulnerabil-

4 Ibid., 419.

ity that on strictly theoretical grounds might in principle seem impossible for the Christian. Which choice one makes – to go forward, step back – it is the possibility of this as a *Christian* choice that matters most.[5]

IV

How far then can I go in learning from another religious tradition, by way of measured, intentional study and reading? I would like to make the preceding reflections more concrete by an example drawn from my own work. For it is in my actual study of Hinduism, after all, that I have come across the difficult possibility I have been describing here. By study, I have been learning to create a freer space wherein what I have already known of God in Christ enables me to learn anew, in the words and images of Hindu traditions.

More specifically: I recently wrote a Christian commentary on the three mantras sacred to the Srivaisnava Hindu tradition of south India:[6]

The Tiru Mantra: Aum, obeisance to Narayana.
The Carama Sloka: Having completely given up all modes of righteousness, to Me alone come for refuge. From all sins I will make you free. Do not grieve.
The Dvaya Mantra: I approach for refuge the feet of Narayana with Sri; obeisance to Narayana with Sri.

These mantras are central to Srivaisnavism's theology, piety and commentarial production. They are short, and, compared with many other mantras, relatively straightforward and easy to remember, simple words expressive of praise of Lord Narayana (Tiru Mantra), of his invitation to the devotee to surrender completely (Carama Sloka), and the devotee's wholehearted response in taking refuge with Narayana and the goddess Sri (Dvaya Mantra). Elucidated with the commentator's acute eye, they condense the ancient, large body of revelation and revered tradition, offering a succinct distillation of teachings that can be explicated as filling out the doctrine, life and practice of the community. They chart the human acknowledgement of dependence on God, the divine and human exchange of commitments, and the divine promise of liberation and ultimate peace. Thus the mantras are

---

5 See also my choice to work with hymns praising three goddesses, addressing them directly, in *Divine Mother, Blessed Mother* (New York: Oxford University Press, 2005), rather than with texts about them.
6 *The Truth, the Way, the Life: Christian Commentary on the Three Holy Mantras of the Srivaisnava Hindus* (Leuven: Peeters Publishing, 2008).

considered by the Srivaisnava tradition to contain, in a particularly condensed and essential fashion, all that needs to be said about the human condition, the goal of life, the way to that goal, and obstacles thereto. To utter them is to say everything at once, and for prayer.

As things became clearer in the course of my study – with the help of traditional commentaries – I learned to see a pattern of worship, response, surrender and promise, such as can be imagined as components of a spiritual conversation:

Praising God: Aum, obeisance to Narayana (Tiru Mantra).
Divine invitation: Having completely given up all modes of righteousness, to Me alone come for refuge . . . (Carama Sloka a).
Surrendering to God: I approach for refuge the feet of Narayana with Sri; obeisance to Narayana with Sri (Dvaya Mantra).
Divine promise: . . . from all sins I will make you free (Carama Sloka b).
Final instruction: Do not grieve (Carama Sloka c).

Words heard, uttered, in divine–human exchange: the mantras are more than theology, they are also meant to be recited, prayed as praise of God, surrender to God – and thus, in their very density and particularity, they are liable to raise particularly difficult questions for anyone who studies them. My sense was that I needed to engage them deeply, understanding them in such a way that I would also be taking them to heart – 'as if' my prayer, as my prayer – uttering the words in a frequency and with an immediacy meant to deeply inculcate their affective and intellectual force within my life, as words foreign to my tradition, yet now too as my words as well.

It may seem nearly impossible for a Christian, as a Christian, to make this choice and to meditate religiously on Narayana as worshipped in the Tiru Mantra, or to surrender to God using the Dvaya Mantra as my utterance; and yet the kind of study described here, an unprotected encounter that gives strange words a new power and familiarity, creates the possibility of praying in just this way, even hearing the Carama Sloka as God's own initiative and response. All of this quickly becomes too much, but this is an ideally awkward position for the Christian to be in, since finally real interreligious learning is at stake. In this way I reached the position of having to choose whether or not to pray with these mantras, finally faced with the real question of deciding whether or not to let go, for a time, of God as I have been accustomed to call upon God. I have hoped that Christ, who calls each of us to our vocation, sends us on particular missions and thus does not object to my appropriating words such as 'Narayana' and 'Narayana with Sri', allowing them for a time to echo in my mind and heart, hearing and responding to God, beyond God, sent by God.

V

Obliquely, though still more fundamentally, I have found inspiration in Luke's version of the Gerasene demoniac story. The possessed man, once cured, wants to stay with Jesus, but is sent away – by Jesus – to head in the other direction, in order to do the work Jesus has in mind for him:

> The man from whom the demons had gone out begged to go with him, but Jesus sent him away, saying, 'Return home and tell how much God has done for you.' So the man went away and told all over town how much Jesus had done for him. (Luke 8.38–39)[7]

This man – freed from his possession and transformed by contact with Jesus – became eloquent in speaking in the name of Jesus, and making known to all what Jesus had done for him. But the price was that he could not exercise this function until he 'went away', returning to a place where Jesus was not – moving away from Jesus to do the will of Jesus. Analogously, it is possible to be profoundly transformed by our contact with Jesus, and then to move away, sent into a new place, unencumbered for a moment by deep and still abiding commitments to Christ. This is what it means, can mean, for any of us who believes that Christ still speaks to us and gives us a mission in life, to learn more deeply another religious tradition, necessarily moving for a time to a distance from the familiar ground on which we would have previously known Christ.

VI

Christians can let go of God with a good sense that this is God's will, as a necessary moment within a Christian life that is attuned to pluralism. Real inter-religious learning, as Christian learning, requires that a space be left open, for some of us to stand at the edge. It is my faith, my hope, that God actually wants some of us to undertake these experiments, even if so dangerous a journey into the heart of another tradition is rarely given to anyone. It would not be good for the Church were we to invite everyone to let go, to seek God beyond Christ yet by Christ's favour; like most vocations, this is for the few.

A believer's task, today, is not only to believe that God is everywhere, but at the same time also to travel, intellectually and affectively, where God seems not to be. To do this requires of us skill in crossing boundaries. Ramakrishna, the early Jesuit missionaries, Jesus himself, show us ways of

---

7 New Revised Standard Version.

imagining this cross-over that is a real letting go, yet within a larger, intact realm governed by God's plan. It is to be sent away by Christ, faithful to a mission that is always and yet again a matter of going elsewhere, where Christ is not, yet where our God surprisingly appears when other names are heard and other faces appear.

To enter so deeply into another tradition for the sake of my faith, for the sake of knowing God differently – to see God in different images and hear God by different words in a different language – still and always carries with it the price of a certain distance from our own tradition. The old and familiar language of Christian faith is not denied, but neither are its terms allowed to preclude continued inquiry and even participation, in worlds where Christian words and images no longer have their accustomed power. While it is certainly possible to be sceptical, for liberal or conservative reasons, about what I am proposing and how I am imagining it, the dynamic I am suggesting is all the more worth considering because it eludes the dichotomies that liberals and conservatives have tended to propose.

8

In Search of Wisdom

MORNY JOY

In undertaking my explorations on the theme for this book, I have to make one reservation at the outset. Basically, this is that I am loath to identify myself with any form of institutional religion. The reason for this is that I have found, with a few minor exceptions, that both in their official policies and attitudes towards women, institutional forms of religion leave much to be desired. While their spiritual legacies are indeed rich, and there are many fine women and men today who exemplify their most revered ideals, I have not been able to affiliate myself in any formal capacity with a specific religion – Eastern or Western. That said, this does not imply that I categorically refuse to attend ceremonies from these respective traditions. Yet, if I am asked to describe my position, I would say, banal as it might sound, that my search in this life is one for wisdom. It has indeed been a challenge in writing this essay to try and be as precise as I can as to what exactly this means – as it is still a work in progress – both theoretically and existentially. As a scholar – trained in philosophy and Religious Studies – or, more specifically, in the approach of *Religionswissenschaft*, I have undertaken the study of both Eastern and Western religions. In this endeavour I have travelled much in the world and experienced in diverse settings what could be termed as both the benefits and liabilities of specific religious orientations – specifically as they relate to women. The question naturally ensues then as to what I understand as 'wisdom'; where I believe it is to be found today; and whether it could be considered to have spiritual implications.

One scholar who has helped me to clarify my understanding of the concept of wisdom is the French philosopher, Pierre Hadot, whose long life and exacting scholarship illustrate his own search which has been both academic and personal. Hadot is known principally for his studies on ancient philosophy and his book entitled *Plotinus*.[1] In another work, *Philosophy as*

---

1 Pierre Hadot, *Plotinus or The Simplicity of Vision*, tr. M. Chase (Chicago: University of Chicago Press, 1993 [1989]).

a Way of Life,[2] Hadot had begun to chart a course that differed somewhat from his earlier investigations into neo-Platonic mysticism. In this book, Hadot describes the ancient philosophical schools as more intent on inculcating a disciplined mode of existence, rather than endorsing a particular doctrine or set of conceptual truths. A philosopher then undertook exercises of a rational, imaginative or intuitive character, which varied according to the school,[3] that set him on a path of self-formation towards the goal of wisdom.[4] Hadot describes ancient philosophy: '[N]ot as a theoretical construct, but as a method for training people to live and to look at the world in a new way. It is an attempt to transform mankind'.[5] Thus, even if this discipline involved theoretical learning, it was always in the cause of a graduated, if not necessarily smooth, path of spiritual formation: 'This procedure is clear in the works of Plotinus and Augustine, in which all the detours, starts and stops, and digressions of the work are formative elements. One must always approach a philosophical work of antiquity with this idea of spiritual progress in mind'.[6]

In this same work, Hadot also describes the way that such an appreciation of philosophy as a journey towards wisdom began to change over time. This was basically due to the incorporation of its requisite spiritual discipline within the burgeoning Christian monastic movement. By medieval times, especially with the establishment of universities, philosophy had become the handmaiden (*ancilla*) of theology. Philosophy was thus reduced to a distinctly rational mode of thinking, essentially divorced from any path to deeper spiritual awareness – a characteristic it retains today. As Hadot states: 'It was no longer a way of life'.[7] Hadot does qualify this description by allowing that modern philosophy has, from time to time, acknowledged certain practices of a personal nature that are akin to the ancient philo-

---

2 Pierre Hadot, *Philosophy as a Way of Life: Spiritual Exercises from Socrates to Foucault*, ed. A. I. Davidson, tr. M. Chase (London: Blackwell, 1995 [1987]).

3 Hadot further explains: 'Each school will elaborate its rational depiction of this state of perfection in the person of the sage, and each will make an effort to portray him. It is true that this transcendent ideal will be deemed almost inaccessible; according to some schools there never was a wise man, while others say there were one or two of them, . . . and still others maintain that man can only attain this state during rare, fleeting moments (ibid., p. 57).

4 Hadot states: 'Every school practices exercises designed to ensure spiritual progress towards the ideal state of wisdom, exercises of reason that will be, for the soul, analogous to the athlete's training or to the application of a medical care' (ibid., p. 59). Hadot also notes: 'Unlike Buddhist practices of the Far East, Greco-Roman philosophical meditation is not linked to a corporal attitude but is a pure rational, imaginative, or intuitive exercise that can take extremely varied forms' (ibid., p. 59).

5 Ibid., p. 107.

6 Ibid., p. 64.

7 Ibid., p. 270.

sophical model. (In this connection he names both Descartes and Spinoza as retaining the appreciation of ancient philosophy as a practice of wisdom).[8]

Hadot reveals glimmers of his own personal views on this change in an interview with Michael Chase that is appended at the end of *Philosophy as a Way of Life*. In the interview, Chase, in attempting to summarize Hadot's own career trajectory, positions him as an expert on the thought and life of Plotinus, as well as other early mystical neo-Platonic philosophers. Hadot, in a self-reflective response, portrays himself as 'naively believing' at the time of his early studies of these mystics, which dated from approximately 1946, 'that I too could relive the Plotinian experience. But I later realized that it was an illusion.'[9] He continues by stating that he had even alluded to such a position in the conclusion of his earlier book on Plotinus where he had suggested that the idea of the 'purely spiritual life' is untenable.[10] This does not amount, however, to a complete rejection of Plotinus. He further observes:

> As I grow older, Plotinus speaks to me less and less, if I may say so. I have become considerably detached from him. From 1970 on, I have felt very strongly that it was Epicureanism and Stoicism which could nourish the spiritual life of men and women of our times, as well as my own. That was how I came to write my work on spiritual exercises.[11]

Hadot is guardedly positive about the possibility of contemporary people being able to take up the practical path towards wisdom. He remarks: 'Personally I believe firmly – albeit naively – that it is possible for man to live, not as a sage (*sophos*) – most of the ancients did not believe this to be possible – but as a practitioner of the ever-fragile exercise of wisdom'.[12] But there have been significant changes philosophically, even for Hadot himself.

From other remarks that he makes in the interview with Chase, it appears that Hadot himself has also been influenced by the work of Bergson, Heidegger, Sartre, Merleau-Ponty, Camus and Gabriel Marcel.[13] Though all of these philosophers could be described as engaged in tasks of self-transformation, and even cultivating a new philosophical way of seeing the world, there were no explicit spiritual practices involved. It was the

---

8 Ibid., p. 272.
9 Ibid., p. 281.
10 Ibid., p. 281. These reflections on the part of Hadot can be found in *Plotinus* (1993, pp. 110–13).
11 Ibid., pp. 280–1.
12 Ibid., p. 211.
13 Ibid., p. 279.

existentially inclined thinkers among them, however, who influenced Hadot to become more aware of the material (social and political), as well as the corporal conditions of life in this world.[14]

It was such insights that I think led Hadot to move beyond Plotinus and in the direction of the Stoic sage, Marcus Aurelius, in particular, on whom he also wrote a book entitled *The Inner Citadel*.[15] He cites this philosopher and emperor with approval, as a man whose deeds are in the cause of 'the discipline of action' in that they consist 'precisely in acting in the service of the human community, in other words, in practicing justice oneself and in correcting injustices'.[16] It would seem that this depiction on Hadot's part signals a subtle shift in his approach towards a revised form of wisdom that he now supports. This approach embraces constructive activity in this world, particularly in securing justice for one's fellow human beings. Although Hadot will still acknowledge that wisdom can involve a detached perception towards this world – i.e., that one can reach a state of trans-formed consciousness by disciplining what would be termed today the egoistic drives for self-fulfilment that govern habitual behaviour – he does not necessarily view it as requiring a concomitant withdrawal from society.

At the same time, Hadot presents two other practical qualities or modes of living, derived from ancient philosophy, that are characteristic of a person who seeks to progress on the path to wisdom. One of these is that of living in accordance with nature, and the other that of living with a focus on the present. Both of these modes of conduct have distinct implications for my own evolving understanding of wisdom.

For Hadot, living in accordance with nature does not involve either Kant's 'natural religion' or a Hegelian 'religion of nature'. Neither does it imply a Rousseau-like innocence, nor a vapid type of 'go with the flow'. Instead, it describes a discipline whereby one seeks to establish a form of coherence and balance in oneself that, at the same time, coincides with that of the larger cosmic dimension. Such a harmonious existence derives primarily from a voluntary personal commitment, rather than the acceptance of an externally imposed metaphysical system. Yet, it would nonetheless appear to incorporate certain principles that testify to the notion of an inter-

14 Hadot also refers to the work of Bergson, Husserl, and Merleau-Ponty, perceiving a certain affinity in different aspects of their work, though he is well aware of their differences. He finds in the phenomenology of Husserl and Merleau-Ponty the laudatory admonition to return to the 'things themselves', as a mark of a much-needed awareness of things in the world, as distinct from the habitual taken-for-grantedness of mundane perception (1995, p. 253). He finds a similar notion in Bergson's description of the 'displacement of attention' (1995, p. 254).
15 Pierre Hadot, *The Inner Citadel: The Meditations of Marcus Aurelius*, tr. M. Chase (Cambridge MA: Harvard University Press, 1998 [1992]).
16 Ibid., p. 283.

related and participatory vision of the universe. As Hadot has come to interpret this instruction, 'to act according to nature', also requires a commitment to contribute to the well-being of the whole. This has two distinct yet inter-related parts. These are: 'On the one hand, then, . . . to act [in accordance with nature is to act] in the service of the human community, and, on the other, to consent to the general movement of the universe.'[17] To appreciate fully these conditions, one needs a basic understanding of the inter-related Stoic universe. In Hadot's depiction, this universe was the result of an initial impulse or force that was associated, among other things, with both Reason and the work of Nature:

> The Stoics not only thought that universal Reason had, by means of its initial impulse, set in motion a law of development of the universe which has as its goal the good of the Whole; but they also admitted that this fundamental law of the universe has, as its primary goal the good of rational beings.[18]

Hadot then proceeds to place this understanding within a contemporary setting in such a manner that it would seem to be one to which he also subscribes.

> The Stoics were saying exactly the same thing as Einstein, when he denounced the optical illusion of a person who images himself to be a separate entity, while he is really a part of that whole which we call the universe. Einstein also declared that it is our duty to open our hearts to all living beings, and to all of nature in her magnificence.[19]

The philosopher in search of wisdom then, for Hadot, cannot presume to be a solitary soul, isolated from fellow human beings, but as a person engaged in a communal enterprise that fosters the well-being of the society and its members, at the same time that he or she affirms the wonders of

---

17 Hadot, *Philosophy as a Way of Life*, p. 283. There is no time to go into further detail of Marcus Aurelius's vision of the Stoic universe – but Hadot provides a succinct summary of its main features: 'Thus, this universe contains within itself its rational laws of development and organization. In this evolutionary process, as in the growth of a living being, everything contributes to the welfare of the entire organism, and everything is brought about as a necessary consequence of the initial impulse, and the rational program which the latter sets in motion' (*The Inner Citadel*, p. 156). Such a view posits the cosmos as containing within itself its own originary impulse and developmental process that bespeaks an immanent world view whereby 'the world possesses its own internal law' (p. 156).
18 Hadot, *Philosophy as a Way of Life*, p. 160.
19 Ibid., p. 283.

existence in this world.[20] In this manner, Stoic philosophy and its cosmology had certain resonances with contemporary process thought.

This affirmative orientation is also supplemented by Marcus Aurelius' advice to live in the present only – for it is here alone that one can find a measure of happiness. This recognition of 'the infinite value of the instant' is premised on the idea that the past can only bring nostalgia or regret, and that the future remains uncertain, if not full of foreboding, especially about death. In contrast, to live in the present means that attention is then centred on each moment. This is because the totality of existence itself is contained in this instant. Hadot expands on this insight: 'The instant is our only point of contact with reality.'[21] At the same time, however, it offers us 'the whole of reality [because] it allows us to participate in the overall movement of the event of the world, and the reality of the world's coming to be'.[22] For this to occur, a certain disciplined conduct is necessary: 'At each instant, we must therefore resituate ourselves within the perspective of universal reason, so that, at each instant, our consciousness may become cosmic consciousness.'[23] It is such a consciousness that then allows an insight into the 'mutual implication of each thing in everything else'.[24]

As Hadot relates with specific reference to the Stoics and Epicureans:

Such an attitude can only be understood if we assume that there was, in ancient philosophy, a sharp awareness of the infinite, incommensurable value of existence. Existing within the cosmos, in the unique reality of the cosmic event, was held to be infinitely precious.[25]

It also needs to be kept in mind that Stoicism was not, as it has often been portrayed, primarily directed towards self-preservation in a society that

20 As Hadot will elsewhere depict this situation: 'The realization of one's self as identical with universal Reason, then, as long as it is accompanied by consent to this will, does not isolate the self like some minuscule island in the universe. On the contrary, it can open the self to all cosmic becoming, insofar as the self raises itself from its limited situation and partial, restricted, and individualistic point of view to a universal and cosmic perspective. At this point, self-consciousness becomes consciousness of the world' (*The Inner Citadel*, pp. 180–1).
21 Hadot, *Philosophy as a Way of Life*, p. 229.
22 Ibid., p. 229. As Hadot explains: 'For them [both the Stoics and Epicureans] each instant and each present moment imply the entire universe, and the whole history of the world. Just as each instant presupposes the immensity of time, so does our body presuppose the whole universe. It is *within ourselves* that we can experience the coming-into-being of the universe and the presence of being . . . For the Stoics, this experience of the instant corresponds to their theory of the mutual penetration of the parts of the universe' (ibid., p. 260).
23 Ibid., p. 229.
24 Ibid., p. 244.
25 Ibid., p. 268.

prized only the rational qualities of the good, and the ethical ideal of justice. There are three tasks that Marcus Aurelius advised as indispensable accompaniments to this concentration on each instant. As described by Hadot, these are: '1. An effort to practice objectivity of judgment; 2. An effort to live according to justice, in the service of the human community; and 3. An effort to become aware of our situation as part of the universe.'[26] For Hadot, as for Marcus Aurelius, it is the second of these three components that constitutes 'an essential element of every philosophical life. In other words, the philosophical life normally entails a philosophical engagement.'[27] Yet all three of these diverse yet inter-related tasks are required for the attainment of wisdom that is at one and the same time a 'wisdom that conforms itself to cosmic wisdom and to the wisdom in which human beings participate.'[28]

There is still one final element, however, that Hadot adds to complete the dynamics of Stoic thought and action. Ultimately, Hadot emphasizes that, in its deepest impulse, Stoicism was both ordered by, and directed towards the service of love, particularly that of one's fellow human beings. 'All of the logic of human action tends to reveal that the prime motive of our activity must be the love of other people, since this love becomes fused with the deepest urges of human nature.'[29] In this way, Hadot depicts the quest for wisdom as one that is intimately related to an affirmation of this world. It reaches out to human beings as part of a commitment to bring about a world that fosters all that pertains to the flourishing of life. Such an attitude attests to the 'the universal love which the parts of the whole feel for one another as well as the cosmic vision of a universal attraction which becomes more intense the higher one climbs on a scale of beings, and the more conscious they become.'[30] Hadot concludes: 'The closer people get to the state of wisdom – in other words the closer they approach God – the more the love which they feel for one another – for all other human beings, as well as for all beings, even the most humble – grows in depth and in lucidity.'[31]

This statement inevitably introduces the notion of God in Stoicism, and in the work of Marcus Aurelius in particular. (It is rather noticeable that Hadot himself rarely broaches this topic.) Obviously, there is no personal God, or father-figure involved. In one sense, in Stoic philosophy God is coterminus with Reason and Nature as a modality of an absolute principle that regulates the Whole. The intention of God also corresponds, as it were, with the originary impulse that sets the world or the cosmos on its creative

---

26 Ibid., p. 212, quotation amended.
27 Ibid., p. 274.
28 Ibid., p. 274.
29 Hadot, *The Inner Citadel*, p. 229.
30 Ibid., p. 231.
31 Ibid., p. 231.

course. At the same time, as Hadot notes, this intention or will of God is always ordered towards the good.

> The unique intention of the sage comes to identify itself with this divine intention, by wanting what divine intention wants: primarily, the good of other rational beings. It, too, transforms every obstacle that opposes the realization of a given action or specific goal into good, insofar as it utilizes such obstacles in order to consent to the will of God or of universal Nature. Thus, for the good will, everything is good.[32]

It is with this divine intention that the sage attempts to align himself – first in the disciplining in his or her desires, and then, second, by accepting all that occurs as good. This is not indifference, rather: 'It is the Whole which, through and by me, loves itself, and it is up to me not to destroy the cohesion of the Whole, by refusing to accept such-and-such an event.'[33] All comes to be because of love, and the seeker of wisdom also needs to act always out of such love, so as to intensify this love manifest in the world.

This somewhat short summary of Hadot's later thought cannot do justice to his immense corpus, and it may well be objected that my reading is selective. (Given the fact that Hadot's work has also been described as not completely faithful to ancient philosophy – as he sought to interpret it for today – my own work may be doubly irregular.) I do not think, however, that I have distorted Hadot's ideas, but highlighted certain preoccupations that are pertinent to my own investigations. What I do detect as crucial in Hadot's more recent work is a turn from a mode of spiritual life that was preoccupied only with matters that pertain to a world other than this one. Such a concern, in and of itself, amounts to a rejection of this world and forecloses any movement of dedication to improving the situation of those whose suffering in this life can be overwhelming to the point of utter destitution.[34]

In contrast, Hadot's reading of Marcus Aurelius supports the notion of a sage who, because of fellow feelings of solicitude, tries to alleviate the suffering of others by a dedication to justice. I find this revision to be especially congenial for a number of reasons. In its portrayal by Hadot, there are definite contemporary resonances, both with engaged Buddhism and the social gospel movement, especially as it evolved in Canada. This was a movement that developed in the late nineteenth century and resulted in the foundation of the United Church of Canada in 1925, which was an amalgamation of

32 Ibid., p. 200.
33 Ibid., pp. 142–3.
34 In this connection, it is apposite to draw attention to a fact that Hadot stresses: '[T]he Stoic believes in the absolute value of the human person. It is too often forgotten, and cannot be repeated too much, that Stoicism is the origin of the modern notion of human rights' (Ibid., p. 311).

progressive members of the Methodist, the Presbyterian and Congregational Churches. This Christian Socialist movement was opposed to the emphasis on personal salvation and the privatization of religion. Instead, it viewed religion and social ethics as inseparable. In Canada it had a strong influence on many social movements, including suffrage for women, a national health system, and finally the New Democratic Party, which is still an active political presence.[35]

I find this orientation to be especially congenial for a number of reasons, and it will be the aspect of compassion and love, combined with the pursuit of righteousness as a characteristic of wisdom, that I will now explore in our contemporary era. I intend to clarify this investigation with reference to the writings of contemporary thinkers and activists. These people may not conform exactly to every aspect of Hadot's depiction of the seeker of wisdom, but what has recommended them to me is their expressions of concern for others. Such people may indeed come from religious backgrounds, but what I have discerned in their work, and what has inspired me, is their affirmation of this world and their unrelenting dedication to protect and to enhance certain conditions that not only make life in this world viable, but also help it to flourish.

In support of this position, I would like first to turn to the work of Paul Ricoeur, especially during the last 20 years of his life. As he aged, Ricoeur became considerably troubled by the unmerited suffering, specifically in the form of violence, that he observed human beings inflicting on one another. In one essay, he reflected on the history of Europe:

> A major feature of the history of Europe is the extraordinary weight of suffering which the majority of states, great or small, taken in pairs or in interposed alliances, have inflicted in the past. The history of Europe is cruel: wars of religion, wars of conquest, wars of extermination, subjugation of ethnic minorities, expulsion or reduction to slavery of religious minorities; the litany is without end. Europe is barely emerging from this nightmare.[36]

In *Memory, History, Forgetting*[37] he reprised such themes on a global scale. He became particularly concerned with contemporary attempts to thwart

35 Richard Allen, *The Social Passion: Religion and Social Reform in Canada 1914–1918* (Toronto: University of Toronto Press, 1971); Nancy Christie and Michael Gauvreau, *A Full-Orbed Christianity: The Protestant Churches and Social Welfare in Canada 1900–1940* (Montreal: McGill-Queens Press, 1996)

36 Paul Ricoeur, 'Reflections on a New Ethos for Europe', in Paul Ricoeur, *The Hermeneutics of Action*, ed. Richard Kearney (London: Sage, 1996) pp. 3–13.

37 Paul Ricoeur, *Memory, History, Forgetting*, tr. K. Blamey and D. Pellauer (Chicago: University of Chicago, 2004).

people's capacities to live well. As a result, his own thoughts turned to the topic of justice as a solution to this tragedy. He wrote a number of essays that proposed possible remedies and which have been collected in two volumes.[38] In these investigations into justice, Ricoeur was adamant about one fact. This was that the solicitude or compassion that he advocated as part of the reciprocal recognition between friends, be somehow transmuted into justice, when it was a question of dealing equally with other people with whom we were not in close relationships.

> *Equality*, however it is modulated, is to *life in institutions* what solicitude is to *interpersonal relations*. . . . Equality provides to the self another who is an *each* [sic] . . . The sense of justice takes nothing away from solicitude, the sense of justice presupposes it, to the extent that it holds persons to be irreplaceable. Justice in turn adds to solicitude, to the extent that the field of application of equality is all of humanity.[39]

Behind this dedication to both solicitude and justice there lay a philosophy that both rejoiced in and promoted life. He recounts his amazement at one day encountering a kindred spirit when he came across the word 'natality' used by Hannah Arendt.[40] In *The Human Condition*, Arendt had stated:

> The new beginning inherent in birth can make itself felt in the world only because the newcomer possesses the capacity of beginning something anew, that is, of acting. In this sense of initiative, an element of action, and therefore of natality, is inherent in all human activity.[41]

In commenting on this, Ricoeur remarked: 'For her, too, birth signifies more than death. That is what wishing to remain living until death means.'[42] Ricoeur himself identified with such a philosophy and poignantly describes his own appreciation of this condition in the last years of his own life. 'I, therefore, project not an after-death but a death that would be an ultimate affirmation of life. My own experience of the end of life is nourished by this deepest wish to make the act of dying an act of life.'[43] It is for this reason

38 Paul Ricoeur, *The Just*, tr. D. Pellauer (Chicago: University of Chicago Press, 2000); Paul Ricoeur, *Reflections on the Just*, tr. David Pellauer (Chicago: University of Chicago Press, 2007).
39 Paul Ricoeur, *Oneself as Another*, tr. K. Blamey (Chicago: University of Chicago Press, 1992), p. 202.
40 Paul Ricoeur, *Critique and Conviction*, eds F. Azouvi and M. de Launay, tr. K. Blamey (New York: Columbia University Press, 1998), p. 157.
41 Hannah Arendt, *The Human Condition* (Garden City, NY: Anchor Books); Lewis Edwin Hahn, *The Philosophy of Paul Ricoeur*, (Peru Ill.: Open Court, 1995), pp. 10–11.
42 Ricoeur, *Critique and Conviction*, p. 157.
43 Ibid., p. 156.

that Ricoeur appreciates that mortality has to be thought *sub specie vitae*, not *sub specie mortis*.[44] Ricoeur also registers his difference from Heidegger's, 'being-toward-death', preferring instead the expression 'being until death'.[45] It is also from this perspective that Ricoeur rejects any attachment to an imaginary that is preoccupied with 'the projection of the self beyond death in terms of after life'.[46] Such a forgoing of the consolations of an afterlife entails for Ricoeur a type of Freudian mourning, or an Eckhartian mode of detachment (*gelassenheit*). In actuality, Ricoeur's own Christianity is akin to that of Kant, where he allows that it is not possible to have knowledge of God in this world. His own hope is that at his death there is a possibility that 'the veils of this language, its limitations and codifications [may be] erased in order to let something fundamental express itself, which perhaps then, effectively, belongs to the order of experience'.[47] Yet all he has undertaken in this life has not been done with the expectation of such activities being tallied at his death and due recompense awarded. It is from Ricoeur's dedicated life, writing in the service of justice, enacted without any expectation of ultimate reckoning, yet with a profound and abiding veneration for the preciousness of life, despite its travails, that I derive my appreciation of this contemporary exemplar of wisdom.

Another person who was very much influenced by Arendt's concept of natality is Grace Jantzen. Before her premature death in 2006, Jantzen had come to the realization that a preoccupation with death, together with a fervent attraction to the notion of a compensatory otherworld, had permeated much religious thought over the centuries. What troubled her about this was the associated fact that women and their bodies had come to signify the temptations of this inferior world, and were designated as the representatives of sexuality, which was regarded as intrinsically sinful. As a result, women came to bear the burden of responsibility for the evils of this world and were disproportionally the subjects of retributive violence. In her writings Jantzen was attempting to provide an antidote to this problematic complex which she diagnosed as 'a symptom of the deep misogyny of western culture, [of] fear, dread and fascination with the maternal body, which is, however, its foundation [in that it is the locus of birth]'.[48]

Appealing to Arendt, Jantzen sought to adapt her idea of natality so as to provide an alternative vision that promoted the value and beauty of life in this world. She proposed that 'Our embodied, gendered selfhood, situated

---

44 Ibid., p. 156.
45 Ibid., p. 156
46 Ibid., p. 156.
47 Ibid., p. 145.
48 Grace Jantzen, 'Feminism and Pantheism', *The Monist*, 80/2, 1998, pp. 266–85.

in the social and cultural web of relationships, delineates our natality; and
it is out of this natality that creativity emerges. If violence is linked with
death-dealing and destruction, creativity is linked with natality.'[49] For
Jantzen, 'natality' invokes the human capacity to create, to begin anew in a
manner that celebrates the wonders of corporeal existence, as well as the
beauty of this world. She declares:

> The possibility of beginning which is rooted in our own beginning, is
> always material, embodied: there is no disembodied natality . . . thus the
> freedom of natality is not the putative freedom of a disembodied mind, a
> mind made as free as possible from bodily shackles, as Plato would have
> it, but rather a freedom that emerges from and takes place within bodily
> existence.[50]

Jantzen's work during the final years of her life on the origins of violence
was primarily an attempt to transform humanity's moribund obsession to
an affirmative one that would cultivate creativity and beauty. It would also
permit women to claim their birthright as co-inheritors of the world. This
world was envisioned by Grace as a place of fecundity where women, as well
as men, are created in the image of a god figure who has symbolized the
ideals of compassion and justice to which both can aspire.

Jantzen herself was brought up as a Mennonite in Canada, then during
her time in England she turned to the Anglican faith. Finally, however, she
became a Quaker and an ardent pacifist. She viewed her own work as
belonging more to philosophy of religion than to theology, although as she
began to explore non-dualist ways of thinking, she wrote a number of times
about pantheism. These non-dualist explorations were part of a project
Jantzen undertook to challenge the traditional Western symbolic structures
that she considered privileged a male god figure within a hierarchical
system. Moreover, in her view this system encouraged a dualist framework
that separated matter from form. Accordingly, 'men were linked with
reason, spirit and form', while women were associated with 'matter, with the
chaotic, and evil'.[51] Instead of this model, Grace proposed a substitute imaginary model that promoted pantheism. Such an alternative perspective
would view the world in a different way. Here the 'divine precisely *is* the
world and its ceaselessly shifting bodies and signifiers'.[52] Here also the material and the spiritual are regarded as inseparable, and various other

---

49 Grace Jantzen, 'A Reconfiguration of Desire: Reading Feminist Mystics in Postmodernity',
Women's Philosophy Review 29 (2002), pp. 23–45.
50 Grace Jantzen, 'Feminism and Pantheism', *The Monist*, 80/2, 1998, p. 145.
51 Ibid., pp. 266–85.
52 Ibid., p. 282.

notions of the divine could then be proposed such as an idea of a god that is 'embodied, earthed, female'.[53] Grace Jantzen's life and work was also a testimony to wisdom, but one that enlarged Ricoeur's witness by confirming the participation of women as an integral element in the restoration or re-enchantment of this world.

In the final section of my essay, I would like to draw upon the lives of several contemporary wise women who are dedicated in similar ways to an activist renewal of the world in situations that the integrity of this life seems to have been forgotten. They are not motivated by any concern for compensation, but simply are attempting to effect a change in the interests of justice so that authoritarianism and/or violence no longer dominate. Their work also provides hope that the powers of inequity and retribution can indeed be opposed – though not without cost – and may even be brought to justice, though this is never assured.

My first example of a contemporary example of wisdom is Shirin Ebadi, winner of the 2003 Nobel Peace Prize, who is a fierce campaigner for justice in Iran. A Shi'a Muslim from a middle-class background, she was the first woman to be appointed a judge in Iran in 1975, when she became the President of Bench 24 of the Tehran City Court. In her autobiography, *Iran Awakening*,[54] she explains her early enthusiasm for the revolution when the Shah went into exile and was replaced by Ayatollah Khomeini. This enthusiasm faded as various members of the new regime began to impose tighter restrictions that were often unjust and arbitrary. The restrictions on women were particularly severe, including a law that only men could be judges. Ebadi relates how she was relegated to be a clerk in the very court over which she had presided.[55]

Eventually Ebadi retired, but in 1992, after a seeming thaw, she again began to practise. It was not long, however, before she realized that the extent of the corruption prevented her from properly representing her clients. As a result, she then elected to work on a *pro bono* basis, taking on cases that, as she describes them, 'illustrated the tragic repercussions of the theocracy's legal discrimination against women'.[56] From then on her life has always been in danger. Her phone is tapped and her life has been threatened – increasingly so since the award of the Nobel Prize. In one particularly shocking episode, when she was reading official files as part of a defence

---

53 Ibid., p. 283.
54 Shirin Ebadi, *Iran Awakening, From Prison to Peace Prize: One Woman's Struggle at the Crossroads of History* (Toronto: Vintage Canada, 2006).
55 Ibid., p. 55.
56 Ibid., p. 111.

team in a case for those who had been murdered by death squads, she came across her own name as one of those to be targeted.[57]

What has saved her thus far has been her growing international reputation – but, even so, she is never free from danger. She remains fearless, however, in her defence of what she understands as justice, particularly in the case of women's rights. She declares:

> In the last twenty-three years, from the day I was stripped of my judgeship to the years doing battle in the revolutionary courts of Tehran, I had repeated one refrain: an interpretation of Islam that is in harmony with equality and democracy as an authentic expression of faith. It is not religion that binds women, but the selective dictates of those who wish them cloistered. That belief, along with the conviction that change in Iran must come peacefully and from within, has underpinned my work.[58]

Ebadi remains firm in her decision to stay and work in Iran for democracy and human rights. She reflects on the criticism she has received that Islam and human rights are incompatible.

> Over the years, I have endured all manner of slights and attacks, been told that I must not appreciate or grasp the real spirit of democracy if I can claim in the same breath that freedom and human rights are not perforce in conflict with Islam. When I heard the statement of the prize being read aloud, heard my religion mentioned specifically alongside my work defending Iranians' rights, I knew at that moment what was being recognized: the belief in a positive interpretation of Islam, and the power of that belief to aid Iranians who aspire to peacefully transform their country.[59]

As a warrior in the name of rights and justice, Shirin Ebadi is a woman who embodies a fierce wisdom, born of her struggles on behalf of those who have been persecuted and killed. In writing her story, her stated intention is that of increasing 'women's self-confidence and self-reliance' so that they will 'disregard obstacles and difficulties and . . . have a strong will for victory'. With such an approach, in her view: 'There is no problem that cannot be solved.'[60]

My second example is that of Venerable Dhammananda of Thailand. I have twice visited her temple, Wat Songdhammakalyani, in Nakhon-

---

57 Ibid., p. xv.
58 Ibid., p. 204.
59 Ibid., p. 204
60 Ibid., p. 218.

pathom, about 60 kilometres to the west of Bangkok. There she has a centre of both education and Buddhist practice, where her major commitment is to help women. In her former life, Venerable Dhammananda was known as Chatsumarn Kabilsingh, a scholar who received her PhD from McMaster University in Canada, who then taught for many years at Thamasset University in Thailand. In 2002, she decided to become ordained as a nun (*bhikkuni*). This, however, was not a single event as, in the intervening years, there have been a number of ceremonies in both Taiwan and Sri Lanka where she has taken different precepts. This process has been necessitated by the fact that the Thai *sangha* does not recognize the ordination of nuns, though the Buddha himself, albeit reluctantly, allowed that this could take place. (Various technical difficulties involving all too familiar appeals to precedence, tradition, etc., are summoned as reasons for this refusal.)

Venerable Dhammananda believes that one of her principal tasks is that of improving the status of Thai women, and thus restoring to Thai women the respect that is due to them. In a chapter in her book, *Thai Women and Buddhism*,[61] she specifically addresses the sex trade in Thailand, demanding an answer to how a Buddhist country can allow its women to be thus exploited. She basically understands this situation to be a result of the low estimation in which women are held. Dhammananda's argument is that if the *sangha* were to accept the ordination of women, then women's standing in Thailand, which is over 90 per cent Buddhist, would improve immeasurably from both a social and spiritual perspective. Dhammananda says: 'In Thailand, women's spiritual potential is belittled, while their physical potential is exploited. The root cause that thwarts the *bhikkuni* revival and enables the prostitution explosion is the negative social attitudes towards women.'[62] In another straightforward statement, she says:

People don't understand what the connection is between this ordinational problem and the problem of prostitutes, for example. I try to bring this out in my presentations. When women cannot become ordained, because the image of women is so negative, that pushes women to the other end of the spectrum. That's why the doors to brothels are open to women. But why are the doors closed for women to become nuns? I talk about the need to see social issues as holistic – you cannot separate them.[63]

61 Chatsumarn Kabilsingh (Venerable Dhammananda), *Thai Women and Buddhism* (Berkeley CA: Parallax Press, 1991).

62 Venerable Dhammananda, *A Feminist Buddhist* (Nakhonpathon, Thailand: Wat Songdhammakalyani Publications, nd).

63 Venerable Dhammananda, *Newsletter on International Buddhist Women's Activities*, 11/3, 1995.

Dhammananda's argument is that the ordination of nuns would help to alleviate the disrespect and abuse to which women are submitted in many aspects of Thai culture. This would strengthen what I have termed elsewhere women's 'symbolic status' – though this is not Dhammananda's own term.[64] (I consider that access to full symbolic status is an essential step for women in many religions in the world.) While Dhammananda's statement may be a particularly graphic one, it does help to bring into focus the many other ways in which male-dominated religions have excluded and denied women access to full religious participation. While I would not recommend this solution of ordination in a Western secular society where other religious battles are being fought for women's symbolic status, and where secularists would find it ludicrous, it does make sense in Thailand. This is because I do not think a simply secular application of human rights to secure equal status for women would suffice to change things in overwhelmingly religious countries. This is because human rights do not even begin to address the deep-seated and pervasive forms of religious prejudice that inform women's inferior symbolic status and the consequent suspicion or even hostility with which women are regarded in many more traditionally religious communities in various countries of the world – though instances of such attitudes have not been eradicated in so-called secular countries either.

The final example of contemporary wisdom is that of the Kenyan, Wangari Matthai, the 2004 Noble Peace Prize winner for 'contribution to sustainable development, democracy and peace'. Matthai has been particularly active in both environmentalism and women's issues. Her memoir, *Unbowed*,[65] provides a vivid portrayal of one woman's struggle both for the reforestation of Kenya and for democracy, which she views as inextricably intertwined. She was educated in a convent in Kenya and then studied in the United States, before being the first woman to obtain a doctorate in Veterinary Medicine at the University of Nairobi, where she then became a Professor.

---

64 By symbolic status, I intend to signify a parity of esteem that pertains either to being respected as a religious authority, or to being invested with a mode of religious agency that is most revered in a particular religion. The term, with its symbolic reference, has both psychoanalytic and religious resonances. The pertinent forms of access and religious agency would include the right to study, interpret and teach sacred texts in their original languages, to officiate at sacred rituals, and to make decisions of a deliberative nature that would have practical applications for adherents of that religion. Such attributes and activities have been mainly the prerogative of men, and many religions still forbid women the means to attain such accomplishments and their accompanying recognition.

65 Wangari Maathai, *Unbowed: A Memoir* (New York: Random House, 2006).

Maathai's battles on behalf of such seemingly basic ideals as democracy and women's rights have been marred by imprisonment and violence. This is because a basic component of her platform is to bring justice to Kenya, a goal that has proved to be particularly elusive. As Maathai observed of a time in 2003, when there seemed to be a brief respite from abuse of the political system, with her own election to parliament: 'The years of misrule, corruption, violence, environmental mismanagement, and oppression had devastated our country. The economy was in ruins and many institutions needed rebuilding. But on that day the future looked bright – not only for me, but for the whole country.'[66] She was nonetheless well aware that democracy alone could not supply the solution for all the continuing problems of poverty and deforestation – but it marked a necessary foundation. Unfortunately, this democratic interlude did not last, and the struggle still continues today.

As a political crusader, Maathai's life has been endangered many times – by police, by the political opposition, by tribal conflict – and she has often had to go into hiding. She has been imprisoned, and only released because of international pressure. She describes the situation:

It is often difficult to describe to those who live in a free society what life is like in an authoritarian regime. You don't know who to trust. You worry that you, your family, or your friends will be arrested or jailed without due process. The fear of political violence or death, whether through direct assassinations or targeted 'accidents', is constant.[67]

It was in 1977 that Maathai had founded the Green Belt Movement as a way to protect lands from illegal privatization by the government, and to protect biodiversity, especially by the reclamation of the forests. In addition, in her work with the National Council of Women in Kenya, she has encouraged women to both produce and sell seedlings in the effort to rehabilitate the forests. This is indeed a literal commitment to renew the earth. In all of these undertakings, Maathai appreciates that it is trees that will make the difference.

As such, their unchecked harvesting is an indicator of the symbolic connection she makes between government abuse of power and environmental degradation as a result of poor policies – the result of which is the price that all Kenyans pay in their poor quality of life. Maathai understands that trees provide a solution, in that:

---

66 Ibid., p. 289.
67 Ibid., p. 206.

The trees would provide a supply of wood that would enable women to cook nutritious foods. They would also have wood for fencing and fodder for cattle and goats. The trees would offer shade for humans and animals, protect watersheds and bind the soil, and, if there were fruit trees, provide food. They would also heal the land by bringing back birds and small animals and regenerate the vitality of the earth.[68]

Trees, then, are also symbolic of a world that is flourishing not just environmentally, but as a place that nurtures all life.

In the Epilogue to her memoir, Maathai reflects on her award of the Nobel Prize and how this recognition has afforded her a measure of security. She now sees her work as linked with many others in the world who are also fighting to make it a place of peace, justice and good governance for all its citizens. In concluding she declares:

> Humanity needs to rethink peace and security and work towards cultures of peace by governing itself more democratically, respecting the law and human rights, deliberately and consciously promoting justice and equity, and managing resources more responsibly and accountably – not only for the present but for future generations.[69]

Conclusion

All of the people that I have selected as exemplars of wisdom for this essay are, I believe, illustrative of a version of wisdom that I hold to be both pertinent and applicable to contemporary life on this planet. This is because each one of them, in diverse ways, both fosters life and strives valiantly – often at great personal cost and danger – to bring a just and compassionate society to fruition in their community or the world at large. Each one is no doubt influenced by the religion in which they were raised, and it has no doubt been a formative influence. The expression of each of their specific programmes, however, does not depend on, or appeal overtly in any way to an ideal of an afterlife where they will be compensated for their labours. Nor does it reflect any allegiance to a belief system of a hierarchical nature or one that imposes dogmatic tenets. Instead, their lives radiate a vibrant compassion for the well-being of their fellow creatures that is motivated by love of this world. If there is a God who informs their lives, it is not one who can be discerned by rational means, nor one that functions as the designer of dualistic divisions that deems this world of matter as inferior to a spiri-

---

68 Ibid., p. 125.
69 Ibid., p. 294.

tual realm. For Dhammananda, there are indeed the teachings and example of the Buddha as inspiration; for Sirin Ebadi, there is the example of Mohammad and the words of the Qur'an; while for Maathai Wangari, there is the life of Christ. Yet where I think that all of them move beyond a traditional religious ethical position is in their passionate drive to fight for justice and to put an end to violence. This is motivated by a love not only for earthly creatures, but also, with certain of them, for the earth that they inhabit. For all of them are committed to the flourishing of life in various guises which a number of them also see as inherently intimately interrelated. In many ways their lives and works are remarkably similar to the description of the conduct of a wise person as portrayed by Hadot:

> [T]he discipline of action attains its culminating point in the love of one's neighbour. All the logic of human action tends to reveal that the prime motive of our activity must be the love of other people, since this love becomes fused with the deepest urges of human nature.[70]

---

70 Hadot, *The Inner Citadel*, p. 229.

9

Agnosticism and Atheism

ANTHONY KENNY

In his book *The God Delusion*[1] Richard Dawkins introduces a discussion of agnosticism with the following words:

> The robust muscular Christian haranguing us from the pulpit of my old school admitted a sneaking regard for atheists. They at least had the courage of their misguided convictions. What this preacher couldn't stand was agnostics: namby pamby, mushy pap, weak-tea, weedy, pallid fence sitters.[2]

In this essay I shall argue that it is misguided to regard agnosticism as a diluted form of atheism. There are significant differences between the two positions; and the differences show agnosticism, if carefully defined, to be both epistemically and morally preferable to atheism. But before defining this desirable form of agnosticism, I must say a few words about atheism and theism.

On the face of it, atheism makes a much stronger claim than theism does. Atheist: no matter how 'God' is defined, there is no God; Theist: there is at least one definition of 'God' which makes it be true that 'There is a God'. If we are to make a realistic contrast between the two, we have to agree on an interpretation of 'God'. Most of us, I imagine, are atheists and not agnostics with respect to the Homeric gods of Olympus. With the possible exception of one or two Oxford professors of Classics, nobody nowadays believes that Zeus, Hera and Aphrodite actually exist in any literal sense. This does not prevent us from enjoying the *Iliad* and the *Odyssey*. Nor does it mean that Homer has nothing to teach us about ourselves and about the world we live in.

The God delineated in the sacred texts of the Abrahamic faiths is obviously very different from the Olympians. I confess, however, to being an

---

1 London: Bantam Press, 2006.
2 Ibid., p. 46.

atheist with respect to the God of traditional Judeo-Christian natural theology: a being endowed with omnipotence, omniscience and supreme benevolence. In a book published in 1979, *The God of the Philosophers*,[3] I argued that these three attributes were incompatible with one another, as could be seen by reflection on the relationship between divine power and human freedom. If God is to be omniscient about future human actions, then determinism must be true. If God is to escape responsibility for human wickedness, then determinism must be false. So there cannot be an omniscient, omnipotent, all-good being. I concluded that there can be no such thing as the God of scholastic or rationalist philosophy. Whatever truth is contained in the Judeo-Christian scriptures is presented to us not literally but metaphorically.

Since then I have not changed my mind on that topic. However, I left open the question whether it is possible to conceive, and believe in, a God defined in less absolute terms. In that sense, I am not an atheist, and I have remained an agnostic.

To give precise and topical content to my discussion, I offer a definition of God as an intelligent designer of our universe. I mean the words 'intelligent designer' to be taken at their face value: I am not interested in the position of those who use the expression as a euphemism for the world-maker described in the first chapters of Genesis. With regard to an intelligent designer of the universe I am agnostic; I do not know whether or not there is such a being. The reason that I am agnostic is that I find equally plausible the arguments for and against the existence of a God so defined.

Let us consider first arguments in favour, such as Aquinas' fifth way, and Kant's physico-theological proof. Kant states it thus. Everywhere in the world we find signs of order, in accordance with a determinate purpose, apparently carried out with great wisdom. Since this order is alien to the individual things which constitute the world, we must conclude that it must have been imposed by one or more sublime wise causes, operating not blindly as nature does, but freely as humans do.[4]

In considering this argument, it is important first of all to recognize that there is a difference between design and purpose. Design differs from purpose because design is purpose preceded by an idea: a thought, or blueprint, in somebody's mind. If the world is designed, then there was a precedent idea in the mind of the creator – what, in the fourth Gospel, is called the *logos* or Word. It was pointed out many years ago that what is called the argument from design would be more appropriately called the argument *to* design – from purpose to design.

---

3 Oxford: Oxford University Press.
4 See *Critique of Pure Reason, Transcendental Dialectic*, Book II, Ch. 3, Section 6.

Unlike Aristotle, who saw the existence and ubiquity of purpose as a basic fact about the cosmos, and Descartes who altogether denied the existence of teleology in the world outside the human realm, Aquinas and Kant were in agreement that purpose in nature needed explanation, and that the explanation must be in terms of design. Kant's argument makes use of the key premise of the Fifth Way: 'Things which lack awareness do not tend towards a goal unless directed by something with awareness and intelligence, like an arrow by an archer.'[5]

Since Darwin, however, such a claim needs more supporting argument than either Kant or Aquinas was able to offer. Darwin agreed with them, against Aristotle, that purpose did need explanation. Against them, he agreed with Aristotle against Aquinas that the world, outside the human realm, contained purpose, but not design. He offered, in natural selection, a recipe for translating teleology into a naturalistic explanation that made no call on design.

But if Darwin undercut the argument from design in biology, more recently a new form of the design argument has made its appearance in physics. Physicists have identified six fundamental constants that are believed to hold throughout the universe. The value of each of these seems, in advance, to be extremely improbable. But if any one of them differed very slightly from its actual value, life in the universe would be impossible. How are we to explain this fine tuning? Is it not *prima facie* evidence that our universe was designed in such a way as to make life possible?

Atheists have adopted two different methods of neutralizing this *prima facie* plausibility. The first is by adopting something called the anthropic principle. Here we are, in this universe. Therefore, our universe must be the kind of universe capable of generating and supporting us. However improbable *a priori*, our universe must necessarily have the features required for our existence, because here we are, thinking about it. Hence the cosmological constants, immensely improbable though they may appear, call for no explanation. Far from being improbable, says the anthropic principle, they are necessary, and necessary truths need no explanation.

We need to look more closely at the use of 'necessary' here. There are three senses of the word 'necessary' in play in this argument, corresponding to three kinds of necessity: causal necessity, metaphysical necessity and epistemic necessity.

First, causal necessity. Certain conditions may be causally necessary if a certain effect is to be brought about: such as the necessity that the cosmological constants should have their actual value if intelligent life is to emerge. But that does not mean that there is any antecedent necessity that

---

5 *Summa Theologiae*, Ia, 2, 2.

they should have the value they do. Their having those values is not a matter of metaphysical necessity. The value of the cosmological constants is not a necessary truth nor anything that follows from necessary truths: it is something discovered by empirical research and scientific hypothesis.

Besides causal and metaphysical necessity there is also epistemic necessity, which is the counterpart of epistemic possibility. P is epistemically possible when we can say 'For all we know to the contrary, p may be the case.' If not-p is not epistemically possible, then p is epistemically necessary. Something may be epistemically necessary without being metaphysically necessary: as I write, it is epistemically necessary, but not metaphysically necessary, that Barak Obama is President of the United States. The anthropic principle argues, fallaciously, from the epistemic necessity of conditions favourable to human life to their metaphysical necessity.

An alternative route that atheists take in order to avoid the *prima facie* evidence for design is to maintain that there are many universes with different laws and different cosmological constants, and that our universe just happens to be the one among them favourable to the development of life and intelligence. This line has been taken by, among others, Giordano Bruno, Martin Rees and Richard Dawkins. As Dawkins puts it, 'We have to be in one of those universes (presumably a minority) whose by-laws happened to be propitious to our eventual evolution and hence contemplation of the problem.'[6]

Though often combined in atheistic apologetics, the two solutions to the improbability of the cosmological constants are quite different from each other. The anthropic principle says there is nothing to be explained – there was no improbability in the case, only necessity. The multiverse thesis says that there is indeed something to be explained, and it is to be explained by *a priori* probability. This can be done if we simply call into existence billions of universes – all, *ex hypothesi*, inaccessible to scientific inquiry.

The first explanation is a fallacy, resting on confusion between epistemic and metaphysical necessity. The second explanation is a piece of extra-scientific speculation. Its only merit seems to be that it provides an alternative to intelligent design. But if an Astronomer Royal tells me there is an infinity of universes, and a fundamentalist preacher tells me there is only one universe designed by an extra-cosmic intelligence, I am faced with two equally metaphysical theses. Science offers me no guidance which to choose.

Let us return for a moment to Kant. He was himself critical of the design argument, as he was of all proofs of God by theoretical reason. His own criticism of the proof concerns not its authority but its scope. The most the argument can prove, he says, is the existence of 'an *architect* of the world

6 Dawkins, *The God Delusion*, p. 145.

who is always very much hampered by the adaptability of the material in which he works, not a *creator* of the world to whose idea everything is subject'.[7] Many religious believers would be very content to have established beyond reasonable doubt the existence of such a Grand Architect. Others would regard the worship of anything less than a creator as being a form of idolatry, and would deny that such an intelligent designer deserved the name of God.

So far we have been discussing the kind of universe we have. But why is there a universe of any kind? The most fundamental reason for postulating an extra-cosmic agency of any kind is surely the need to explain the origin of the universe itself. Most philosophical arguments for the existence of God are only sophistications of the cry of the simple believer, 'God must exist, else where did the world come from?'

At a time when philosophers and scientists were happy to accept that the universe had existed for ever, there was no question of looking for a cause of its origin, only of looking for an explanation of its nature. But when it is proposed that the universe began at a point of time measurably distant in the past, then it seems perverse simply to shrug one's shoulders and decline to seek any explanation. We would never, in the case of an ordinary existent, tolerate a blithe announcement that there was simply no reason for its coming into existence, and it seems irrational to abandon this principle when the existing thing in question is all pervasive, like the universe. If an intelligent creator can really be conceived, he would surely be a more persuasive solution to the problem than the arbitrary invocation of a multiverse.

My own difficulty with the arguments we have considered is in giving sense at all to the notion of an extra-cosmic, superhuman intelligence. I emphasized earlier the difference between design and purpose. Design differs from purpose because design is purpose preceded by an idea: a thought, or blueprint, in somebody's mind. In our kind of mind, the idea that precedes an artefact is not anything simple or timeless, but something that gets built up by research and experiment. The argument from design can only establish its conclusion if it is possible for there to be a quite different kind of mind: a divine, extra-cosmic, simple and eternal mind. That, to my mind, is the greatest difficulty with the argument.

If we are to attribute intelligence to any entity – limited or unlimited, cosmic or extra-cosmic – we have to take as our starting point our concept of intelligence as exhibited by human beings: we have no other concept of it. Human intelligence is displayed in the behaviour of human bodies and the thoughts of human minds. If we reflect on the actual ways in which we

---

7 Kant, *Critique of Pure Reason*, A 627.

attribute words such as 'know', 'believe', 'think', 'design', 'control', 'intelligence' to human beings, we realize the immense difficulty there is in applying them to a putative being which is immaterial, ubiquitous and eternal. With a degree of anthropomorphism we can apply mentalistic predicates to animals, computers, institutions, to organisms that resemble us or to artefacts that are our creations; but there are limits to anthropomorphism, and an extra-cosmic intelligence appears to me to be outside those limits. It is not just that we do not, and cannot, know what goes in God's mind; it is that we cannot really ascribe a mind to a God at all. The language that we use to describe the contents of human minds operates within a web of links with bodily behaviour and social institutions. When we try to apply this language to an entity outside the natural world, whose scope of operation is the entire universe, this web comes to pieces and we no longer know what we are saying.

My reaction to the difficulty of either proving or disproving God's existence is agnosticism: to say that we do not know either way. Often both theist and atheist philosophers, instead of offering arguments, adopt a strategy that might be called grabbing the default position – that is, a tactic of throwing the burden of proof on the opponent. But it is agnosticism that is the true default position. A claim to knowledge needs to be substantiated, ignorance only has to be confessed. Moreover, a claim to know that God exists, or a claim to know that God does not exist, is an absolute commitment. The profession of doubt is no such thing.

Agnosticism differs from dogmatic atheism as much as it differs from dogmatic theism. Unlike atheism, agnosticism is, or can be, provisional. In my book *What is Faith?*[8] I made a distinction between necessary and contingent agnosticism. Necessary agnosticism is the belief which many philosophers such as Kant have had that knowledge whether there is a God or not is in some sense impossible because of the limits of the human mind. There are several philosophical arguments to the effect that agnosticism about the existence of God is something that is built into the human condition rightly understood. I find the arguments for that kind of agnosticism as unconvincing as either the arguments for theism or atheism. Contrasted with necessary agnosticism is the contingent agnosticism of a man who says, 'I do not know whether there is a God, but perhaps it can be known; I have no proof that it cannot be known.'

My own agnosticism is of this kind. That is, I am open to the idea that some proof or disproof may convince me, though I haven't yet come across one. Contingent agnosticism of my kind involves not knowing whether other people know, or only think they know, there is a God. Of course I

8 Oxford: Oxford University Press, 1992.

think that they do not know – but for this belief of mine I would not claim the status of knowledge.

This brings out a second distinction between atheism and agnosticism: the latter allows for a greater respect for other people's opinions. Many atheists suggest that all those who believe in God are unreasonable in so doing. I disagree. Those who claim to know that there is a God, I have agreed, are making a claim that is not justified; but so too are those who claim to know there is no God. But a belief in God, falling short of certainty, is not open to the same objection. A belief may be reasonable, though false. If two oncologists tell you that your tumour is benign, then your belief that it is benign is a reasonable belief even if, sadly, it is false. In the case of many people in many cultures, I maintain, religious belief, even if false, may well be reasonable. (So, too, may tentative, non-dogmatic atheism.) But I think belief in God is reasonable only if it is based on considerations available to all humans: not if it is claimed on the basis of a special message to oneself or to the group to which one belongs.

Because I think belief in God can be reasonable, I think it is wrong to object to bringing up children with a belief in religion. The education of children is impossible without narrative and ceremony, and growing up is a matter of knowing what to discard and what to maintain. I see nothing wrong in telling children about Santa Claus; it does not lead to an adult society of bigoted Santaclausians. Many intellectual Christians, as they mature, abandon other bits of the Christmas story: I know priests in good standing who do not believe that Jesus was born in Bethlehem. Disbelieving in religious narratives, however, does not necessarily mean discarding them: it means, as I suggested earlier, removing them from the history section of one's mind into the poetry section. Faith, as an irrevocable commitment, is not reasonable when given to a false proposition. But I see nothing unreasonable in believers having the degree of commitment to their church, synagogue or mosque that they might have to a political party or social community.

Finally, agnosticism, unlike atheism, makes room for prayer. Being agnostic does not mean that one cannot pray. In itself, prayer to a God about whose existence one is doubtful is no more irrational than crying out for help in an emergency without knowing whether there is anyone within earshot. But if, as I have argued, statements about God in the indicative mood cannot be interpreted literally, likewise equally prayers to God cannot be taken as literal uses of the imperative mood either. With that qualification, I would still subscribe to what I wrote 30 years ago in *The God of the Philosophers*.[9]

---

9 Page 129.

There is no reason why someone who is in doubt about the existence of God should not pray for help on this topic, as in other matters. Some find something comic in the idea of an agnostic praying to a God whose existence he doubts. It is surely no more unreasonable than the act of a man adrift in the ocean, trapped in a cave, or stranded on a mountainside, who cries for help though he may never be heard, or fires a signal which may never be seen.

Such prayer seems rational whether or not there is a God. Whether, if there is a God, it is pleasing to him or conducive to salvation is quite another question. Religious people, no doubt, will have their own views on that. But if there is a God, then surely prayer for enlightenment about his existence and nature cannot be less pleasing to him than the attitude of a man who takes no interest in a question so important, or in a question so difficult who would not welcome assistance beyond human powers.

10

Ideals Without Idealism

CLARE CARLISLE

As a 'poet of the religious', Søren Kierkegaard sets before his reader a con-
stellation of spiritual ideals, exquisitely painted with words and images that
evoke their luminous beauty. Among these poetic icons are ideals of purity
of heart; love of the neighbour; radiant self-transparency; truthfulness to
oneself, to another person, or to God. Such ideals are what the 'restless
heart' desires, and in invoking them Kierkegaard refuses to compromise on
their purity – while insisting also that they are impossible to attain. It is the
human condition which makes them impossible, and he is willing to
describe this in dogmatic terms as original sin – sin being the refusal and
loss of God, and thus also the loss of a self that has its ontological ground
in its relationship to God – but he is more concerned to explore it in psychological terms. The human condition is for Kierkegaard characterized
not merely by ignorance, but by wilful self-deception.

One of the most striking aspects of Kierkegaard's philosophy of religion is
his elucidation of a tension at the centre of Christian teaching: between an
insistence on the limits of the human being, and an unconditional command
or an irresistible impulse to transcend these limits. This would render the
human situation utterly tragic were it not for grace, and indeed the difficulty
of recognizing and receiving this grace makes it tragic enough. The religious
life seems to be a sort of spiritual rollercoaster: the beautiful ideals are
glimpsed, and they elevate and inspire; one falls short of them, and despairs;
a gift is offered and despair is transfigured; the gift slips away and leaves one
empty-hearted. 'Christianity is as paradoxical on this point as possible', writes
Kierkegaard: 'it seems to be working against itself by establishing sin so
securely as a position that now it seems utterly impossible to eliminate it
again – and then it is this same Christianity that by means of the Atonement
wants to eliminate sin so completely as if it were drowned in the sea.'[1]

---

1 Søren Kierkegaard, *The Sickness Unto Death*, tr. Howard V. Hong and Edna H. Hong (Princeton: Princeton University Press, 1980), p. 100.

In this essay I will reflect on the structure as well as the content of the kind of impossible ideals that are invoked in many of Kierkegaard's texts. I want to consider the shape of a life lived in relation to these ideals, to trace the twists and turns of the spiritual path as it gains and loses sight of God. There is perhaps something specifically 'religious' about the structure of the ideals in question: on the one hand an absolute impossibility, tied to an interpretation of the human condition as such; and on the other hand an absolute demand, an irresistible claim exerted by these ideals that admits of no compromise. I think that this kind of logic can be found in Buddhist teachings, too, and I suspect that it may be shared by other traditions; Jacques Derrida has found the same paradoxical structure in ideals such as justice, democracy, forgiveness and so on – and it may be that these ideals are in some sense religious, perhaps the apparently secularized residue of an essentially theological way of thinking.

In considering the structure of impossible ideals, I will try to respond to the important and influential critique advanced by Friedrich Nietzsche. Nietzsche famously criticizes the content of Christian ideals: he regards them as symptoms of *ressentiment*, and as hypocritical insofar as their valuation of pity and compassion masks a covert will to power – but he also criticizes idealism itself as a negation of the world we live in. Put in very general terms, this critique rests on the view that if we live according to ideals that could not be instantiated in this world, then we subject this world to values that are not *of* it, and when life inevitably falls short of these impossible standards it is, as a whole, denigrated. This is an important aspect of what Nietzsche calls nihilism, the essence of Western metaphysics, of idealism, of Platonism, of Christianity: 'A nihilist is a man who judges of the world as it is that it ought *not* to be, and of the world as it ought to be that it does not exist.'[2] In his lectures on Nietzsche during the late 1930s, Martin Heidegger explained that

the cause of nihilism is morality, in the sense of positing supernatural ideals of truth, goodness and beauty that are valid 'in themselves'. The positing of the highest values simultaneously posits the possibility of their devaluation, which already begins when these values show themselves to be unattainable. Life thus appears to be unsuitable and utterly incompetent for the realization of these values.[3]

2 Friedrich Nietzsche, *The Will to Power*, tr. R. J. Hollingdale and Walter Kaufmann (New York: Vintage, 1967), §585.
3 Martin Heidegger, *Nietzsche*, tr. David Farrell Krell (San Francisco: Harper and Row, 1979–87), Vol. III, p. 206.

This Nietzschean analysis should be taken seriously, and one way of responding to it would be to compromise on the purity of moral and religious ideals, or on the desire or demand for them, and thus to find a new and less difficult logic of becoming, for example, a Christian – to straighten out the spiritual path. But this is certainly not Kierkegaard's way, for he seeks to accentuate the difficulties – both intellectual and existential – of Christianity. I want to suggest that Kierkegaard is right to regard the invocation of impossible ideals as an indispensable aspect of Christian teaching, and I also want to argue that this does not make it, nor any other teaching that is structured in this way, nihilistic. The Kierkegaardian version of ethico-religious idealism can be interpreted as aiming precisely at understanding and enhancing *this* life, *this* world. Setting aside Nietzsche's attack on the content of Christian morality, then, we can read Kierkegaard in a way that addresses the general, structural issue of idealism.

*   *   *

The theme of impossible ideals pervades Kierkegaard's authorship, although it is naturally most prominent in his more explicitly religious texts. In *Fear and Trembling* (1843) the pseudonym-poet Johannes de Silentio expresses his awe and admiration of Abraham, the 'father of faith', and repeatedly confesses his own inability to do what Abraham did: 'The poet or orator can do nothing that the hero does; he can only admire, love, and delight in him ... I cannot make the final movement, the paradoxical movement of faith.'[4] Johannes de Silentio suggests that Abraham's greatness consists precisely in the absolutely paradoxical character of his response to God's command to sacrifice his son Isaac: 'He who expected the impossible became the greatest of all',[5] writes the pseudonym in his 'Eulogy on Abraham'. When a person 'examines the conditions of his life', these 'explain that [faith] is an impossibility', but the Kierkegaardian Christian is a 'knight of faith' who 'acknowledges the impossibility, and in the very same moment ... believes the absurd, for if he wants to imagine that he has faith without passionately acknowledging the impossibility with his whole heart and soul he is deceiving himself'.[6]

Kierkegaard thought that the assumption that one is a Christian easily and as a matter of course was the most pervasive and dangerous malaise within Christendom, and in *Fear and Trembling* he seeks to challenge this

---

4 Søren Kierkegaard, *Fear and Trembling/Repetition*, tr. Howard V. Hong and Edna H. Hong (Princeton: Princeton University Press, 1983), pp. 15, 51.

5 Ibid., p. 16.

6 Ibid., pp. 42, 47.

perceived complacency by raising the question of whether faith is even possible. The implicit question posed by his interpretation of the story of Abraham is: *Would you, could you do what Abraham did? Could anyone? And if not, do you really have faith? Could you? Could anyone?* Johannes de Silentio presents the reader with a beautiful ideal of faith, but at the same time he shows it to be so monstrous, so repellent, that it becomes impossible not only to attain it, but even to wish to attain it. 'Let us then either cancel out Abraham, or learn to be horrified by the prodigious paradox that is the meaning of his life, so that we can understand that our age, like every other age, can rejoice if it has faith.'[7]

The 1846 discourse *Purity of Heart is to Will One Thing*, written in Kierkegaard's own name, invokes the ideal of a pure heart – and yet most of the text is devoted to detailing all the different forms of *impurity* of heart. Desire for reward, fear of punishment, pursuit of a personal victory over impurity, and fluctuations in persistence and effort are all variations of the self-interest that prevents a person from willing the good 'in truth', solely for its own sake. Kierkegaard emphasizes that 'the separation of sin lies in between' a person's resolution to live purely and the successful realization of this ideal: 'each day, and day after day, something is placed in between: delay, blockage, interruption, delusion, corruption.'[8] Similarly, in *Works of Love* (1850) he outlines only to deconstruct a distinction between pure and impure love; between Christian, agapeistic love and preferential, erotic love.[9]

Another important example of the impossible Christian ideal is the characterization of faith in Kierkegaard's 1849 text *The Sickness Unto Death*. Here the pseudonym Anti-Climacus insists that faith, rather than virtue, is the opposite of sin, and of the despair which constitutes the spiritual 'sickness' of sin. He describes faith as a state in which 'the self rests transparently in the power that established it' – that is to say, in God. But Anti-Climacus goes on to suggest that despair is universal, implying that the clear, untainted, self-present, restful state of faith is never actually reached: 'anyone who really knows mankind might say that there is not one single living human being who does not despair a little, who does not secretly harbour an unrest, an inner strife, a disharmony, an anxiety about an unknown something or a something he dare not even try to know, an anxiety about some possibility in existence or an anxiety about himself . . .'[10] The real author of the text

---

7 Ibid., pp. 52–3.
8 Søren Kierkegaard, *Purity of Heart is to Will One Thing*, tr. Douglas V. Steere (New York: Harper and Row, 1956), pp. 31, 218.
9 See Vanessa Rumble, 'Love and Difference: The Christian Ideal in Kierkegaard's *Works of Love*', in Elsebet Jegstrup (ed.), *The New Kierkegaard* (Bloomington: Indiana University Press, 2004).
10 Kierkegaard, *The Sickness Unto Death*, p. 22.

certainly includes himself among those who suffer from despair; this is why the pseudonymous voice of Anti-Climacus is needed, for faith can only be known, and thus described, from this fictional perspective. Kierkegaard, who is named as the editor of *The Sickness Unto Death*, considered emphasizing his distance from his pseudonym by including an editorial note in which he states that the book's description of despair and sin 'applies to me in many ways . . . I, the editor, am not the physician, I am one of the sick'.[11]

But why offer a description of faith if such faith is impossible to attain? Why invoke the ideal of purity of heart if this is unrealizable? What purpose is served by these ideals of transparency and purity? What do these ideals *accomplish*?

The obvious answer to this question is that 'resting transparently in God' presents the reader with a goal to strive after. But surely the profound 'rest' of faith must be the opposite of all striving? It is true that Kierkegaard sometimes emphasizes the importance of striving. However, if we interpret his ideals as merely regulating a striving for perfection, in the way that Kantian ideals are regulative, this does not respond to the Nietzschean accusation of nihilism – for why should we 'regulate' or judge this life according to ideals and standards that can never be found within it?

Kierkegaard's ideals are not just untouchable guiding stars that help us progress from bad to better. The light of these ideals is not a reminder of a remote heaven, but a means of illuminating *this* world, *this* life, *this* human condition. The notion of transparent rest in God, for example, works to bring into relief essential features of sinfulness: the anxiety and restlessness, the concealment and deceit. It is in living with the ideal, in the light of the ideal, that these phenomena of sin come into view – and they need to be uncovered, pointed out, because otherwise the ubiquity and totality of sin, and therefore of its symptoms, hides it from view. (The theological doctrine of original sin conveys precisely this ubiquity and totality; another way of putting this is to say that the condition of sin, and its concomitant suffering, is ontological rather than psychological.) Kierkegaard suggests in *Purity of Heart* that the chief reason for practices such as prayer and confession is the exposure of the individual's sinful condition: 'The all-knowing One does not get to know something about the maker of confession, rather the maker of confession gets to know about himself . . . The prayer does not change God, but it changes the one who offers it . . . Much that you are able to keep hidden in darkness, you first get to know by your opening it to the knowledge of the all-knowing One'.[12] As Kierkegaard observes in this discourse, delusion 'is unable to check itself'.[13] Continual anxiety is like a low

---

11 Ibid., p. 162.
12 Kierkegaard, *Purity of Heart is to Will One Thing*, pp. 50–1.
13 Ibid., p. 39.

continuous sound – the humming noise of a refrigerator, for example – that is usually unnoticed until it stops. The concealment inherent in sin deceives itself as well as others. Anti-Climacus's description of rest and transparency serves to expose, by delimiting and rendering recognizable, an inability to rest and to see clearly. In fact, *the notions of rest and transparency serve to expose the condition of their own impossibility*: the condition of sin. Similarly, the ideal of 'willing one thing', crystallized in *Purity of Heart*, exposes the many different varieties of 'double-mindedness' which contaminate even the sincerest attempt to live a good Christian life.

This exposure, this detection of sin, is accomplished by a kind of *testing*: the ideals of rest and transparency *test* the anxiety and opacity of sin; the concept of purity of heart *tests* 'double-mindedness'. 'Testing' here means tapping against something to sound it out for faults and weaknesses, to find whether or not it 'rings true' – what Nietzsche, in fact, describes as 'philosophizing with a hammer' in order to 'sound out' idols.[14] While Nietzsche uses tools such as vigorous critical thinking and, in the 1880s, the doctrine of eternal recurrence to test ideals and values in the name of 'life' and 'affirmation', Kierkegaard uses ideals to test human life. But the aim of this testing is not to *judge* life in accordance with a transcendent value, but rather to *know* life, to gain a more intimate and honest acquaintance with one's own inner life. Both Kierkegaard and Nietzsche exhibit a critical brilliance that has its roots in a much older religious tradition of scrupulous self-examination before God.[15]

To some extent, Kierkegaard's view of ideals echoes Luther's view of the law, which the German reformer presents in his interpretation of Romans 3.20: 'By the law is knowledge of sin'. For Luther, the law is 'impossible of attainment', and thus 'the entire design and power of the law is just to give knowledge, and that of nothing but sin'. Kierkegaard follows Luther in emphasizing the delusion and self-deception that characterize the human condition, and which thus provide the conditions of Christian practice. Luther writes that 'the Scripture sets before us a man who is not only bound, wretched, captive, sick and dead, but who, through the operation of Satan his lord, adds to his other miseries that of blindness, so that he believes himself to be free . . . But the work of Moses is the opposite of this – namely, through the law to open to man his own wretchedness.'[16] Kierkegaard, however, seems to be far more conscious than Luther of the possibility that his writing might be an exercise in testing or sounding out

---

14 See the Foreword to Nietzsche's *Twilight of the Idols*.
15 See Don Cupitt, *Above Us Only Sky* (Santa Rosa: Polebridge Press, 2008), p. 15.
16 See Martin Luther, *The Bondage of the Will*, tr. J. I. Packer and O. R. Johnston (London: James Clarke, 1957), pp. 158–62.

the hidden weaknesses in the reader's inner life, and indeed in his own life too; the impossibility of Christian ideals not only preoccupies his reflections on 'the task of becoming a Christian', but often also dictates the style of his texts, especially his use of pseudonyms. As Vanessa Rumble writes, 'Kierkegaard sets the Christian standard so high that no human could work to attain it and no human consciousness really wish it, so high that . . . so many of his pseudonymous texts disintegrate into the paired roles of . . . the observer/poet caught up in submissive wonder before the inaccessible hero of immediacy.'[17] We have seen how this literary structure is exemplified in *Fear and Trembling*.

If ideals merely served to expose the human condition as it really is, they might yet seem to be nihilistic, to be orientated to the condemnation of life in the name of an impossible ideal. The important question here is the quality, the 'how' of this exposure; the attitude or spirit of the testing, the bringing-to-light. If an ideal helps a person to understand herself and others better – and this involves grasping precisely why the ideal is impossible – then this knowledge can promote compassion, toleration, forgiveness, humility . . . the very ideals that are impossible to realize in their purity. In all its formulations, the Christian ideal is basically the ideal of love: self-love, love for the neighbour, love for God. There must be, then, a kind of 'double movement' involved in the invocation of the Christian ideal: first, an uncompromising questioning in the name of an ideal that has to be preserved in its pristine purity; and second, a profound and loving acknowledgement that *this is where we are, this is who we are*: it is here, now, under these less-than-ideal conditions that one tries to practise justice, or Christianity, or selflessness, and indeed it is these very conditions that invite or even impel one to practise them. Kierkegaard's attack on Christendom – the worldly instantiation of Christianity – is certainly harsh and uncompromising, and it is tempting to regard this as evidence of an intolerant refusal to give this world, this life, a chance. But on the other hand, his insistence that we are absolutely mired in the state of sin, so much so that only a god can save us, means that we are stuck in Christendom and that therefore our 'practice in Christianity' *has to* take place here.

Practising Christian love involves a double gesture: of challenge and forgiveness, of discrimination and open-hearted welcome, of vigilant self-examination and unconditional acceptance. This implies doublemindedness, and thus impurity, only if the first gesture does not already contain the second, and draw its energy and motivation from it. There is certainly a *moment* of condemnation when the ideal of purity is invoked: in *Purity of Heart*, for example, Kierkegaard states that 'the apostolic

---

17 Rumble, 'Love and Difference', p. 164.

admonition "purify your hearts ye double-minded" is condemning, namely, *double-mindedness*.[18] However, he also implies that any condemnation (or even testing) in the name of an ideal of pure love *violates the ideal*, since the judgement exhibits precisely the 'double-mindedness' that purity of heart is supposed to exclude. This very scenario is, in fact, described in *Works of Love*:

> With the one ear you hear what he says and whether it is wise and correct and penetrating and brilliant etc., and, alas, only with the other ear do you hear that it is the beloved's voice. With the one eye you look at him, testing, searching, criticizing, and, alas, only with the other eye do you see that he is the beloved. Ah, but to divide in this way is not to love the person one sees.[19]

The second moment of the double gesture of testing in the name of the Christian ideal, then, means *looking with love* on imperfection, on impurity. One can only look with love on what has been made visible, exposed by the first moment of testing. It is important to recognize that this compassionate attentiveness is just as opposed to *over*looking faults indulgently as it is opposed to criticism and condemnation.

Sin, for Kierkegaard, is the reality of human life, and as such it has the highest claim on our attention. The purpose of the ideal of purity is to shed light on sin, helping Christians to see it more clearly within themselves. Kierkegaard knew that focusing on the ideal of purity, rather than on the reality of sin, can be one of many ways to overlook – and in overlooking, to avoid – one's own sinfulness. A genuinely Christian ethic, he insists, 'does not ignore sin, and its ideality does not consist in making ideal requirements, but ... in the penetrating consciousness of reality, of the reality of sin ... The new ethics ... presents ideality as a task, not however by a movement from above down, but from below up.'[20] According to Kierkegaard, the task of Christianity is not primarily a matter of believing that certain historical events took place, nor even a non-rational confession of faith, but the continual deepening of a person's inward, heartfelt understanding that she is a sinner. This bare self-identification is given by dogmatics, but Kierkegaard's communicative task is to explore more fully the condition of sin: its phenomenology and its psychology; its modes of operation and its

---

18 Kierkegaard, *Purity of Heart*, p. 53. He is commenting on James 4.8.

19 Søren Kierkegaard, *Works of Love*, tr. Howard V. and Edna H. Hong (Princeton: Princeton University Press, 1987), p. 165.

20 Søren Kierkegaard, *The Concept of Anxiety*, tr. Reidar Thomte (Princeton: Princeton University Press, 1980), p. 18.

effects; its various manifestations and disguises. The self-discovery of sin does not just accomplish greater intellectual truthfulness, but opens up *within sin itself* the possibility of becoming a Christian, the possibility of faith, the possibility of a loving life – the possibility of loving life itself in its weakness, its blindness, its impurity.

*   *   *

I find in Kierkegaard's works an insight into the religious life that is not confined to a Christian context. Or, to put it another way, if this insight is specifically Christian, it expresses a truth that applies to anyone who aspires to live in accordance with ideals that surpass their present human condition. Philosophers outside the Christian tradition, such as Plato and Spinoza, have also recognized that an essential aspect of the task of living in such a way is to bring together love and knowledge, kindness and understanding, accept-ance and awareness, compassion and wisdom (*philo-sophia*). These qualities are like the wings of a bird: they must be equal in size and equal in strength, for otherwise the bird will not fly. Neither knowledge without love, nor love without knowledge, will allow what Kierkegaard calls the human 'spirit' or 'inner being' to grow and flourish.

But doesn't this just present us with yet another impossible ideal? Isn't the perfect balance of awareness and acceptance the narrowest of narrow paths, like a walk along a tightrope that requires super-human precision, delicacy and concentration? Is anything in nature perfectly symmetrical?

From Kierkegaard's point of view, acknowledging the impossibility of such an ideal effects the transition from a merely human 'ethical sphere' of existence to a 'religious sphere'. In the religious sphere the individual is 'before God', and the movement into this sphere is one of surrender and receptivity to God's love. Kierkegaard insists that this movement must be continually renewed, constantly repeated, since sin comes into being afresh at every moment. By oneself, one cannot maintain the balance of knowl-edge and love – either of oneself or of others – but to exist before God is to be known and loved infinitely, and thus in equal measure. It is in this light that the traditional doctrine of divine omniscience, benevolence and omnipotence comes to life, gains an existential meaning: God knows all, loves unboundedly, and saves what seems irredeemable.

Here, however, we find ourselves in a circle, because this relationship to God, which constitutes the religious sphere, is precisely what is defined as faith – the faith that is impossible, humanly speaking. And how can we speak other than humanly? People sometimes ask me how I can be a Kierkegaardian without being a Christian, and this is not an easy question to answer, but perhaps it is equally difficult to say how one might be a

134   CLARE CARLISLE

Kierkegaardian *and* a Christian. Not only does Kierkegaard follow the Lutheran interpretation of the Sermon on the Mount, according to which Jesus does not teach an ethic that we can actually live, here and now, but rather sets an impossible standard that exposes the depth of sin and thus shows us that salvation can come only by faith and by an unmerited gift of grace – but he seems to go even further in accentuating the paradox and impossibility of faith itself. To know and love others is difficult enough, but, according to Kierkegaard, 'it is far more difficult to receive [love] than to give [it]'.[21]

Faith as Kierkegaard describes it can seem to be an abstract vanishing-point, so highly spiritualized that it is more divine than human. However, his remarks about the practices of prayer and confession, quoted earlier in this essay, indicate a way out of the circle that philosophical thinking alone cannot follow. These practices can bring a person – whether in solitude or in a community – before a knowing, loving God in a more concrete sense, for they involve the whole being in an attitude of the body as well as of the mind, and engage the imagination and emotions as well as the intellect. Likewise, in the Buddhist tradition meditation practices bring together *sati* (mindfulness) and *metta* (loving-kindness). For example, the technique of *metta-bhavana* (cultivation of loving-kindness) meditation involves a kind of attentive well-wishing: the practitioner seeks to channel love to herself, to friends, to those whom she has harmed or been harmed by, to all beings; the technique of *vipassana* (insight) meditation is the practice of attentive awareness of whatever arises from moment to moment, combined with acceptance of this. In the case of both these techniques, the inevitable failure to maintain mindfulness and *metta* or acceptance is just another aspect of the self, or just another passing phenomenon, to be observed with understanding and love. The Christian and Buddhist traditions are alike in incorporating very powerful human figures – Jesus and Gotama – who not only symbolize the qualities of wisdom and compassion, but overflow with them in an excess that transcends their historical existences, repeating itself in lineages of teaching, and in liturgical, devotional and meditative practices.

Kierkegaard writes that 'in order to pray, there must be a God', but he immediately adds that (in other words) 'there must be a self plus possibility'.[22] Here, a 'self' is conceived as determinate, limited, while its 'possibility' transcends its limitations and yet is in some way related to it. Possibility in this sense is difficult to distinguish from *im*possibility; that is, from what

---

21 Kierkegaard, *Fear and Trembling*, p. 104.
22 Kierkegaard, *The Sickness Unto Death*, p. 40.

the individual cannot reach or accomplish by herself. I cannot say what is possible; I do not know what *my* possibilities might be. I do not even know who I am. But I have encountered in other human beings qualities of wisdom and love that at once reflect back to me my own limitations and show me, with an ephemeral clarity and certainty, that there is much more than I now know beyond them.

11

The God of the Prophet Jesus of Nazareth

JAMES P. MACKEY

It has long been a commonplace in that strange philosophical game of proving and disproving the existence of God to find devotees of certain religions complain that, whatever the intrinsic merits or demerits of this peculiar philosophical pastime, the definition of God agreed by both theist and atheist teams of worthy philosophers bears little or no recognizable resemblance to the God who occupies the central place in the religion of the complainant. This complaint in itself may then represent no more than a local move or a minor battle in a more widespread war between the champions of religious faith and the champions of plain human reason. Nevertheless, this complex context is the ideal one in which to set and see the uniqueness of the God that appeared in the preached and practised faith of the historical Jesus. For that God appeared in certain detailed differences from the portrait of God painted at the time and by the leaders of the religion into which Jesus himself was born, and as a prophet of which he was condemned and went to his death. Yet Jesus never gave any indication that the knowledge of this true God came to him in any way other than through the natural world and its history; and in particular in his case the natural history of his own people, and more particularly still in the history of preceding prophets in Israel (the original and true image of the prophet is that of seer, not that of stenographer of divine dictation) – and despite the fact, as he also knew and said, that the history of Israel and even the history of Israel's prophets was littered with incompletion, corruption and downright falsification of the revelation of God in nature and in that same history. And indeed, as any careful reader of what Christians call the New Testament can see, the picture of God painted in the life, death and teaching of the seer Jesus, was tampered with, and it was reduced to their measure and sometimes corrupted, even from the very outset of his public mission, by the closest and most trusted of his followers who called themselves 'sons of the prophets'; even as some of these also recorded faithfully in their memoirs of him, in the course of revealing their resistance to the most challenging of

137

these, the gist of his own words and the import of his deeds. In all of this
there is surely detectable in the biblical story of Jesus a clash of Gods; but
equally surely this is not a clash of a God of philosophers with a God of religious observers. Quite to the contrary, the God that Jesus revealed as the
common Father of all is the God who is revealed to all in the whole history
of the creation. And that is the first thing that must be realized by any who
would try to re-draw from available sources a true portrait of the God of
the prophet Jesus.[1]

Jesus, the prophet who was God?

The task of describing the God who stands at the heart and centre of the
faith of the historical Jesus cannot even begin, never mind succeed, without
some close analysis of the common Christian confession that 'Jesus is God'.
Now this very common confession at best represents a radically condensed
form of a definitive truth about Jesus. But at its worst, and it is only too
frequently used at its worst, this extremely foreshortened résumé of ancient
Christian theology and the dogmatic definitions in which that theology
became crystallized can be just as extremely misleading about the true relationship of Jesus to the God he prayed to as Father. For the name Jesus
(classically, Joshua or Jehoshua) was a common name for an Israelite in his
time. It names a man, for there are no such names, indeed no names at all,
for God. And to make a man, any man or woman, God or equal to God is
the epitome of idolatry and blasphemy combined. In fact, the blasphemy of
posing as the equal of God is the original sin of the whole race, in the sense
that it is the mother and father of all other sin and of all of man's ever pullulating inhumanity to man. The Genesis story of the Fall offers that insight
at the very beginning of the Bible; and the famous hymn in Philippians
praises Jesus for (alone?) not falling: he 'did not think equality with God a
thing to be grasped', as Adam/Everyman did (Philippians 2.6). John too in
his Gospel has Jesus plead not guilty to the charge of the capital crime of
blasphemy brought against him, namely, that 'you, being a man, make yourself God'; the evidence for which was his alleged using or accepting such
titles as 'son of God', and saying such things as 'I and the Father are one', and
'the Father is in me and I am in the Father' (John 10.22–39).

---

1 The theological and exegetical arguments that are necessary for the adequate support of
most of the positions taken here on the faith of the historical Jesus and on the God that can be
seen at the centre of that faith may be found in much fuller form in the twin books: James
Mackey, *Christianity and Creation: The Essence of the Christian Faith and its Future Among Religions* (New York and London: Continuum, 2006); and *Jesus of Nazareth: The Life, the Faith and
the Future of the Prophet* (Dublin: Columba Press, 2008).

For the Bible applies the title of 'son of God' to many people and to the Israeli people itself. The oneness of Jesus with God then refers to the fact that the recipient of that title is and acts towards the creation as does the Creator Spirit itself, and in doing so is the spitting image of the Father as mediator of the reign of God in the world. And as for the cruder forms of the language of transcendence and immanence as contraries to which philosophy of religion has long been addicted, it is well past time that contemporary practitioners of that noble branch of philosophy should consider the wisdom of the double immanence language that the Bible always uses when engaging the best imagery available for the relationship of God, world and humanity in particular. For then it would be easier for them to see that the all-too-common phrase is potentially a very misleading way of saying what the Bible really does say, that the fullness of God dwelt in Jesus (as Jesus lived and moved and had his being in the Spirit of God – the double immanence once again), and God was thereby bodied forth into the world in all of his life, death and destiny (Colossians 1.19).

The principal locus of this idiom of sons of God, sometimes also called simply gods, or divine men, was the ideology of sacral kingship in that ancient world; although that idiom was by no means confined to sacral kingship; Moses, the founding prophet of Israel to whom Jesus compared himself most favourably, was a divine man according to later Israeli tradition. This ideology of sacral kingship the Israelis borrowed, together with the institution of kingship, from Egypt and other surrounding nations, and nowhere in the Bible does one glean the impression that the phrases associated with that ideology are used in Israel with any other range of meaning than that borrowed from the ancient world. When Mark has a Roman centurion, seeing how Jesus died, say 'truly this man was a son of God', he need have had no fears that the Israelis all around might have thought he was mistaking the condemned man for God (Mark 15.39). And when John has doubting Thomas finally confess on encountering the risen Lord, 'My Lord and my God', the informed reader will remember a coin of a contemporary emperor, Domitian, inscribed with the legend, *Dominus et Deus,* 'Lord and God'; and will remember also that the most these Roman emperors ever wished for was the modest apotheosis of a place among the stars (John 20.28).

Incidentally, if it is misleading to the point of being potentially untrue to say that the man, Jesus, is or was God, it is equally a misrepresentation of the Bible to say that God became man in the case of Jesus. That last phrase is often put forward as the content, if not indeed as an equivalent translation of the so-called 'incarnation' text in John's Gospel: 'And the Word became flesh and dwelt among us' (John 1.14). But that text cannot be taken as in any way the equivalent of the proposition, God became man.

The term 'flesh', in its native Hebrew idiom, refers not to human nature as such, but to the human being trying to survive and flourish on its own, as creator of its own life and world in reliance on its own wisdom. And it is into that primordial and permanent human temptation to fall from grace in the manner that the very first chapters of Genesis describes, that the Word of God comes in the case of its coming into Jesus also. The image of the Word of God in what Christians call the Old Testament functions as the equivalent to the image of the Wisdom of God, or even the image of the Spirit of God. Therefore the 'incarnation' text in John is fully the equivalent of a baptismal text, for example, in which the Spirit of God is said to come upon or into Jesus so as to make him a true son of God; and neither in these texts nor in any similar ones is it ever suggested that Jesus is God, or that God became a man in Jesus (Matthew 4.16–17).

The most famous dogmatic definition on the matter of this relationship between Jesus and God, issued at the Council of Chalcedon in AD 451, would equally resist reduction to such statements as 'Jesus is God' or 'God became man'. For, in rough translation, this defined doctrine proclaims that in Jesus our Messiah and Lord we encounter one who was fully of the same human nature and substance as us, 'like us in all things except sin'; and one who is simultaneously of the very nature and substance of God. Or, as the Council itself puts the matter, Jesus as Lord is 'made known (to us) in two natures without confusion (of these), without change (of either), (but also) without division or separation, the difference of the natures being by no means removed because of the union, but the property of each nature (human and divine) being preserved and coming together in one individual'.[2] This definition secures the view that in Jesus we encounter a man who does not change into God, and God who does not change into a man. And the union of the two in one individual is adequately accounted for by the formula used by Jesus himself: Jesus lives and dies and has his eternal being 'in the Father', and the Spirit of the eternal Father lives most fully in this world, in and through the man Jesus; and in and through his true followers, in so far as they do truly follow him.

The God of Jesus, the prophet

If Jesus was not God then, who or what was he? The Christian Bible answers that question by portraying Jesus, as he understood himself, as a prophet of the Lord in Israel; and his first company of followers took themselves to be 'sons of the prophet(s)' – a kind of community of followers of individual prophets well known from what Christians call the Old Testament, but this

---

2 J. N. D. Kelly, *Early Christian Doctrines* (London: Adam and Charles Black, 1958), pp. 338ff.

time organized around a leadership group of the Twelve in order to symbolize the arrival of the (re)new(ed) Israel.[3] And the question that must interest philosophers with their gods then is this: of what kind is the God that appeared in the prophetic words and deeds of Jesus of Nazareth?

The quickest route to a vantage point from which this God can be seen is through the trial of Jesus before the Israeli High Priest. Jesus was tried before the High Priest on a charge of blasphemy, and found guilty and condemned to the obligatory sentence of death. On evidence recorded in the Bible, he had put himself forward as a prophet; but more, much more than that, he regarded himself as the prophet of the age of fulfilment, the prophet like himself that Moses had foretold would come. And then worse, much worse even than that, Jesus had proclaimed himself a prophet greater than Moses, who the Israeli's have always insisted gave them the perfect and eternal Torah. And Jesus had made this highest-risk claim despite the fact that it had been laid down in that same Torah that if any such future prophet differed from the Mosaic Torah, that false prophet must die (John 5.46; Deuteronomy 18.15–20). Presumably because such a foolish man would be representing a divinity different from the one who gave the Torah to Moses, a false god preached by a false prophet, a blasphemy against the one true God, a piece of plain idolatry that consisted essentially in the act of some prophet setting himself up as the true image or son of a God that could only be considered an opponent, an adversary of the one true God; the whole evil affair an exercise in pure Satanism. (For some sense of the equivalence of these phrases see John 8 again and other similar scenes from that most historical of Gospels.) Yet to represent a divinity different from the one that 'the Jews' believed Moses represented was just what the prophet Jesus did, and it is in doing this that he was deemed to have blasphemed. And so his judgement, sentencing and execution were unquestionably valid and legal, in accordance with the Torah revealed through Moses.

What then were the differences between the God of the prophet Jesus and the God of the prophet Moses? The quickest route to the kind of short answer to that question that this context can offer is through Matthew's Sermon on the Mount, through the conceit of having Jesus handing down the new Torah from another mountain, just like Moses handed down the old Torah from a holy mountain (Matthew 5—7). 'You have heard that it was said to them of old ... but I say to you', Jesus repeats in different ways. Matthew rather brazenly regards this move by Jesus to reform the Mosaic Torah as fulfilment of the old; but as the High Priest would illustrate rather graphically later on, one man's fulfilment is another man's contradiction,

---

3 The fuller evidence for Jesus as primarily a prophet, and neither a priest nor a king, is to be found once again in Mackey, *Jesus of Nazareth*. See Acts of the Apostles 3.25.

and any objective and fair-minded referee in this affair would find it difficult to side with Matthew rather than Caiaphas. For in the foremost of these
contrasts Jesus insists that we must not kill anyone, where the Mosaic law
had permitted capital punishment on many counts, as well of course as the
killing and uprooting sometimes of whole populations that characterized
the advance by Moses and Joshua in the trek to take the allegedly promised
land (a practice enthusiastically pursued by Israelis to the present day).
Indeed, we must not even get angry with another, nor mock nor diminish
anyone, not even those who are our sworn or perceived enemies, who do us
wrong and injure or rob us. Instead, we must love our enemies, give and do
good to those who rob or injure us, so that every case of forgiveness – and
we must always forgive those who do us wrong – becomes a case of creative
and loving forgiveness, in that we do an actual and extra good in response
to the evil suffered. We do not satisfy ourselves with some formal declaration of forgiveness that all too often succeeds only in making us seem
superior, without any thought for the more complex motives and circumstances that so commonly characterize the murky mess of human moral
relationships.

This prophetic theme of doing only good to those who do evil is seen to
be particularly prevalent as soon as our attention is drawn to the second
manner in which Jesus of Nazareth, like other prophets, in addition to the
proclaimed word, presented the true image of God and of God's ways with
the world: the use of symbolic action or drama. Throughout the mission of
the prophet Jesus two main classes of these symbolic activities are in evidence: eucharistic meals and healings. In the former he used the oldest and
most natural sacrament in the world, the meal, in order to dramatize God
the Creator's giving of life and of all the supports and enhancements of life,
symbolized in the bread and wine, to all without distinction; and thereby to
inspire them to respond with a gratitude – hence the name, Eucharist – that
should further inspire the recipients of this utterly free and ultimately
boundless gift to share this with others rather than treat it as a private possession to be amassed and enjoyed at the expense of others. And in the very
first eucharistic meal recorded at the beginning of the very first Gospel,
written by Mark, and said to have taken place in the home of Jesus himself
and at his own table, it is reported that Jesus demonstrated and insisted that
the wrongdoers (as society saw them) were as unconditionally entitled, if
not more entitled to a place at that sacramental table, as those who thought
themselves righteous before God (Mark 2.15–17).

The same point is put constantly in the ever-active healing ministry;
making life whole again for those who suffered its diminution and despair,
and with no regard whatever as to whether the beneficiaries were good or
evil. But this time the point is put in a more roundabout manner, though

none the less powerful for that. For so often Jesus takes the occasion of a healing event in order to break the link that traditionally held in most people's minds, the link between someone's suffering and injury and some evil done by that person or her family that must explain the suffering or injury as divine punishment for it. On all such occasions Jesus insists that God does not punish people for their evil-doing. Sometimes this is stated more or less directly; sometimes it is more obliquely suggested, as when people who come to be healed – for instance in the story of the healing of the paralytic at the beginning of Mark's account of the ministry – are told by Jesus that their sins are already forgiven before they have even thought to ask for forgiveness (Mark 2.5). But the insistence of Jesus is constant on this point; as he once put the principle of this matter in one plain and simple sentence to the effect that the ills and injuries that people suffer in this life, far from being occasions of God punishing the evils they them-selves have committed, are instead occasions for the true nature of the true reign of God to come clear in the plain light of day. 'It was not that this man sinned, or his parents, but that the works of God might be manifest in him'; so Jesus himself said when healing a man born blind, as his disciples asked him, 'Rabbi, who sinned, this man or his parents, that he was born blind? (John 9.1–17).

In all of these ways, then, the prophet Jesus persistently and imaginatively portrays the one, true God as one who reigns through the continuous creation and advance of life for all, abundantly and eternally. This true reign of the one true God is a reign in which the creative healing of the ills that humanity has inflicted on itself and all of its kind must be further advanced by the overcoming of the dying to certain forms of life that are a necessary, intrinsic part of God bringing life to higher and higher forms until it achieves a derivative eternity for all. Only God can provide the latter, for that finally consists, in our case, in the continuously creative act of bringing safe out of the inevitable disintegration of our current and gross material bodies the 'spiritual bodies', as Paul calls them, in which God can allow us to share in the divine eternity (1 Corinthians 15.44). The former, however, the prevention of the sufferings of life in this age, and the healing of what cannot be prevented, together with the enhancement of life for all, can and must be supplied, within their capacity to do so, by human beings who in their fallen state are, ensemble, the perpetrators of all the ills and dyings that are truly incomprehensible and unacceptable.

Human beings must be prepared to share life and the necessities and enhancements of life, and indeed to sacrifice their own lives for others, in order that the true reign of God makes of this cosmos again the paradise it is as it comes daily from the hands of the Creator. So they exercise the stew-ardship of the creation to which by their very nature they are called; and in pursuit of this reign in God's cosmic kingdom they must do good and only good to all, to the evil-doers as much if not more than the virtuous; forgiving all unconditionally, but doing this creatively in imitation of the one they call their Christ. All of this Matthew summarizes in some sentences placed on the lips of Jesus in his fabled Sermon from the Mount, and binds it all together in the Bible's ideology of sonship of God. He has Jesus point out that God sends the heat and light of the sun, and water in the form of rain, the twin cosmic sources of life on this earth and originating sources then of all the necessities and enhancements of life, to the just and the unjust, the good and the evil alike, without distinction or discrimination. So we must do likewise; for we are to be perfect in the manner in which our heavenly Father is perfect; true sons and daughters of God, mediating God's reign on earth as it once was and can still be when earth is paradise regained (Matthew 6.43–47).

The God of the prophet Jesus versus the God of the priest Caiaphas: the clash of faith and religion

So much of so many of the truest and most revealing of the religious myths of the race takes the form of theomachy, a battle of the gods; and that is certainly the case with the biblical story of the God of the prophet Jesus. A very brief résumé of the battle must suffice for our purposes; as that is crystallized in the continuing row between Jesus and the Temple officials concerning his practice of healing on the Sabbath. To Jesus, healing was an essential part of divinely initiated and indeed enjoined human co-operation in the ongoing creation of life, and life more abundant that was at the centre and of the essence of the reign of God itself. Therefore, whatever it was that the code of Sabbath observance was meant to embody and express about God and humanity – for example, that humanity, by refraining from working on the Sabbath, should dramatize the fact that it was primarily God who continued to make the good world, something that humanity could not take on to do on its own without wrecking its world and itself with it – that should not involve neglecting, or even postponing the quintessentially catch-up part of that work called, quite literally, healing, salving, salvation. In short, the best way of summing up all these rows about Sabbath observance is to say that it was all a matter of striking the balance between symbolizing and effecting the unavoidably derivative nature of humanity's natural role in creating life, and life for ever more abundant for all, and yet holding to the view that this role must be played out through all the days that God gives us.

Left at that of course, that account of the running rows about Sabbath observance might not have amounted quite yet to a sense that the God that the prophet of Nazareth represented was a different God from the one whose reign and rule the Temple authorities believed they shared and imposed. All of that could have been gathered into that ever-changing area in which great ideals are concretized in specific rules and regulations, and where much room remains for differences of interpretation between priests, prophets and scribes, without any suspicion arising that some are dealing with a different God. But wait for and examine the principle in which Jesus himself summed up this whole matter of dispute about Sabbath observance, and then the difference does certainly amount to a clear sense of a different God. The principle as formulated by Jesus was this: 'the Sabbath was made for man; not man for the Sabbath; so the son of man is lord even of the Sabbath' (Mark 3.27). For when the principle is stated and generalized in this manner, then Sabbath immediately comes to stand for all the rules laid down for what to believe about God (creed), how to live life as God wills (code), how to acknowledge God in gratitude, praise and above all, worship (cult). And, finally, Sabbath rules come to stand for the rule that says we must obey those who would insist that God has entrusted to them the formation and imposition of all of these other rules about creed, code and cult (constitutional churches, institutional religion). Then the difference between the God that Jesus knew both from the world around him and from the very centre of his divinely inspired being, and the God whose alleged rule was imposed by the Jerusalem authorities for the glorification of that God rather than for human benefit and under pain of punishment in this life and possibly in the next, was considerably greater than that between chalk and cheese. It was, and remains, the difference between, on the one hand, the God who created the world for its own sake, as a pure act of grace, and continuously creates it in all of its evolutionary elan, and all for the end and purpose named *shalom*, the perfection of life for all, unthreatened by even the shadow of death; and, on the other hand, a God who created humankind in particular to obey God under pain of punishment and death, and to praise and glorify God for all eternity.

Thanks (Eucharist) and praise are certainly called for in the case of a God who, to the contrary, creates the world for the eternal peace and prosperity, the eternal *shalom* of all creatures. But in this other context of the God of the prophet, thanks and praise are as much and more for the good of humanity as they are for the glorifying of God. For the gratitude in particular, as is shown in the one religious ritual that Jesus certainly used in the course of his prophetic mission, the Eucharistic meal, can do more than anything else to make us feel how much of a gift, a grace, a gift utterly freely and unconditionally given, is the world in which we live and all that is continuously and creatively evolved in it. And if that sense of being so enriched without any merit on our part, and despite any demerit of any amount we may have amassed, does not inspire us to create life, its supports, healings and enhancements, just as liberally for others and at whatever expense to ourselves, in imitation and continuance, within our powers, of the same rule of God operative in the whole world, then nothing will: no promise of a distant reward in some other world (of the existence of which we have no evidence or reliable testimony, apart from string theory and other forms of metaphysical physics); and certainly no threat in an equally remote and improbable place of punishment, like the traditional Christian hell.

The main difference between the God of Caiaphas the priest and the God of Jesus the prophet emerges once more when one considers their contrasting attitudes to the Temple, the twin pillar with Torah of Israelite religion at the time of Jesus. Although the account of the trial of Jesus reveals a failure to establish a case against Jesus with respect to his attitude to the Temple, the trial of Stephen on identical charges of attacking both Torah and Temple reveals in detail evidence to support the capital charge as it related to the Temple. For Stephen, arraigned before the priestly bench, insists that the only house that can be regarded as the true and permanent house of God is heaven-and-earth; that is to say, the cosmos of which God is simultaneously creator and paterfamilias, with the clear implication that the Jerusalem Temple, or indeed any other Temple, must be seen only, if also helpfully, as a symbol of that real temple of God; a sentiment virtually echoed by Jesus in a discussion of the relative merits of the temples in Jerusalem and on Mount Gerizim (Acts 6.8–14; John 4.21–23).

The house of creation is the house of God, every part and level of it; in which God is directly encountered, most particularly in the provision of life, and of all the necessities and enhancements of life, and all the healing of life's reversals, a provision that is always and eternally extended to all alike, irrespective of their moral or other merits. This is the true house of God, the true sons and daughters of the paterfamilias of which will provide for each other, even those who do evil and do them wrong. This is the eternal Eucharistic meal of the world, in which the rule of the creator/paterfamilias consists wholly and entirely in the carrying out of the duties of that office, and of which each and every daily meal must be both a participation and a symbol. The temple, every temple was made for man, for everyman, in order to symbolize and effect the eternal divine provision of life for everyman without distinction or respect of persons. (Jesus did not sum up this matter in these words, as he did with respect to Torah; but he could have done.) Man was not made for the Temple, to serve God and glorify him in that particular Temple or set of temples, and to make satisfaction there for offending God by not doing this and other things that God has specifically ordered; and to offer both service and satisfaction through the priests of the Temple that stand between God and the rest of humankind, so that God, through the good offices of the priests, might restore life and grace once more, where otherwise the punishment of pain, deprivation and death would be dealt out, here and hereafter, for as long as hereafter may last.

In view of this plain position of the Bible, it is more than depressing to note that within three centuries or so the self-declared followers of Jesus, who was neither a priest himself nor had he ever ordained any, had erected temples, and had turned the death of Jesus into a human sacrifice required and arranged by God in satisfaction for the sins of humankind. Of course the death of Jesus was a sacrifice, and a human sacrifice at that, since Jesus was a human being and he was the only one who died on that Calvary cross on that Friday afternoon long ago. And it was a sacrifice for the sin of the race in two senses: first, in that the killing of Jesus was the very paradigm of that sin of humans who would play God and so attempt to guarantee their lives, always at the expense of their fellow humans. And second, in the sense that by dying for that other life of mutual love and service, Jesus achieved the very height of inspiration of others to take up such a way of living and thereby send their sin into remission and achieve *shalom* for all, in place of the war of all against all.

But Calvary was not a cultic sacrifice offered by a priest in a possibly vain attempt either to acknowledge God's ownership and lordship over all or to turn away the punitive wrath of God against human sinning; a primitive practice of human sacrifice that even the Israelite religion had long abandoned, as the Bible story of God thwarting Abraham's intended sacrifice of Isaac probably reminds us (Genesis 22). Neither did Jesus himself take such a primitive view of his role and fate on Calvary. It is clear from the Gospels that he regarded his death as the execution of the prophet, and as such as an act attributable not to his Father in heaven arranging for a required satisfaction for sin, but attributable rather to a satanic power acting through the Temple authorities, thereby making them sons of the devil, 'a killer from the start', rather than true sons of the one true God (John 8.39–47). Calvary had to be the one or the other; it could not have been both.

The question does then arise: if Jesus presents in word and deed and for our imitation a God who reigns eternally in no way other than through creating and healing and enhancing life for all, and enjoining on all of us to do likewise, how is it that the Bible also presents us with a God, and Jesus as his plenipotentiary, who does return evil for evil, including threat of eternal torture, as a means of imposing his will and reign on this world and any other world there may be? For the Jesus of Matthew's great last judgement scene is certainly somewhat different from the Jesus who delivered the Sermon from the Mount (contrast Matthew 5—7 with 25.31–46). The only credible answer to that question must be: the biblical writers did indeed record faithfully the true account of the true reign of God that Jesus lived, preached and died for; but they are equally faithful to the facts in recording their own resistance to it from beginning to end, for they simply could not take it. They preferred another kind of reign of another God, one who would act more like the kings they knew, enforcing sovereign will by force and threat; and so some of them would have Jesus come again (certainly Paul and Matthew, not John or Mark, and Luke is a bit 'iffy'), this time to be the kind of son of God they wanted, the kind the crowd who supported Jesus entering Jerusalem so clearly identified when they shouted 'Blessed is the kingdom of our father David that is coming' (Mark 11.10). King David redivivus and triumphant was the son of God they wanted, here now or coming soon; the son of a God who would destroy those who would oppose his reign and kingdom. Nothing less would do.

All of which should remind the Bible reader that the prophets from the beginning had spoken against such earthly sons of God. The prophets of Israel spoke for God to the people of Israel, telling them that they should not have a king like the surrounding nations; God was the only King whose reign they should embrace. They told the people that they should not attempt to domicile God in a house built for that purpose. And when the people insisted on having kings and temples, the prophets ranted on God's behalf at having palace and temple 'lintel to lintel' in the same sacred compound, as was then the convention; for then the secular ethos of the king would undoubtedly corrupt that of the Temple, and their God would be made into the image of one who reigned by sovereign will and force and threat, and would extend his kingdom also by such means: a composite message that the prophet Jesus repeated in warnings to the would-be leaders of his own followers, the 'sons of the prophets', that they should not lord it over their brethren like the rulers of the Gentiles did, but should serve them like slaves. This prophetic vision of God, of the true reign of the one true God, has been betrayed in one respect or another by some of the earliest leaders of the followers of Jesus, by some biblical writers, and by most of the mainline churches that sprung up after the close of the age of biblical writers, and to this day. And in some of these respects, it has to be said, the Jewish faith and the Muslim faith, mother and offspring of the faith that came to be called Christian, are still closer to the faith of the prophet Jesus than is the Christian faith.

Philosophers and the gods

The standard dishes on the menu for courses in the philosophy of religion have long consisted of proofs of God's existence, miracles and the problem of evil, although these can be reduced to two standard dishes, of proofs and disproofs; for miracles are proofs based on distinctive events rather than the existence of the cosmos as a whole, and the so-called problem of evil functions as the best disproof on offer by argumentative atheists. On these two matters there is space, and indeed need in the present context for but two sets of brief remarks.

First, in the matter of proofs it is puzzling, to say the least, that they seem to start with a definition of God and then set out to prove that such a God, so defined, exists. But how could one define or even describe with the least specificity something one had not already encountered; especially in the case of God who, those who claim to encounter It, declare to be indefinable? Second, it was always to features of the natural world and its history that the prophet Jesus pointed people in order that they should have each their own experience of an encounter with this otherwise indefinable One and even of Its characteristics as the eternally good and indiscriminately benevolent origin of all existence and life: the kind of direction to an experience of God that the prologue to John's Gospel summed up in the proposition that the continuously creative Word (of) God, through that creative activity, enlightens everyman in the world. The prophet Jesus therefore has the same access to God through the world as the best of philosophers have – it is the worst philosophers who dumb the whole matter down to so-called proofs and disproofs – an access that is ethical and therefore personal, rather than merely theoretical, as Stephen Clark's chapter in this book illustrates. Or since science seems to have taken over from philosophy the task of disapproving of God, the words of a physicist might be preferred: 'the commitment to truth which leads a scientist like myself to the laboratory is, ultimately, not different from that commitment which issues forth in the reasonable commitment known as worship'.[4] For the prophet is the seer, as is the contemplative philosopher, and not some kind of town crier of verbal messages received verbatim and direct from God.

If the so-called proofs of God's existence are bedevilled by conceptual and logical ineptitude, the same is true with bells attached when the major disproof of God's existence is thought to consist in the deployment of a certain so-called problem of evil. Here the conceptual ineptitude consists in the vacuity of the concept of omnipotence (and indeed all the other omni's) when applied to God, as Hegel was wont to insist. Then add the uncertainty as to whether the evil referred to in this theodicy argument is a moral or a

---

4   In Poon's review of Keith Ward's god-of-the-gaps approach, *Studies in World Christianity* 4.2 (1998), pp. 255–8. There are other examples of this similarity between the God of the philosophers and the God of religion: for example, in John Dillon's collection, *The Great Tradition* (Aldershot: Ashgate, 1997). See also T. L. S. Sprigge, 'The God of the Philosophers', *Studies in World Christianity* 4.2 (1998), pp. 149–72.

physical entity – the problem of evil is often glossed as the problem of suffering or the problem of pain. The logical ineptitude consists in the fact that divine omnipotence does not imply that God should do everything that is possible for God, like ridding the world of free wills so that moral evil should have no place in it; just as incidents of pain and suffering are not in themselves morally evil, as part, for instance, of the shedding of old forms of life in the course of the creative elan of life to higher forms. In any case, there is something distinctly odd about there being a problem concerning the pullulating evil we know in the world, which would be a problem for a God if such did exist, but a problem that could be expected to conveniently appear to disappear only if God were to be solemnly and definitively denied existence. The problem of evil then would disappear if the principal culprit were declared dead or gone. Only the juvenile simplicity of John Lennon's imagination could get away with such a suggestion, and then only by singing it to an attractive tune. Imagine!

No; there is a real problem of evil in this world, and we well know what it is. It consists in an apparently insuperable predominance of human evil in the world, growing if anything as we evolve in knowledge. It is diagnosed in the Bible as stemming from the tendency of individuals or whole nations of us thinking that we are the creator gods of this world, thereby creating gods in our own image, and most particularly in the image of the kings and lords who gain life and the supports and enhancements of life for themselves and their people; grasping for themselves the wisdom of God, while really knowing how to gain their ends only by the twin violence of trade and the arms of war; threatening with suffering and death all who would resist their sovereign wills (Genesis 1—3; Ezekiel 28). The practitioners of theodicy could be right if they realized that it is such gods bestriding the earth that are responsible for the real problem of evil. That problem would then be solved if people turned away from such gods, the gods of too many priests and would-be kings; and turned instead to the God of the prophets, the God that the prophet Jesus assured us was Father to us all, and as such was the paterfamilias who presides at the eucharistic table of life, not in order to lord it over all, but to serve life ever more abundant to all – as Luke has Jesus the son do in symbolic imitation of his Father and ours, in his particular account of the so-called last supper; never to return evil for evil, not even in the form of well-deserved punishment, either here or hereafter, but only to do good; healing and advancing life for each other, since in a material world all exist and live at each other's expense; instead of all of us in every place and time doing so much violence to lives and livelihoods for our own selfish and hopeless ends.

There can be little doubt about the fact that the philosophy of life expounded and lived by Jesus of Nazareth is as humanist as any humanist philosophy of life could ever hope to be. The reason why many self-styled humanists in the West feel that they have to be atheistic or at least agnostic is because they think that the eternally violently punitive God with which Christianity, the dominant religion of the West, eventually replaced the Father of the prophet Jesus, is the only God that is credible enough to reject. Yet even the atheistic or agnostic humanists should feel welcome to join with any band of true Jesus followers they might be lucky enough to meet. For in that studiously ignored scene painted in John 10, in which he rejects the accusation that, as the Philippians hymn would put it, he grasped at equality with God, Jesus himself offers the hand of fellowship to such people. To paraphrase his words on that occasion, he says: if you will not accept my claim to be son of the Father but not God as he is, and you will not keep faith with him through me, then leave all that aside and keep faith with the works of creation as I describe and promote them, and we will find peace and paradise together. For it is not those who simply bow down and call me and the Father 'Lord' who enter paradise regained, but those who live by the rule of that reign, doing only good to good and evil alike.

Similarly with the more philosophically minded atheistic humanists who base both their atheism and their prospects for humanity's best future on science, the ones whose messiah and world missionary is Richard Dawkins: there is little or no point in undermining his scientific disproofs of God's existence – an easy enough thing to do[5] – as long as both sides in this modern debate between religion and science are talking about the same divine demand for human sacrifice and the same eternal torturer of unrepentant sinners. The majority of his millions of readers will not fully understand either Dawkins' scientific argument or the vast over-simplification of the scientific evidence on which it is based. Rather, happy with the general impression he conveys that modern science with its massive prestige is on

---

5 See Emma Young, 'Strange Inheritance', in *New Scientist*, 12 July 2008, pp. 29–33; especially the cover legend: *'Forget Genes: the surprising power of the other side of evolution'* and the inset on p. 31 entitled, 'Rewriting Darwin and Dawkins'. See Stefan Helmreich, 'Recombination, Rationality, Reductions and Romantic Reactions', *Social Studies of Science* 28 (1998). See Amanda Gefter, 'Which Way Now?', *New Scientist*, 3 May 2008, pp. 29–31, in which, with the quest for a theory of everything facing a possible dead end, radical new routes are proposed that together see the emergence of the material cosmos from mathematical, through geometric forms. See also Philip Ball, 'Quantum All the Way', *Nature*, Vol. 453, pp. 22–5, describing how scientists begin to see how, rather than forcing a dichotomy between the counter-intuitive ways in which the sub-atomic level behaves, and the ways in which the classical world appears, a comprehensive account of the universe can show how the classical world continuously emerges from quantum phenomena. So the process by which the world we know comes to be is vastly more complex and creatively unpredictable in detail than Dawkins' John Lennon-type fairytale of the bright but selfish little genes that finally produced and propagate *homo insipiens* could ever manage to imagine.

their side, Dawkins' readers will find the capstone proof of their preferred atheism in the conviction that the God portrayed in such violent and vindictive character truly is unworthy of worship; for on this point Dawkins is quite correct. And then the Christian defenders of the faith who man the barricades against the hordes of Dawkins will have no option but to throw down the idol they have fashioned in their own likeness, and then to live and act once more in the image of the Father of the prophet Jesus. Otherwise they must sooner or later be overcome. Sooner, probably.

12

Humanism and Spirituality:
or How to be a Good Atheist

MICHAEL McGHEE

After the slow, soft undermining, then the abrupt and devastating loss of what the priests used to call the precious gift of the Faith, I had, after some years in which a sense of absence and mourning was quietly haunting me, turned towards Buddhism, first in my reading, then in my practice. After the contortions I had undergone in my passage out of the Church about whether I was still a Catholic, where the measure was what I did or did not 'believe', I felt some relief at last when I realized that the measure of whether I was a Buddhist was whether I was a practitioner, a member of a *sangha*. In later years I realized that this was an aspect at least as important within Christianity, though by then I no longer considered myself by any means Christian, even though I was prompt to correct misconceptions of that tradition and remained inspired by some of its language, images and metaphors. Nevertheless, there is some sort of cyclical movement in my life in which I feel compelled from time to time to re-examine these life-choices, to look again at my Catholicism and see how it moves me and where I now stand.

Meanwhile, although I had visited it after a brief phase of logical posi-tivism had brought down, as it seemed, the whole house of metaphysical-theological-ethical-aesthetical cards, secular humanism had held little or no appeal, had seemed arid, defining itself negatively – God is in his grave, morality is not grounded in his Will. It did not otherwise appear to have a distinctive ethical position that could be called 'humanist'. Secular human-ism seemed to be a negative position, not a positive movement. But as it happens, a renewed interest in secular humanism has coincided with one of those periodic reassessments of my former Catholicism.

I recently came across a book on humanism by Richard Norman,[1] a philosopher whose work I respected – it was a measured and sober, almost sombre piece of work. Norman did not, as some more conspicuous

---

1 Richard Norman, *On Humanism* (London: Routledge, 2004).

secularists have done, lay all our human ills at the door of religion, and neither did he adhere to an easy belief in human progress, which seems a charge routinely and sometimes rightly made against humanists. On the contrary, Primo Levi's *If this is a Man* was for him a crucial text for humanism, which he saw as 'an attempt to think about how we should live without religion', as the search for 'some alternative set of beliefs to live by'. His rejection of 'religious belief' was grounded in the thought that it is false rather than always harmful. Thus Norman writes: 'Humanism as I understand it involves not just the rejection of religious belief but, at the very least, the positive affirmation that human beings can find from within themselves the resources to live a good life without religion.'[2]

It is important to avoid a misconception here, one that sees humanism as valorizing human beings above and over against the rest of the natural world. On the contrary, one would expect that any conception of a good life would involve recognition of our interconnectedness with other animals and a proper respect for our place in nature, and Norman's brief definition is consistent with such a view. However, it is also pretty minimalist. It seems likely that there will be more than one answer to the question, What would constitute a good life without religion? Presumably these would be broadly secular humanist answers just to the extent that they conceived the moral life as having a human motivation independently of any reference to a transcendent ground. But Norman's definition also provides an example of what is almost a routine conflation, of 'religious belief' with 'religion'. The assumption must be that the terms are roughly equivalent or at least mutually implied. I was not sure that one could live a good life without *religion*, in the sense at least of the availability of some of the practices, perspectives and human insights[3] found in our religious traditions, although I thought that one *could* live a good life without 'religious belief' – though that did rather depend on what one was calling 'religious belief'. When Western philosophers talk these days about 'religious belief' they generally have in mind something they also call 'belief in God', a phrase which is, however, much more slippery than it might appear. Thus it is easy to think of it as the expression of an opinion that there is a God, as opposed to something both more difficult and more profound, something more like a conversion, a transforming realization of God's presence.[4]

---

2 Ibid., p. 18.

3 See Norman's own excellent discussion of Piero della Franscesca's *The Resurrection* in his 'The Varieties of Non-Religious Experience' in John Cottingham (ed.), *The Meaning of Theism* (Oxford: Blackwell, 2007).

4 For a previous attempt to discuss this issue see my 'Seeke True Religion. Oh Where?' in Cottingham (ed.), *The Meaning of Theism* (Oxford: Blackwell, 2007) in which I try to develop the view that 'belief in God' is a specific form of the more generic 'religious belief'.

Also quite by chance, and as part of my 'periodic review', I had been reading an article by Nicholas Lash[5] with the provocative title, 'The Impossibility of Atheism' – provocative if only because the position it announced seemed in the current climate unfashionable and reactionary,[6] a rearguard and hopeless action against a now ascendant secularism. It seemed when I first glanced through it that the article argued that one could *not* live a good life without belief in God (and Lash was quite rightly emphatic that this phrase did not refer simply to an opinion about what is the case) – or at least that one's conception of what constitutes a good life is seriously impaired by the absence of this belief.

As I have already implied, talk of 'rejecting religious belief' tends to be understood as talk of rejecting theism or belief in God, and theists and secular humanists alike incline towards this assimilation. This makes it difficult for either party to take seriously the idea of a 'religious' attitude or perspective not explicitly or surreptitiously theistic, even though, as I should want to say, and here I follow Simone Weil, such a perspective is not directed, as it were, towards the heavens, but towards life on earth.[7]

I

The exasperation of theologians has been mightily aroused lately by secularists who believe they are attacking religious belief and theology *as such* when, in reality, and unawares, it is alleged, they are attacking a form of religious belief contaminated by bad theology: the secularists fail to understand the nature of religious belief and so their rejection of it is suspect, even though it should be admitted that the bad theology is widespread in its influence, perhaps more than many of them care to admit, and humanly damaging to those believers whose lives are informed by it.

Now, if secular humanists see their project as founded on the rejection of religious belief and it is shown that they misconceive belief, then this must have consequences for their self-understanding. But it does not follow that the project itself is misconceived. The secular humanist project can start simply from the *absence* of belief, and how this absence comes about is secondary: after all, it is possible to raise the question, How should we live? in an entirely secular atmosphere. The project is not undermined even if it is articulated in terms of the rejection of a misconceived notion of belief. We

5 See his *Theology for Pilgrims* (London: Darton, Longman & Todd, 2008) and his essay elsewhere in this volume.
6 'Daft' as he puts it himself.
7 Since it is so widespread I shall go along with this usage in this essay, though it should be repeated that the term 'religious belief' is actually wider than the specifically theistic 'belief in God'.

should at least need to explore further the founding idea that one can live a good life *in the absence of* belief, even if, as I have hinted, there is some reason for demurring about a good life without *religion*.

The possibility of *rapprochement* between secularists and religionists has been enhanced by recent work by the Irish theologian James Mackey, who repudiates the forms of belief and bad theology rejected by the secularists, but also claims, in accord with the secularists, that the bad theology, in the form of discredited doctrines of God and creation, still flourishes in the ranks of believers and their ecclesiastical hierarchs, and stands in need of correction by the great secular philosophers of the last two centuries.[8] Perhaps this kind of overture can be reciprocated – perhaps secular humanism can acknowledge a need to be corrected or augmented by some religious modes of thinking, though with no implication in favour of 'belief'. But, as we might have seen, there is a complication. Nicholas Lash follows Karl Rahner in what looks like the claim that any conception of the good life cut off from belief in God is disastrously flawed. The message to the secular humanist trying to develop a conception of the good life appears to be quite blunt. Not only are you wrong in your understanding of the religious belief that you reject, you cannot have an adequate conception of human nature or what it is to live a good life except under the condition of belief. Well, perhaps that is too strong a version of the claim. The Rahner position cited by Lash[9] says that 'keeping the word "God" in play, even if only as a question,[10] is part of the very definition of what it is to be a human being', and, more trenchantly: 'The absolute death of the word "God" including even the eradication of its past, would be the signal, no longer heard by anyone, that man himself had died.'

One gets a general impression here, rather than a precise thesis and, although those of us who are non-believers might be tempted to sigh, shrug and move on to other things, perhaps with a slight shiver at that Heideggerian signal no longer heard by anyone, I should prefer to pause and dwell on just what Rahner thinks is *secured* by the use of the word 'God' and to see how much of what is thus secured can be appropriated independently of its use, notwithstanding the further comment that the 'use of this word, *and this word alone*, brings a person face to face with the single whole of reality and the single whole of their own existence' (my italics).[11]

---

8 See in particular his *Christianity and Creation: The Essence of the Christian Faith and Its Future Among Religions* (London: Continuum, 2006).

9 Lash, *Theology for Pilgrims*, p. 24.

10 This qualification seems to imply that at least a positively directed agnosticism is part of what it is to be a human being. I assume this is shorthand for something like being *fully* human.

11 One can, after all, simply *wonder* at the existence of the world without thinking that the world itself must be *produced*, though the wonder itself might be productive of a fundamental reorientation of attitude. Cf. David Cooper's chapter in this volume.

There are two things here: one could perhaps *agree* that the use of this word could bring a person face to face with the single whole of reality and of their own existence, and yet *disagree* that it is through the use of this word *alone* that a person might be brought to this pitch. But first let us return to the alleged misrepresentation of belief in God that brings the self-understanding of the secular humanist into question. If *that* is what is involved in belief in God, Rahner seems to imply, then we should all be atheists. He writes as follows:

> . . . *that* God really does not exist who operates and functions as an individual existent alongside other existents, and who would thus be a member of the larger household of all reality. Anyone in search of such a God is searching for a false God. Both atheism and a more naïve form of theism labour under the same false notion of God, only the former denies it while the latter believes it can make sense of it.[12]

The passage places the 'atheist' on the same footing as the 'more naïve theist' – as labouring under the same false notion of God, though despite this condescension it offers a reason for abandoning one kind of justification for non-belief. However, to repeat an earlier point, just as few people come to belief through the traditional arguments for God, so it may be that non-belief can survive damage to its own critical narrative about the nature of belief, if indeed it has one – and then find little to attract it, even if it finds nothing to condemn, in a *corrected* account of its nature. Not all religious belief is contaminated by a false notion of God, and nor need all atheism be so contaminated, though it would then have to give a different account of itself.

What of the true God, the God of sound doctrine? Rahner's remarks, and those by Lash in support of his position, should remind us of two crucial and connected remarks in Aquinas. St Thomas has told us that we can know by the light of reason *that* there is a God but not *what* he is. He goes on to say that God, whom he calls 'that great ocean of being', is not *a* being, one among others, but is, rather, *supra ordinem omnium entium*, beyond the order of all beings – so not part of the 'household of all reality', to use the Rahner phrase. He is beyond our understanding, so that 'every way we have of thinking about God is a particular way of failing to understand him as he is in himself'. This thought is echoed centuries later by an entry recorded in one of Newman's notebooks and brought to our attention by Lash, that in talking about God we can only set right one error of expression by another. This is not a God that can be searched for as an 'existent' within the

---

12 In Lash, *Theology for Pilgrims*, p. 20.

'household of reality', but is rather the condition or ground of that house-hold and a condition, therefore, of the possibility of any kind of investigation into what belongs within it.

II

But if these grammatical remarks about 'God' are in the classical tradition of St Thomas, they also bear a striking resemblance to the work of the Wittgensteinian philosopher, Dewi Phillips, whose sustained critique of much contemporary philosophy of religion appears continuous with the Thomistic/Rahnerian tradition. If God is not a being among others but beyond the order of all beings, if God does not belong within the household of all reality, then it is a mistake to superimpose upon discourse about God a form of discourse that belongs to our understanding of the natural order. The main burden of Phillips' work, as I understand it, is that we are constantly tempted to import an alien model into our thinking about God and belief, superimposing on religious discourse a methodology of evidence, hypothesis and probability (precisely the methodology that Richard Dawkins seeks to impose) that belongs to empirical, particularly scientific investigation.

Once one claims that 'God' is not the name of an 'existent', where the most general characteristic of an existent is its contingency, the question whether there is anything that would constitute an inquiry, let alone a method of inquiry, into the existence of God becomes conceptually problematic – not on the grounds that it isn't true that God 'exists' but because the nature and form of God's existence must determine the nature and form of what, if anything, would constitute an inquiry. The very contingency of 'existents' determines the possibilities and direction of inquiry, into the conditions upon which their existence depends. But if we are talking of an eternal and necessary being, one whose necessity implies that it is not within the order of beings which come into and go out of existence (and might not have existed at all) then the notion of 'an inquiry into existence' must at best be radically altered, and perhaps dismissed as the wrong kind of question, no matter how tempting (come on, there's a God or there isn't a God, let's just sort it out). All we can do as philosophers, I suggest, is to inquire into the *conditions* under which that concept of eternal being is *formed*, and then follow such promptings of the heart as may be there occasioned. This would not be an inquiry into the alleged *existence* of something in the manner and in the terms of an empirical investigation. It is rather a matter of reflecting on what it is like to have that sense of wonder that there is a world at all and the way that this wonder might inspire a vision of – some will talk of a felt encounter with – a creative source that lies beyond the world. It seems to me to be grammatically and doctrinally correct to say that this vision unfolds in the form of *worship* of a sustaining and loving power. And that this is what constitutes belief in God. It is not well described as a belief that something exists (to which one had better then adopt a reasonably respectful attitude, as it were), since that kind of language misleads us into modelling the discourse on what belongs to science and empirical inquiry. By that token it is also emphatically not the conclusion of an *argument* for the existence of God. This is not to deny that we can *ask* whether such a being exists – only to deny that any answer is available other than in the form of whatever in the contemplation of the very existence of the world prompts this confession of faith and adoration. However, one has to say that there is a great gulf between the profound nescience of this approach and the detailed familiarity with the mind of God evinced in so many pulpits.

To put all this in another way, I have some sympathy with a remark made by Phillips,[13] that any 'inquiry' would take the form of whatever leads to 'finding God' rather than of finding out whether there is indeed a God (though believers often talk of God finding *them* – and 'finding God' has of course a pejorative ring to it). Nor is this, I think, the infamous 'Wittgensteinian fideism' just because we are talking about the conditions of concept formation rather than about an inexplicable and ungrounded 'commitment' to a propositional 'belief', and this must lead us back to Rahner's reference to the single whole of reality.

But first, Phillips has often been dismissed, wrongly in my view, as an 'anti-realist' who simply reinterprets religious language in 'humanist' terms, and it will help our progress if we can look at a recent example of this criticism, made by John Haldane, who, in an assessment of Phillips' contribution to the philosophy of religion, writes that 'His approach to religious discourse is reminiscent of that of a tradition of theologians who have sought to interpret Christian belief and practise in ways that free them from the presumption of realities existing apart from human thought, language and action.'[14]

And he concludes that 'Phillips is right to refer the sense of religious claims to human practice, but wrong in not allowing them the possibility of "transcendent" reference; or put another way, wrong to think that their full meaning is exhausted by their practice-constituted sense.'[15] Presumably this is because their 'full meaning' must also embrace the 'transcendent

13 In 'At the Mercy of Method' in Timothy Tessin and Mario von der Ruhr (eds), *Philosophy and the Grammar of Religious Belief* (Basingstoke: Macmillan, 1995), p. 3.
14 In 'Phillips and Eternal Life: A Response to Mikel Burley', *Philosophical Investigations*, Vol. 31, 2008, p. 252.
15 Ibid., p. 253.

reference', though this seems to me confused – that there is a reference to God is a function of the *sense* of theological discourse. To talk of the *possibility* of transcendent reference here is to introduce a different topic, that of religious scepticism (whether there is *really* a God that we thus refer to[16]). Haldane has just accepted as fair an account of his own position on the resurrection of Jesus, that 'the belief cannot be reasonably understood in any way other than as involving a metaphysical commitment'. Now, it seems plausible, initially, to say that you fail to understand the religious claims of believers if you do not see that those claims involve a metaphysical commitment. It seems plausible because it is a concession that doesn't require you to take a *view* about the commitment but simply to acknowledge its presence – it would be a failure to realize something about *believers* (they are committed to the belief in God) and you do not need to be a believer yourself or to share that commitment, in order to acknowledge its presence.

But when Haldane says that Phillips is wrong not to allow religious claims 'the possibility of "transcendent" reference', the complaint appears to be a rather stronger one – that he fails to see something, not about believers, but about the status of their *religious claims*. It is only *initially* plausible to say that you fail to understand the religious claims of believers if you do not see that they involve a metaphysical commitment. But to make such a claim is to fail to acknowledge that the kind of reductionist that Haldane takes Phillips to be is actually making a *revisionist* move, offering an intellectual reappraisal of religious discourse. The reductionist doesn't fail to understand that the religious claims involve a metaphysical commitment but rather sees that very commitment as itself a misunderstanding of the discourse. The point is that the reductionist is already a non-believer and as such they offer an *explanation* of the religious belief they do not or no longer hold, and reinterpret it as, really, and despite appearances, about human life *rather than* about a divine being. What helps their claim is that such discourse is *also* about human beings, whatever the status of the claims about God. In the light of that explanation the reductionist sees believers as having a false belief, not about God, but about the nature of their own discourse. The claim is emphatically not that the believers are mistaken *in* their metaphysical commitment, but that they are mistaken in supposing *that* there was a metaphysical commitment involved at all. Well, these explanations are often found compelling – they exert over us what Wittgenstein once called 'charm'. But it is hard to see what would count in favour of the verdict that they are *right*.

A better route for the secular humanist is to refuse the revisionist theorizing of reductionism altogether and simply say that while they do not

---

16 Are there really unicorns of the kind we refer to in our stories?

share the metaphysical commitment, there are plenty of insights about human life to celebrate within religious discourse, about how to live, about the interior conditions of action, the subjectivity of moral life and so forth.

But, to return to Haldane, he seems to charge Phillips with a refusal to concede, not that religious claims are about a divine reality, but that there *could be* a divine being that they are about. This seems close to wanting him to concede that believers could be right in believing in God. And it is surely a modest enough concession. And if Phillips is not, after all, a reductionist, then presumably he would concede that Haldane could be right to believe in God. However, I think that what Phillips *ought* to reply is that such a concession would be an empty gesture – and to say this is not to take a reductionist line after all. It is an empty gesture because there is no procedure for determining that the believer is 'right' to believe in God. What has happened is that we have slid back to a model of quasi-empirical inquiry.

III

I should like now to return to the idea that the philosopher of religion can inquire only into the conditions of concept formation and to the idea espoused by Rahner that the word 'God' brings a person face to face with the single whole of reality and their own existence. In the preceding article in his book, 'Where Does *The God Delusion* Come From?' Lash had remarked of the question, Why is there anything at all?, that it is often said that God is 'the answer' and he comments that it a 'very *strange* answer because it does not furnish us with information: it simply names the mystery'.[17] This is a significant and helpful comment, not least because this question – Why is there anything at all rather than nothing? – has been used by many thinkers as part of what looks like an argument for the existence of God, a form of cosmological argument revived and made familiar by the late Herbert McCabe. This argument depends on a series of questions asking why *this* state of affairs obtains rather than *that*, questions which are answered by showing that what happens to obtain is contingent upon some particular condition, which already obtains; and the series culminates in the great question, Why is there anything at all rather than nothing?, as though *that there is anything at all* were *one* state of affairs and *nothing at all* another. We are then invited to find the presence of anything at all *as itself a contingency* that depends upon and is explained by a divine condition or ground.

One problem I have always had with this argument is that the principle of sufficient reason is already an *expression* of our assumption of contingency,

---

17 Lash, *Theology for Pilgrims*, p. 16.

and has its application in a world of contingent objects, that could have been otherwise, that depend upon conditions which explain why things are thus and not so. The principle impels us forward in particular cases to look for the explanatory condition that we believe must be there: even when we cannot find it, we wait for it with confidence. But as many philosophers have pointed out, it begs the question to claim that the totality of contingent things is itself a contingency waiting upon an explanation.

What the 'argument' misrepresents is a particular kind of religious quest which resolves itself in a transforming experience of contingency, of one's own dependence and that of all things upon a loving and sustaining power that lies beyond the world and yet is suffused within and throughout what is then thought of as creation. This experience can arise from a sense of wonder at the existence of the world *or* visit us and bring *about* the sense of a dependent totality,[18] which those of us who are non-believers do not share, though we can have plenty of experience of the contingency of human life, as I shall come to later, not in the sense simply of encountering and suffering it, but rather of having the universal displayed in the particular in a vivid and life-changing apprehension of the human condition.

Part of the problem, then, if we think of it as an argument, lies in seeing the very existence of things *as a contingency* in the first place. This is not a problem for the believer because they are already schooled in such a view, a view with a history in the imaginative responses of past ages; but it is certainly a problem for the non-believer. As I have said, someone can have an experience of contingency that amounts to an access of faith – the access of faith is, if you like, a conversion to the sense that all is contingent – and perhaps this is the real force of the 'argument', that it is a kind of *vademecum* by which someone is led to acknowledge contingency where previously they had not, and where to acknowledge contingency is already a confession, not a condition, of faith.

I find it difficult to grasp one particular response, though, to us unamenable non-believers. This says that to refuse to acknowledge the contingency of things is to commit oneself to the absurd idea that it is all a 'brute fact'. Now there are plenty of contexts in which one is properly indignant if someone claims that some state of affairs is just a 'brute fact' and has no explanation. But we do not have the stage-setting in *this* context that makes it *arbitrary* to insist that something is a brute fact: it *is* arbitrary so to insist in the face of obviously available, determining conditions. Perhaps this was the point of the famous Wittgensteinian remark in his *Tractatus* about *das Mystische* – that our language, at least as he then conceived it, has its foothold in *how* the world is, and not in *that* it is. But *that* it is – is the

18 See Janet Soskice's chapter for an intense and eloquent expression of this experience.

occasion for *poetry*, wonder, gratitude, *ecstatic song*. And the spirit of God moving over the waters is *one* song, later turned into cruel and ghastly prose.

IV

Nicholas Lash does not, as I said, rely on that argument in the comments we have looked at, but, rather, makes a grammatical remark about how the word 'God' is used and misused, a grammatical remark which seeks to correct typical secularist misrepresentation of the doctrine of God. The God of the orthodox believer is *not* of the kind that Rahner claims is denied by the atheist and accepted by the more naïve theist.

But it is in the context of this grammatical remark that we should try to understand Rahner's controversial claim that the death of the word 'God' would also be the signal for the death of man, and to reflect on how the secular humanist ought to respond. To start in a positive spirit, it seems to me that Rahner's comments significantly augment the account of the grammar of the word 'God'. To understand their significance we should look at two further, helpful claims made by Lash. The first is that the notion of God is better understood by analogy with the term 'treasure'; and the second, that the notion of a god is the notion of what is worshipped, of what one's heart is set on.

This juxtaposition of the words 'heart' and 'treasure' recalls the Gospel saying that where your treasure is, there your heart is also, a saying with an *ethical* implication – that one's treasure and therefore one's heart can be set, as it were, in the wrong place. Whatever one's view of God, one's heart (and treasure) is, in point of hard fact, located somewhere or other. One is, to change the idiom in a way that might reassure the humanist without alienating the believer, in some particular state of *eros*: there is a point of convergence here where the secular humanist and the believer can engage in a conversation about what it is to live a good life.

Lash's remarks are consistent with the idea that our conception of human nature is to be traced along the whole possible trajectory of desire, around the formations and deformations of the heart, around the shifts in one's estimates of where one's treasure lies. The point about the genuine worship of God for those of us who are non-believers is that it rules out other forms of worship, eclipses former idolatries from which one has now turned away, of which one now repents, so it carries an essential reference to *metanoia*, a turning away from unregenerate forms of conduct.

If I may return to my initial scepticism about the assimilation of 'religious belief' and 'religion', and to the idea that one can live a good life without religious belief but not perhaps without religion, I should want to say here that 'religion' in the sense of our religious traditions is one of the repositories of human wisdom, as exemplified just now by the saying about where one's heart is. We can, I think, find a *use* for the term 'religious', though perhaps only a passing use, which carries no commitment to belief in God, though the term is dispensable. I suggested, near the beginning of this essay, that a religious perspective is not a perspective upon a transcendent object, but rather a perspective upon the earth and the human condition. Perhaps that was to go too far, *except* that the nature of any supposed perspective upon the transcendent object – the heavenwards direction, as it were – is determined very crucially by the nature of the perspective upon the earth and the human condition. After all, and to draw again on the New Testament, 'by their fruits ye shall know them'. The latter perspective is in this sense itself transcendent (and 'religious', perhaps), and is better perhaps seen as essentially twofold, as the vision of a possibility of liberation that at the same time and integrally looks back at human suffering and its causes. When Siddhartha has had his first shattering vision of the human condition through encountering the sick man, the old man and the corpse, the universal mediated by the particular, he famously becomes aware of the fourth sight, that of the mendicant disappearing into the forest. This becomes for him the image of possible liberation, again a particular image that represents a universal possibility. We all of us more or less participate in such visions and perspectives, brief expansions of consciousness, represented perhaps by the figure of the Bodhisattva or the Christ, or of Rilke's Angel, and they visit and then leave us; but we recall them as embodying standards of judgement as we continue our progress through mortal life, even if we also acknowledge that we can never possibly measure up to these standards, which are also in a way the object of a sort of worship, their visitations a profound and enveloping transcendence. I can see no reason why a secular humanist should not celebrate such perspectives, even if they are properly wary of using forms of language that owe their origin to traditions they no longer find tenable – except that it is not the *tradition* that is untenable, but rather that certain aspects of it, possibly misunderstood, possibly not, have been let go of. There is a whole language of interiority, with its own distinctions and articulation of possibilities of human experience, that needs nevertheless to be kept hold of.

But according to Rahner it is the use of this word 'God', and this word alone, that leads us to the single whole of reality and the single whole of our own existence. Actually, in one sense Rahner is right – it is the *use* of this word that leads us to the contemplation of our condition, rather than, as it were, the use of the word *God*. If I understand Lash, the claim is that the adequacy of our conception of what it is to be a human being depends upon the extent to which we come fully to realize our creatureliness and radical contingency, and I use that phrase 'fully to realize' as my own gloss on his comment that learning the word 'God' is a matter of lifelong learning, and that the worship and adoration of God is the fundamental form not just of one's knowledge of God but also and therefore of one's knowledge of oneself as creature. But that formulation is already too individualist, of course, and in a way that is instructive also for the secular humanist – we are talking about the fundamental form of *our* knowledge of God and of *ourselves* as creatures. One is not talking of one's own, personal, private, dependence on the mystery of the Godhead, but our *common* dependence, and a vital aspect of this realization is the growth of our mutual solidarity and sense of kinship. And one reason why Lash is right to talk about lifelong learning is presumably that we are confronted by all the egocentric and partisan obstacles to realizing this solidarity – realizing in the sense both of coming to see and making real. This would also explain the Johannine criterion for whether someone genuinely loves God – that they love and do not hate their brother – and it also explains St Paul's explosive comment about stupid Galatians – since the gifts of the flesh and the gifts of the spirit determine forms of community, and the community that is supposed to represent the Church is intended precisely as an image of human solidarity, and a bulwark against the gross cruelties that undermine and destroy it. But surely, *surely* at this point one needs to say that the whole project of humanism is not an exercise in *hubris* but a compassionate solidarity with one's fellow mortals,[19] from a point of view that visits us, though not in obedience to our will, and leaves its traces in our memory, our standards of judgement and in our *imagination* – hence those representations of the Bodhisattva figure or the Christ. It seems to me that the growth of this compassionate solidarity, as I have called it, naturally reorders our priorities and emerges with and through the quietening of desires that conflict with it. This seems to me to represent a vision which one may or may not want to call religious, but is entirely available to the good atheist. It is a vision of a possibility that is secured by its embodiment in practice and by the keeping alive a language of poetic evocation that expresses the horrors and suffering of humanity in a spirit of compassion.

I should like at this point to respond to some perceptive comments on a draft of this essay by Gordon Graham (and see also his essay in this book) in private correspondence, in which he asks whether the humanist vision can 'invoke notions of the sacred and the holy, or, consequently, related attitudes of veneration and worship' and goes on to remark that although the humanist might dispense with these notions, 'what this means is that they must, in the end, subscribe to the Protagorean doctrine that "Man is the measure of all things". Whether you want to use the term "God" or not, the basic religious perception, as I understand it, denies precisely this – and for good reasons.'

---

19 Again, cf. Mackey's comments on humanism elsewhere in this volume.

There is not really enough space to do more than acknowledge that here is a significant locus of future debate and dialogue. However, I would agree that it is not true that Man is the measure of all things – and this because he does not have the measure of himself. This measure unfolds before us and is embodied precisely in those representations that I have mentioned, representations which are surrounded by an aura that inspires veneration.

V

I said that the visitations of this perspective did not depend upon our will, and I did so because I had in mind a serious and related reservation that John Haldane had about the whole reductionist enterprise that he wrongly associated with Phillips, 'a certain de-spiritualization . . . a form of naturalized pelagianism'.[20] But I wish to end with a defence of Phillips, as a kind of *In memoriam*.

Haldane cites the example of Phillips' treatment of the expression 'eternal life', and comments as follows:

> . . . a noun phrase such as 'eternal life' that might have been taken to refer to an existential state or condition is transformed into a series of verbal expressions such as 'participating in the life of God', 'dying to the self', 'seeing that all things are a gift', with these in turn being referred to such activities as forgiving, thanking and loving.[21]

I think that the point of Haldane's drawing our attention to the transition from the 'noun phrase' to the 'series of verbal expressions' is that the latter seem evasive of the idea that there is some reality, some condition of existence, that the noun phrase stands for, which exists (or doesn't exist) quite independently of our beliefs about the matter, and is not reducible to our attitudes and activities. Such a transition *would*, I think, be evasive in the way Haldane suggests. But it seems to me that the whole point about eternal life, to use the noun phrase, is that what belongs within the series of verbal expressions actually *constitutes* the condition of existence that is called 'eternal life'. But the orthodox view is that such a condition of existence may be enjoyed and anticipated here, as well as being the hope and promise of the life to come. Phillips has no need to deny, and nor does the secular humanist need to deny, that Christians live in the expectation of this promise. But if this condition of existence is available here, whatever one may think about lives to come, then it is also available to the secular humanist.

---

20 Haldane, 'Phillips and Eternal Life', p. 259.
21 Ibid., p. 252.

13

A Turn to Spiritual Virtues in Philosophy of Religion: 'The Thoughtful Love of Life'

PAMELA SUE ANDERSON

Introduction

I would like to propose a turn to 'spiritual virtues' in philosophy of religion. This turn would aim at transforming both the focus and the conceptual scheme in contemporary philosophy of religion. I will draw support for this transformation from an unconventional range of philosophers from modern to contemporary, with a key reference to an ancient tradition of spiritual practice. In recent years, John Cottingham has sought to define 'a spiritual dimension' drawing on conceptual relations between analytic philosophy and the fields of religion, psychology and morality. Similar to feminist philosophers of religion, Cottingham attempts to bring together categories and domains which have tended to be separated or opposed in the field; he relates emotion and cognition, religion and science, praxis and belief, interiority and religious language, morality and epistemic conditions, human values and spirituality.[1] In this context, it is worth looking more closely at how Cottingham locates contemporary philosophy of religion in the history of modern philosophy after Kant and within the analytic tradition.

---

1 See John Cottingham, *The Spiritual Dimension: Religion, Philosophy and Human Value* (Cambridge: Cambridge University Press, 2005); 'What Difference Does It Make? The Nature and Significance of Theistic Belief', *Ratio* XIX, 4, December 2006, pp. 401–20; cf. Pamela Sue Anderson, *A Feminist Philosophy of Religion: The Rationality and Myths of Religious Belief* (Oxford: Blackwell, 1998); 'An Epistemological–Ethical Approach to Philosophy of Religion: Learning to Listen', in Pamela Sue Anderson and Beverley Clack (eds), *Feminist Philosophy of Religion: Critical Readings* (London: Routledge, 2004), pp. 87–102. Also see Harriet Harris, 'Struggling for Truth', in Anderson and Clack (eds), *Feminist Philosophy of Religion*, pp. 73–86; 'On Understanding that the Struggle for Truth is Moral and Spiritual', in Ursula King and Tina Beattie (eds), *Gender, Religion and Diversity* (London and New York: Continuum, 2004), pp. 51–64; and Grace M. Jantzen, *Becoming Divine: Towards A Feminist Philosophy of Religion* (Manchester: Manchester University Press, 1998); *Foundations of Violence. Vol. 1 Death and the Displacement of Beauty* (London: Routledge, 2004); *Violence To Eternity. Vol. 2 Death and the Displacement of Beauty* (London: Routledge, 2009).

First, consider Cottingham's assessment of the need to broaden the method and focus of analytic philosophy:

> . . . there seems little to be said for the judgement, still sometimes heard among contemporary cultural pundits, that analytic philosophy has run aground, stuck in the shallows of scholastic pedantry and the dissection of language. The ship is afloat, and sails a wide sea. Yet for all that, there remains a sense that the philosophical voyage has somehow become tamer, more predictable, than it used to be – more like joining a carefully planned cruise than venturing forth on the uncharted ocean. Humanity has always had a deep need to raise the kinds of 'ultimate' question to which the great religions have in the past tried to supply answers, and one might suppose that philosophy ought still to have some role to play here.[2]

> . . . it is important to remember that there are vast swathes of human life where understanding and enrichment does not come through the methods of science: these include . . . the entire domain of human emotions and human relationships as they are experienced in the inner life of each of us, and in our complex interactions with our fellows.[3]

A definite subtext for the imagery of 'a wide sea' and 'venturing forth on the uncharted ocean' (above) is the well-mapped-out land which Kant describes in the *Critique of Pure Reason*.[4] Second, consider Kant's account of the secure ground of knowledge:

> an island, enclosed by nature itself within unalterable limits . . . surrounded by a wide and stormy ocean, the native home of illusion, where many a fog bank and many a swiftly melting iceberg give the deceptive appearance of farther shores, deluding the adventurous seafarer ever anew with empty hopes . . . Before we venture on this sea . . . it will be well to begin by casting a glance upon the map of the land which we are about to leave, and to enquire, first, whether we cannot in any case be satisfied with what it contains . . . and, secondly, by what title we possess even this domain, and can consider ourselves as secure against all opposing claims.[5]

---

2 Cottingham, *The Spiritual Dimension*, pp. vii–viii.
3 Ibid., p. viii.
4 Immanuel Kant, *Critique of Pure Reason*, tr. Norman Kemp Smith (London: Macmillan, 1933), p. 257 (A235–6/B294–5). This is the key passage for the metaphor of the island, or territory of pure understanding, in Kant's 'Transcendental Analytic', Book 2: 'Analytic of Principles', ch. 3: 'The Ground of the Distinction of all Objects in General into Phenomena and Noumena', ibid., pp. 257–75.
5 Ibid., p. 257 (A235–6/B294–5), underlining added.

Kant's imagery portrays an island which is secure but is left by 'the adventurous seafarer' who is deluded with 'empty hopes' on a stormy ocean of 'illusion'. According to Kant, reason drives this seafarer to seek the unknowable, notably the practical concept of freedom and the indeterminate horizon of aesthetic ideas.[6] Third, Cottingham's reference to Kant's island recalls both the safety of empirical knowledge and the danger of going beyond the island. Basically, trying to do speculative metaphysics won't get us anywhere:

> We leave the firm 'island of [knowledge]' and launch ourselves onto the 'wide and stormy ocean' of illusion. . . . This Enlightenment position is widely seen as heralding the effective end of speculative metaphysics in general and **religious metaphysics** in particular. By mapping out the 'land of truth', the conditions under which we are able to lay claim to possible knowledge of reality, . . . Kant [is] seen as ushering in a new framework for human cognition.[7]

We might agree that contemporary philosophy of religion has been located on this 'land of truth' insofar as its claims to knowledge have been restricted to the well-mapped-out empirical world. However, Anglo-American philosophy of religion has not accepted the Enlightenment position, dismissing the claim that religious metaphysics had come to its end. In fact, *A Feminist Philosophy of Religion* picks up Kant's imagery, but then follows Michèle Le Doeuff's use of the philosophical imaginary[8] to challenge contemporary readings of Kant's imagined parameters to knowledge. In doing so, a feminist philosopher questions what Kant meant by the bounds (*Grenzen*) or limits (*Schranken*) of sensibility and reason.[9] We can

---

6 To explore Kant's aesthetics ideas further, see Michael McGhee, '(Sailing to) Byzantium the Kantian Sublime', 2008: http://www.liv.ac.uk/Philosophy/staff/articles/mcghee/kant_aesthetics.pdf.

7 Cottingham, *The Spiritual Dimension*, p. 108; also, pp. 107–9, 117–20, 124 (emphasis added).

8 I draw on Michèle Le Doeuff's conception and use of the philosophical imaginary in her argumentation about philosophy, women and 'the spirit of secularism'; see Michèle Le Doeuff, *The Philosophical Imaginary*, tr. Colin Gordon (New York and London: Continuum, 2002); 'The Spirit of Secularism: On Fables, Gender and Ethics', Weidenfeld Lectures, University of Oxford, Trinity Term 2006.

9 P. F. Strawson, *The Bounds of Sense: An Essay on Kant's Critique of Pure Reason* (London: Methuen, 1966); Katerina Delgiorgi, 'Kant, Hegel and Bounds of Thought', *The Bulletin of the Hegel Society of Great Britain* 45/46, 2002, pp. 56–71; A. W. Moore, 'Bounds of Sense', *Philosophical Topics*, 34, 1 & 2, Spring–Fall 2006, pp. 327–44; and Pamela Sue Anderson, 'Feminism in Philosophy of Religion', in Chad Meister (ed.), *The Philosophy of Religion Reader* (New York and London: Routledge, 2008), pp. 657–8.

push the limits of what is known to gain knowledge of the previously unknown. But can we transgress the boundary to the unknowable? Is it an empty hope to strive to change the questions which have preoccupied contemporary philosophy of religion? Perhaps we can, in Kant's terms, 'think' rather than 'know' what is beyond the bounds of sense.

This line of questioning of Kant and his epistemological map is meant to guide my attempt to change – by expanding – the conceptual scheme of philosophy. In the context of more contemporary imagery than Kant's, a ship has come to represent philosophy's conceptual scheme which must be rebuilt plank by plank at sea: but there is no island! This post-Kantian imagery of a ship at sea is found in Otto Neurath and taken up by W. V. Quine and those who follow Quine, illustrating how change happens to the existing system of knowledge.[10] The philosophical imaginary can help us to see how imagery has and can function in the transformation of philosophical concepts and conceptual relations. And I am eager to employ it in order to begin to change the even more restricted map of argumentation which has made up analytic philosophy of religion since the mid-twentieth century in the Anglo-American world. The island imagery portrays what has given a secure philosophical ground and focus: i.e., knowledge. The move beyond this security to the dangers of the open sea portrays more possibilities. I suggest that these possibilities include, even in Kant, ethics and spiritual practices.

In recent months I have returned to Kant's imagery of the island of understanding, or land of truth, in the Critique of Pure Reason in order to place it not only in relation to contemporary philosophical concerns with our changing conceptual scheme, but in relation to an earlier philosophical tradition which goes back to Plato's lost island-kingdom of Atlantis (in the Timeaus) and Francis Bacon's New Atlantis.[11] Le Doeuff points out that, in order to understand the relation between concepts and images, between knowledge and thought, Kant himself employed imagery which was already

---

10 W. V. O. Quine, 'Identity, Ostension and Hypostasis', From a Logical Point of View (New York: Harper and Row, 1953), pp. 78–9; Anderson, A Feminist Philosophy of Religion, pp. x–xii, 11–12 and 215–21; cf. Otto Neurath, 'Protocol Statements', Philosophical Perspectives 1913–1946, R. S. Cohen and M. Neurath (eds), (The Netherlands: Dordrecht, 1983).

11 On this tradition, see Le Doeuff, The Philosophical Imaginary, pp. 8–20 and 172n8–15; cf. Francis Bacon, La Nouvelle Atlantide, tr. Michèle Le Doeuff and Margaret Llasera. Suivi de Voyage dans la pensee baroque (Paris: Payot, 1980). For discussion of Le Doeuff's contribution to reading this tradition, see Pamela Sue Anderson, 'Michèle Le Doeuff's Primal Scene: Prohibition and Confidence in the Education of a Woman in Philosophy', paper delivered at the 'Michèle Le Doeuff at 60' Conference, University of Oxford, Regent's Park College, 14 July 2008; 'Spatial Locations Understood After Kant: A Post-Kantian Debate about Thinking Space', paper delivered at the Kant Society Conference, University of Sussex, 28 August 2008.

well known within the philosophical tradition at least since Plato. It is this longer tradition from Plato to Kant and beyond which has been taken up by twentieth- and twenty-first-century philosophers from Neurath to Quine and Le Doeuff. The imagery of the ship at sea, and also the Kantian mapping of 'the bounds of sense', are taken up in various branches of analytic philosophy.[12] I would readily recognize the ongoing significance of post-Kantian imagery for the space in which we do philosophy; this space is not limited by the constraints of empirical knowledge alone. In this light, we could insist that philosophy of religion in particular should no longer focus strictly on epistemological questions to do with belief, knowledge or the truth of a claim that God exists or that we are free agents. Moreover, this remains consistent with Kant's insistence upon thinking beyond what cannot be known:

> ... though I cannot *know*, I can yet *think* freedom; that is to say, the representation of it is at least not self-contradictory, provided due account be taken of our critical distinction between the *two* modes of *representation*, the sensible and the intellectual, and of the resulting limitation of the pure concepts of understanding and of the principles which flow from them.[13]

In the above, Kant is clear: we cannot know beyond the bounds of our sensible world, but we can think beyond the island. So why have Anglo-American philosophers of religion feared moving beyond cognitive questions concerning the truth of theism to think freedom? Why not move to questions of virtue and the spiritual practices which would generate (goodness) in love, trust, respect and hope?

Spiritual virtues and the space for enlarging thought

It is my contention that philosophers of religion after Kant should become bold by enlarging thought. They should concern themselves not only with knowing (the empirical world), but with thinking (freedom), acting (virtuously) and making reflective (aesthetic) judgements which would be creative spiritually. This would mean creativity for a world in need of *love*, *trust*, *respect* and *hope*. In an earlier chapter written for a collection in feminist philosophy of religion I advocated uniting knowledge and ethics, in order to cultivate certain intellectual virtues for the field. I argue as follows:

---

12 See Sabina Lovibond, *Ethical Formatio* (Cambridge, MA: Harvard University Press, 2002), pp. 136–50; and Moore, 'Bounds of Sense', pp. 327–44.
13 Kant, *Critique of Pure Reason*, p. 28 (B xxviii) underlining added.

When it comes to women in relation to both epistemology and ethics [knowledge and thought in Kantian terms] they have been excluded, notably, from being credible witnesses or informants, from demonstrating knowledge of their ethical practices, from seeing reality objectively, and from acting autonomously as equally rational agents. Yet my proposal is that these exclusions can be avoided with the free cultivation of four [feminist informed] intellectual virtues: *reflexive critical openness, care-knowing, strong objectivity* and *principled autonomy*. These virtues are meant to unite ethical and epistemological components in a form of virtue epistemology;[14] that is, our perspectives and practices would be shaped by the development of certain virtues with capacities for cognition. Guided by reflexive, imaginative and interactive capacities for discerning truth, a feminist philosophy of religion would aim for practical wisdom.[15]

Yet this aim (above) falls short of the spiritual virtues which I now think should be cultivated both in and for the practices making up philosophy of religion. The 'spiritual' nature of virtues would, as I understand the adjective, render a certain concept of love 'thin' in Bernard Williams' sense of not being embedded deeply in a social location (so not 'world-guided').[16] In contrast, the intellectual virtue which I called 'care-knowing'[17] (above) would have to be 'thick' in Williams' sense of world-guided and action-guiding under fairly specific conditions; this latter action-guiding concept, once cultivated as an intellectual virtue, would intend to eliminate epistemic injustice in local contexts.[18] But now, what I will take to be the spiritual

---

14 For a brief account of the recent emergence of virtue epistemology, see Linda Zagzebski and Abrol Fairweather, 'Introduction', in Fairweather and Zagzebski (eds), *Virtue Epistemology: Essays on Epistemic Virtue and Responsibility* (New York: Oxford University Press, 2001), pp. 3–14; and Miranda Fricker, *Epistemic Injustice: Power and the Ethics of Knowing* (Oxford: Oxford University Press, 2007).

15 Anderson, 'An Epistemological–Ethical Approach to Philosophy', p. 88, emphasis added.

16 On 'thin', as opposed to 'thick' ethical concepts and on the 'world-guided' nature of the latter, see Bernard Williams, *Ethics and the Limits of Philosophy,* with a commentary on the text by A. W. Moore (London: Routledge, 2006), pp. 128–30, 142–55; also see Moore's 'Commentary', pp. 217–19; cf. A. W. Moore, 'Williams on Ethics, Knowledge and Reflection', *Philosophy: The Journal of the Royal Institute of Philosophy* 78, 2003, pp. 338ff.

17 Obviously there are concepts of love, say, agape, which, like 'care-knowing', are thick ethical concepts; but I would like to maintain that love can be a thin concept if taken in a sense that is not restricted to a 'world' or specific social location.

18 Anderson, 'An Epistemological–Ethical Approach', pp. 88–94; 'What's Wrong with the God's Eye Point of View: A Constructive Feminist Critique of the Ideal Observer Theory', in Harriet A. Harris and Christopher J. Insole (eds), *Faith and Philosophical Analysis: A Critical Look at the Impact of Analytical Philosophy on the Philosophy of Religion* (Aldershot, Hampshire: Ashgate Publishing; Oxford: Oxford University Press, 2007), pp. 117–28.

virtues of love, trust, respect and hope are thin, so share-able despite various local differences in their conception and practice. And yet like the afore-mentioned list of thick intellectual virtues, these spiritual virtues will also be characterized by reflexive, imaginative and interactive capacities. In brief, they become characteristics of subjects who reflect, imagine and interact with their every activity. In some sense, we all already share as humans basic dispositions for love, for trust, for respect and for hope.[19]

An additional and crucial element of the four spiritual concepts, which I have singled out, is their power to expand or enlarge the self in relation to other selves and to a global world. I draw this last element from Robert Solomon's account of spiritual passions.[20] In Solomon's own words,

> Spirituality . . . is ultimately social and global, a sense of ourselves identi-fied with others and the world. But ultimately, spirituality must also be understood in terms of the transformation of the self. It is not just a conclusion, or a vision, or a philosophy that one can try on . . . How we think and feel about ourselves has an impact on who we actually are. The grand thoughts and passions of spirituality do not just move us and inform us, or supplement . . . They change us, make us different kinds of people, different kinds of beings.[21]

> Some brands of spirituality insist on the abandonment of the self. Conversely, I want to say that spirituality is the *expansion* of *the self*.[22]

In the above, Solomon reflects a post-Kantian tradition insofar as the self has the capacity for enlarged thought – a capacity to which I will return in discussion of Kant's principles of human thought in the *Critique of Judge-ment*.

Yet Cottingham again offers the relevant context for what I propose as a broadly construed contemporary turn to things spiritual:

> . . . our philosophical discourse about religion may be in need of a certain supplementation . . . it may help if we shift the emphasis slightly, moving

---

19 Paul Ricoeur's fundamental account of 'human capability' could help us to make (more) sense of these *dispositions for* certain spiritual virtues; see Paul Ricoeur, *The Course of Recog-nition*, tr. David Pellauer (Cambridge, MA: Harvard University Press, 2005), pp. 89ff, 139–49.
20 Robert Solomon, *Spirituality for the Skeptic: The Thoughtful Love of Life* (Oxford: Oxford University Press, 2002), esp. chs 2–3; *True to Feelings: What Our Emotions Are Really Telling Us* (Oxford: Oxford University Press, 2007), pp. 268–9.
21 Solomon, *Spirituality for the Skeptic*, pp. 6–7.
22 Ibid., p. 7; emphasis added.

from the domain of religion to the closely related, but distinct domain of spirituality . . .[23]

Even the most convinced atheist may be prepared to avow an interest in the 'spiritual' dimension of human existence, if that dimension is taken to cover forms of life that put a premium on certain kinds of intensely focused moral and aesthetic response, or on the search for deeper reflective awareness of the meaning of our lives and of our relationship to others and to the natural world. In general, the label 'spiritual' seems to be used to refer to activities which aim to fill the creative and meditative space left over when science and technology have satisfied our material needs.

. . . Spirituality has long been understood to be a concept that is concerned in the first instance with activities rather than theories, with ways of living rather than doctrines subscribed to, with praxis rather than belief.

Moving the focus back . . . Pierre Hadot[24] . . . has repeatedly underlined what we might call the practical dimension of the spiritual. There were many Stoic treatises entitled 'On Exercises', and the central notion of *askesis*, found for example in Epictetus, implied not so much asceticism in the modern sense as a practical programme of training, concerned with the 'art of living'. Crucial also was the mastery of methods for the ordering of the passions – what has been called the therapy of desire. The general aim of such programmes was not merely intellectual enlightenment, or the imparting of abstract theory, but a transformation of the whole person, including our patterns of emotional response . . . in the Roman Stoic Seneca it appears as a 'shift in one's mentality' (*translation animi*) or a 'changing' (*mutatio*) of the self. 'I feel' says Seneca 'that I am being not only reformed but transformed (*non tantum emendari sed transfigurari*).'[25]

So how do the above references to ancient forms of asceticism and spiritual exercises, notably Pierre Hadot's practical dimension of the spiritual, square with my sources in Kant, Ricoeur and Le Doeuff – to name only a few thinkers from a tradition of modern philosophy? Cottingham includes a reference to Seneca's focus on a 'shift in one's mentality'. Perhaps this

---

23 Cottingham, *The Spiritual Dimension*, p. 3.

24 To gain greater insight on the highly significant role which Hadot can play not only in the elucidation of spiritual practices for philosophers today, but in exposure of the more *personal* dimensions for contemporary philosophy of religion, see the chapter by Morny Joy in this book. Also see Pierre Hadot, *Philosophy as A Way of Life*, tr. Michael Chase, with an Introduction by Arnold I. Davidson (Oxford: Blackwell Publishing, 2008).

25 Cottingham, *The Spiritual Dimension*, pp. 3–5.

reference could support a shift back to some more ancient tradition; or at least it could be a move away from Kant's island and so away from the safety of empirical knowledge to the sea and so to the dangers of thinking empirically empty, yet ethically significant concepts such as practical freedom and the particulars of aesthetic ideas. In the spirit of the Roman Stoic, then, we might not only be reformed but transformed.

Now, if we read Kant in the light of the philosophical imaginary made evident by Le Doeuff in his first *Critique* but, also, in the light of the principles of human thought made more evident (at least for me) by Hannah Arendt in the third *Critique*, we can recognize that Kant himself advocates programmes not only of intellectual reform and Enlightenment on the basis of scientific knowledge, but also of practical and aesthetic transformation.[26] Crucially, Kant's programmes advocate the enlargement of thought which would transform the self by thinking from the standpoint of others.[27] In the end, this shift in thinking, however complex, does bring our discussion back to Cottingham's spiritual dimension. Crucially, Cottingham describes spirituality (above) for us in terms of 'forms of life that put a premium on certain kinds of intensely focused moral and aesthetic responses' and 'activities which aim to fill the creative and meditative space left over when science and technology have satisfied our material needs'.[28]

At the same time, I insist that something like what Solomon has called 'the thoughtful love of life' should be the focus of intelligent debates by philosophers of religion. My contention is that a passionate love of life gives renewed content to the discipline by focusing on an active participation in cognitive, conative and virtuous pursuits. This passion for a thoughtful love of life is not irrational (but perhaps, non-rational) in motivating reason's capacity to shape a life thoughtfully. Yet there is here a more radical proposal than Kant's own Enlightenment philosophy; that is, a *spiritual life directs reason* (and not the other way around with reason directing us)

---

26 Pamela Sue Anderson, 'A Case for a Feminist Philosophy of Religion: Transforming Philosophy's Imagery and Myths', *Ars Disputandi: The Online Journal for Philosophy of Religion* 1 (2001), pp. 1–35; 'Liberating Love's Capabilities: On the Wisdom of Love', in Norman Wirzba and Bruce Ellis Benson (eds), *Transforming Philosophy and Religion* (Bloomington, IN: Indiana University Press, 2008), pp. 201–26; 'Michèle Le Doeuff's Primal Scene: Prohibition and Confidence in the Education of a Woman in Philosophy', paper delivered at the 'Michèle Le Doeuff at 60' Conference, University of Oxford, Regent's Park College, 14 July 2008; and 'Spatial Locations Understood After Kant: A Post-Kantian Debate about Thinking Space', paper delivered at the Kant Society Conference, University of Sussex, 28 August 2008.
27 I will say more on the technical role of 'standpoint' below; cf. Pamela Sue Anderson, 'Standpoint: Its Proper Place in A Realist Epistemology', *Journal of Philosophical Research* xxvi (2001), pp. 131–53.
28 Cottingham, *The Spiritual Dimension*, p. 3.

towards a *telos*. Thus, spiritual living would move our reasoning towards the exploration of these thin concepts:

1. of 'love' as an openness to others, the world and our natural being;
2. of 'trust' as a coming together of uncertainty and confidence;
3. of 'respect' as an active responsibility to join love and trust in attention to life; and
4. of 'hope' in past, present and future.[29]

Of course, these thin concepts could and are further embedded in life in highly specific ways by the specific spiritual practices of religious institutions. But my concern in the essay is the new philosophical picture which emerges of the conceptual core for those women and men who practise philosophy of religion; this draws on an ancient conception of *reason* as *generated* in a way of *life*, but also on modern rationalists as different as Spinoza and Kant.[30] Together passion and reason would generate the ethical dimensions of love, trust, respect and hope. In turn, these ethically cultivated and spiritually nurtured dispositions would enable those agents who exhibit them to confront uncertainty with a new confidence in philosophical practices which bind life together from birth to death – and possibly, depending on the thickness of one's concepts, beyond this life.

In a time when the world is increasingly aware of global diversity, the tradition of philosophy of religion seems disinclined (or, is it simply afraid?) to scrutinize its own practices not only for epistemic injustice, but more positively for the passion implicit in yearning for the virtuous life. Obviously not every philosopher of religion will be drawn to the passions which could be shared as spiritual virtues. Nevertheless I would still insist that love, respect, trust and hope be treated, due to their fundamental reflexive structures between self–self and self–other, as human capability.[31] In turn, a reflexive capability ensures that we each possess that which can be cultivated as cognitive dispositions. Notice that faith is not included in my list of shareable concepts, but trust is. My reason assumes that faith is a theological virtue and as such is a thick concept that remains deeply embedded in Christianity and in a certain way of living which I find highly

---

29 These thin concepts require a much more detailed account, but I leave this for a later essay. In this chapter, my intention is to introduce the conceptual relations and to argue that these virtues should be recognized; this twofold intention is strongly supported and informed by Solomon, *Spirituality for the Skeptic*, pp. 32–52.

30 Gilles Deleuze, *Spinoza: Practical Philosophy*, tr. Robert Hurley (San Francisco: City Lights, 1988); Pamela Sue Anderson, 'Liberating Love's Capabilities'; Anderson, 'Spatial Locations Understood After Kant'.

31 Ricoeur, *Course of Recognition*, pp. 89–93.

problematic as a feminist. Yet I think that trust is the thin virtue which women and men can share equitably. Faith may come later, but I am not sure about how its embeddedness avoids epistemic forms of injustice. So, instead the proposal is that shared (thin) spiritual virtues become the vital heart of the broadly construed thoughtful love of life. This love of life is precisely what Solomon advocates in 'a spirituality for the skeptic'.[32]

Furthermore, my proposal addresses a contemporary disillusionment with traditional theism and its lack of attention to any shared forms of human spirituality. I'm not simply speaking about myself here, but about the disillusionment I see in highly intelligent, passionate and eager philosophy students. These are students whose passion for justice, beauty or goodness has been alienated when it comes to, for instance, gender and sexuality: this alienation comes from the strict normative constraints of Protestant, whether Anglican or Nonconformist, and Catholic theological practices. For this reason, I propose that a turn to consider our spiritual practices creates the possibility of defining a domain for philosophers and philosophy students which can be shared across traditional divisions. This is to share in a transformation of the field, but also in the transformation of self–other relations. In other words, this means an expansion of how we understand ourselves and others. 'Spiritual' as an adjective would, then, describe a domain of critical activities, including spiritual practices or exercises. This would be a domain of freedom for greater self-understanding and greater reciprocal reflections. The goal would be mutual relations.[33] In this way we would begin to see a significant shift in the conceptual scheme for both philosophy of religion and contemporary moral philosophy, insofar as those fields have been informed by Western Christianity. The movement would be away from an exclusive focus on a transcendent God and would be to a focus on the immanent passions incarnate in self-transcending relations between oneself and others. The concepts of love, trust, respect and hope would be thin enough to be recognized across differences of religion, race, class, ethnicity, gender and sexual orientations. Despite other differences, these spiritual virtues could be recognized globally.

To give a preliminary summation of the philosophical support on which I have drawn so far, those philosophers who are engaging in a broadly spiritual quest for the transformation of ourselves and our practices include Cottingham who also mentions Hadot and Solomon. I also draw on

---

32 Solomon, *Spirituality for the Skeptic*, p. 43.
33 Ricoeur, *Course of Recognition*, pp. 150–246; Pamela Sue Anderson, 'Life, Death and (Inter)-Subjectivity: Realism and Recognition in Continental Philosophy', *International Journal of Philosophy of Religion*, special edition: Issues in Continental Philosophy of Religion 60, 2006, pp. 1–3: 41–59; 'Liberating Love's Capabilities', pp. 201–26.

feminist philosophers Le Doeuff, Lovibond and Fricker, along with the pair Arendt and Ricoeur. These philosophers may not, however, locate themselves in the domain of philosophy of religion; but this again enables shared concepts which are evident in practices, so to speak, at sea!

The past ten years: a turn to the spiritual

At this point, a more personal reflection will help to explain how and why a turn to spiritual virtues seems natural and, in this sense, right. Ten years ago an 'author meets critic' conference took place at the University of Sunderland: on that occasion I was the author of the work criticized: *A Feminist Philosophy of Religion*. My main critics were Grace M. Jantzen and Graham Ward, with a panel of respondents including Harriet Harris, Gerard Loughlin, Paul Fletcher and Beverley Clack; the chair and postgraduate organizer was Hanneke Canters. As it turned out, this philosophy of religion conference could be better described as a workshop because of the formative ideas which were hotly debated and put forward on that occasion. Yet more than formative for thinking in the field, the participants in that workshop became part of my spiritual life, teaching me about love and loss. Tragically Hanneke Canters, Grace Jantzen and Paul Fletcher have each died in the past ten years.[34] My turn to spiritual virtues has been deeply shaped by their deaths (as well as the death of my own partner of 20 years) and the passions which – I now recall – each of them exhibited for life. The lesson is that passions for life motivate spiritual practices of love, trust, respect and hope.

When it comes to philosophy of religion as an academic field of study and practice – in which I teach and have been taught at the interface of philosophy and of theology – my experience has been that generally the discipline has failed to address, let alone cultivate, what I have tried to articulate as spiritual virtues: love, trust, respect and hope. The grounds for these virtues are recognized in the fundamental reflexivity of, in Ricoeur's terms, human capability. This personal reflection suggests that philosophy of religion, if it is to be fair to life and life's relations, should take seriously the recognition of human capability and then the cultivation of the proposed virtues. In doing so, we would at the same time initiate a transformation of the discipline of philosophy of religion into the thoughtful love of life.[35]

---

34 Pamela Sue Anderson, 'Forever Natal: In Death as In Life', *Literature and Theology* 21:2, June 2007, pp. 227–31.
35 This phrase is found in Solomon's *Spirituality for the Skeptic* which was published in 2002 not long before his death; Solomon can be added to the list of those philosophers who have died within these ten years.

For more than a decade in the UK, feminist philosophers of religion have sought a transformation of those epistemic practices which have been unjust in the field. To expose epistemic injustice as a feminist philosopher I myself have turned to ground-breaking work by Fricker, especially her articulation of how a woman can suffer epistemic injustice in philosophy[36] and have drawn more significantly on the philosophical writings of Le Doeuff.[37] But it should be made absolutely clear that my 'feminist standpoint' in philosophy differs significantly from those feminists who assume that 'feminist' means a 'feminine' perspective in theology or in philosophy of religion.[38] The distinction between a feminist standpoint, which is an achievement, and a feminine perspective, which is possessed as a fact of nature, is highly significant for debates in the field. It helps to address the failures of certain feminist theologians to understand in particular a conceptual scheme which has evolved from the practical and theoretical debates in modern philosophy.[39] It perplexes some philosophers of religion that as a feminist I insist upon a Kantian-informed or Enlightenment position on philosophy of religion. But this positioning makes the feminist standpoint, which I've advocated, strongly anti-essentialist. I assume no fixed essential sexual difference between men and women, or even fixed feminine and masculine qualities, when it comes to doing philosophy or cultivating spiritual virtues. Basically, the island imagery might have been employed to exclude women from knowledge, but any such ban on women (besides being immoral) is simply a limit (Kant's *Schranken*) which can and must be moved forward as knowledge increases. There can be no reason to prohibit women from gaining knowledge as mapped out on the land of truth. Women cannot be (absurdly) banned from knowing the very conditions under which we can lay claim to possible knowledge of reality. But the fear might be that women will transgress this limit, but also the bounds to the unknowable in thinking freedom.

So let us return with hope to the recent history of the transformation in the field. Eight years ago, in a published correspondence about transforming the discipline, Jantzen challenged me philosophically to be 'much

36 Fricker, *Epistemic Injustice*, pp. 1–8.
37 Michèle Le Doeuff, *Hipparchia's Choice: An Essay Concerning Women, Philosophy, Etc.*, 2nd edn with an Epilogue, tr. Trista Selous (New York: Columbia University Press, 2006); Le Doeuff, *The Philosophical Imaginary*.
38 Pamela Sue Anderson, 'Standpoint', pp. 131–53; Sarah Coakley, 'Feminism and Analytic Philosophy of Religion', in William Wainwright (ed.), *The Oxford Handbook of Philosophy of Religion* (Oxford: Oxford University Press, 2005), ch. 20, pp. 494–525.
39 Coakley, 'Feminism and Analytic Philosophy of Religion', pp. 511–15.

bolder' in my thinking and writing. Her words continue to provoke me when it comes to a passion for life rather than a mere acceptance of death.[40] A passion for flourishing in this life would seem to motivate Jantzen's challenge to me, but also to the whole field of philosophy of religion: 'I often found myself wishing that you would be bolder, and following the cutting edge of what you say [about] yearning';[41] and 'Just think what a difference it would have made to the history of modernity if the Philosophy of Religion had taken as its emphasis and aim a yearning for beauty and goodness, and fostering their discernment, rather than the justification of a list of beliefs about [God]'.[42]

In fact, the conception of yearning in *A Feminist Philosophy of Religion* has opened the way at least for me to seek more transformative and creative practices in philosophy.[43] Yearning is conceived as a passion moving reason to the heart of religion. Today I would acknowledge that yearning exhibits a similar restlessness to what Harriet Harris describes as the provocation of faith (see her chapter in this book). This provocation is experienced as a feature of a deeply developed disposition, in Harris' case Christian faith which endures even while it is honed and shaped by spiritual and non-spiritual practices. However, at the same time that yearning moves to the heart of religion and sustains interest in a feminist philosophy of religion, I must admit to becoming (even more) seriously disillusioned by traditional debates about God, as well as the traditional Christian virtues, including the thick concept of faith.

The transformation or enlargement of our thinking

A critical question remains concerning the relations between oneself and another which are at the heart of love, trust, respect and hope (as conceived above). Further readings, this time of Kant's third *Critique*, can help with these relations. His principles of human thought, from the *Critique of Judgement*, make communication from and between our different individual perspectives, possible. Now, these principles are:

---

40 Grace M. Jantzen, 'Feminist Philosophy of Religion: Open Discussion with Pamela Anderson', *Feminist Theology* 26 (January 2001), pp. 102–9; also Jantzen, *Foundations of Violence*; and *Violence To Eternity*.
41 Jantzen, 'Feminist Philosophy of Religion', p. 104.
42 Ibid., p. 106.
43 Anderson, *A Feminist Philosophy of Religion*, pp. 21–3, 200–3 and 214–16; cf. Jantzen, 'Feminist Philosophy of Religion', pp. 102–9.

1. to think for oneself which is a necessary standpoint for any thought;
2. to think from the standpoint of everyone else which is necessary, as 'an enlarged mind', for having sharable thoughts; and
3. to think consistently (i.e., in accord with oneself) as 'the maxim of reason' to be attained with the effort of bringing the other two standpoints together.[44]

So, how does the standpoint from which one thinks work with the standpoint of everyone else? Does Kant conceive of a third dimension which is not merely occupied by either oneself or another self alone? Arendt claims a role for 'the spectator' bringing together Kant's principles (1) and (2) so that (3): spectators possess an enlarged mentality which is not solitary. Again, achieving a shared, critical standpoint captures a crucial dimension of what I've sought for a feminist standpoint.[45] Consider Arendt's spectator:

> The spectator's verdict, while impartial and *freed from the interests of gain or fame*, is not independent of the views of others – on the contrary, according to Kant, an 'enlarged mentality' has to take them into account. The spectators, although disengaged from the particular characteristic of the actor, are not solitary.[46]

Arendt helps us to understand how Kant enables the enlargement of thought. She invokes imagery for the spectator, while giving a unifying role to metaphor in thinking after Kant:

> If the language of thinking is essentially metaphorical, it follows that the world of appearances inserts itself into thought quite apart from the needs of our body and the claims of our fellow-men, which will draw us back into it in any case. No matter how close we are while thinking to what is far away and how absent we are from what is close at hand, the thinking ego obviously never leaves the world of appearances altogether. . . . Language, by lending itself to metaphorical usage, enables us to think,

44 See the three maxims of understanding, judgement and reason in Immanuel Kant, *Critique of Judgment*, tr. and with Analytical Index by James Creed Meredith (Oxford: Clarendon Press, 1952), para. #40, pp. 150–1. Also see Hannah Arendt, *Lectures on Kant's Political Philosophy*, ed. and with an Interpretative Essay by Ronald Beiner (Chicago: University of Chicago Press, 1982), pp. 42–4; A. W. Moore, *Noble–9*.
45 Anderson, 'Standpoint', pp. 131–53; 'A Case for a Feminist Philosophy of Religion: Transforming Philosophy's Imagery and Myths', *Ars Disputandi: The Online Journal for Philosophy of Religion* 1, 2001, pp. 1–35.
46 Hannah Arendt, *The Life of the Mind*, one-vol. edn (London and New York: Harcourt Brace & Company, 1977), p. 94, emphasis added.

that is, to have traffic with non-sensory matters, because it permits a carrying over, *metapherein*, of our sense experiences. There are not two worlds because metaphor unites them.[47]

Arendt articulates a provocative proposal for accepting Kant's distinction between the sensible and the intelligible, but not allowing this to be an ontological distinction.[48] A better way to read the two things which are, first, distinguished from each other, and then united, is in terms of judging. Kant states in his third *Critique* that reflective judgement is under obligation to ascend from the particular in nature to the universal arguably by analogy. Or in Paul Guyer's translation of Kant's words from the third *Critique*: 'If, however, only the particular is given, for which the universal is to be found, then the power of judgement is merely reflecting.'[49] For Kant, this *reflecting* (or, depending on the translation, *reflective*) power of judging is creative.[50] As seen above, when done as reflective judgement, this thinking is not a solitary activity.[51]

The relation of metaphor and concept: indeterminate judgements

In another paper I have argued that there is a significant sense in which the imagery which Kant employs forces the reader to agree, stage by stage, with a certain philosophical relationship between metaphor and concept.[52] I rely upon Le Doeuff who establishes a dynamic, dialectical relationship between metaphor and concept in her account of the philosophical imaginary which puts Kant within the long history of philosophers and their evolving imagery and conceptual scheme. Yet questions remain for Le Doeuff, but also for Arendt on Kant. How exactly does judgement move analogically from spatial imagery to conceptual thinking? How, in Kant's case, does the

---

47 Arendt, *The Life of the Mind*, p. 110.
48 Arendt, *Lectures on Kant's Political Philosophy*, p. 44. Cf. Kant, *Critique of Pure Reason*, pp. 257–9 (A294–5/B350); *Critique of Judgment*, pp. 18, 179.
49 Immanuel Kant, *Critique of the Power of Judgement*, tr. Paul Guyer (Cambridge: Cambridge University Press, 2000), p. 67 (5:179); cf. Moore, *Noble in Reason*, p. 88.
50 The struggle to create and achieve communal thinking embraces Kant's three principles of human thought. See Anderson, 'A Case for a Feminist Philosophy of Religion': Appendix.
51 Hans Blumenberg, 'Prospect for a Theory of Nonconceptuality', in *Shipwreck with Spectator: Paradigm of a Metaphor for Existence*, tr. Steve Rendall (The MIT Press, 1997), pp. 101–2. Blumenberg insists that Kant both denies that freedom as an idea cannot be represented as a metaphor and assumes that freedom must be represented as a 'transcendental action of the understanding'; but the latter is incomprehensible as theoretical so it must be practical. Yet if practical, then is there anything theoretical? To avoid this contradictory position Blumenberg contends that Kant's freedom must be taken as a(n absolute) metaphor.
52 Anderson, 'Spatial Locations Understood After Kant.'

image legitimate the confidence of secure knowledge, while the under-standing is rendered unstable by the constant striving of reason in its dangerous pursuit of the unknowable? In one sense, a critique of reason generates a loss or lack of ethical confidence in one's own secure knowledge. Yet, in another sense, this loss leads desire to draw reason onto the sea and to seek the fulfilment of an ancient promise. This historical imagery of ful-filling a promise recalls the metaphor of another island of (lost) bliss where confidence is not an issue.

With this retrieval of ancient metaphors (to express, say, bliss), let us return to the Analytic of Principles in the first *Critique* where Kant reflects back upon what he has demonstrated in the Transcendental Aesthetic and Analytic and also looks forward to the Transcendental Dialectic to come. First, he seems secure: 'We have now not merely explored the territory of pure understanding, and carefully surveyed every part of it, but have also measured its extent, and assigned to everything in it its rightful place. This domain is an island, enclosed by nature itself within unalterable limits.'

Second, he is not secure:

If the understanding in its empirical employment cannot distinguish whether certain questions lie within its horizon or not, it can never be assured of its claims or of its possessions, but must be prepared for many a humiliating disillusionment, whenever, as must *unavoidably* and con-stantly happen, it oversteps the limits of its own domain.[53]

Where exactly are the bounds of sense for this empirical employment of the understanding? Kant demonstrates that the limits (*Schranken*) of our knowledge continue to be worked out as we gain more knowledge, even though what is beyond the bounds (*Grenzen*) of sense will remain unknow-able. Even if the concept of freedom is empty of content, we can think freedom, and indeed we can even imagine, by analogy, another space. For Kant, determinate judgements, i.e. claims to knowledge, depend upon a distinction between, on the one hand, the empirical employment of the concepts of understanding merely to appearances or phenomena: 'that is, to objects of a possible experience' and, on the other hand, the transcendental employment of a concept to things in general and in themselves.[54] But a third dimension of thought is informed by the analogical movement of the metaphor in reflective judgements which bridge the cognitive and the non-cognitive in the creative power of what remains indeterminate. For example, although particular and lacking a universal concept, ideas of

---

53 Kant, *Critique of Pure Reason*, pp. 257–9 (A235–6/B294–5).
54 Kant, *Critique of Pure Reason*, p. 259 (B298/A239).

beauty rest in what we share as human; and this enables us to communicate and to create.

The question of aesthetic ideas and beauty directs us back to Jantzen's feminist philosophy of religion. In our published exchange of letters in *Feminist Theology*,[55] Jantzen writes: 'although we are different in approach, we very much share the urgent wish for the discipline to be more life-giving and whole-making.'[56] Jantzen believes passionately that a Western philosophical and cultural preoccupation with death had displaced any concern with beauty.[57] Spiritual practices would be transformed, according to Jantzen, by the life-giving possibilities in attending to beauty.[58] Her voice on this is highly significant, but it also provokes us to rethink our spiritual practices. With this provocation in mind, I find support in a turn to spiritual virtues in philosophy of religion, urging a new confidence in the power which we each have to affirm our own existence at the same time as approving of another's.[59] Of course, this form of approbation, or mutual recognition, would be risky, if not wise in an ancient sense of practical rationality, but also in a modern sense of communicable and creatively shared. Here an exercise in imagination is absolutely essential for the *corporate* picture emerging at the heart of feminist philosophy of religion. In Kantian terms, imagination must take on a highly positive role in uniting particulars when the universal is lacking. A critical question remains: how does one ensure optimism in the face of death, loss, suffering and so the ongoing struggle to discern and maintain communicable corporate relations between oneself and another? In other words, (how) can the discipline not only become but remain life-giving and whole-making?

---

55 Unfortunately our letters were published in the wrong order. Instead of my first letter appearing followed by Jantzen's response to it; and then, each of our replies to the other, my letter and reply to Jantzen were published together in September 2000 before Jantzen's first letter to me and her subsequent reply to my second letter. So the September 2000 issue of *Feminist Theology* (25) should be read alongside the January 2001 issue (26) going from my first letter and then to Jantzen's and then back to my reply and Jantzen's (see Anderson, *A Feminist Philosophy of Religion*; Jantzen, *Becoming Divine*; cf. Jantzen, 'Feminist Philosophy of Religion, pp. 102–7). Also see Pamela Sue Anderson, 'The Urgent Wish: To Be More Life-Giving', in Elaine Graham (ed.), *Redeeming the Present: The Legacy of Grace M. Jantzen* (Aldershot: Ashgate Publishing, 2009).

56 Jantzen, 'A Feminist Philosophy of Religion,' p. 102.

57 Jantzen, *Foundations of Violence*.

58 Jantzen, *Violence To Eternity*.

59 For an account which supports this new confidence in our power to affirm ourselves and to approve others, I strongly encourage study of Deleuze on Spinoza and Spinoza's *Ethics*, see Deleuze, *Spinoza*; Benedictus de Spinoza, *The Ethics and Selected Letters* (Hackett Publishing Co., 1982).

Conclusion

The experience of more than ten years of critical reflection on the field with feminists and more than twenty years with other contemporary philosophers has encouraged engagement with a long line of philosophers. This includes Plato, Spinoza, Kant, Arendt, Ricoeur, Deleuze, Le Doeuff, Jantzen, Lovibond, Hadot, Cottingham, Harris, Fricker and Moore. Each of these thinkers helps in the working out of a revised form of practical rationality for philosophy of religion which has a critical role to play. To educate our emotions and passions is to motivate reason, especially in meditation on living a life and not merely on death or immortality.[60] Given the time, I will do more specific work with the articulation of each of the spiritual virtues and their practices: of love, trust, respect and hope. The expression of these virtues in spiritual practice would enlarge our thinking beyond empirical knowledge in the thoughtful love of life. After reading Kant, with the help of Le Doeuff's philosophical imaginary, an enlarged mentality will become a practical, but also a spiritual vision for women and men.

---

60 In the concluding pages of *Becoming Divine*, Jantzen admits that she is willing to explore the possibilities in 'a pantheist symbolic' (Jantzen, *Becoming Divine*, p. 274). The present chapter is proposing one way in which to develop Jantzen's vision of 'a symbolic of natality' as 'a flourishing of the earth and those who dwell upon it' (ibid., p. 275, also pp. 272–5).

14

Secularism and Shared Values

RICHARD NORMAN

The discussion of secularism tends to be bedevilled by problems of definition, and by the running together of different definitions. In this essay I am
primarily interested in secularism as a normative view about society: the
view that social and political institutions should be independent of religion
or religious institutions. It is the advocacy of what has traditionally been
referred to as *the separation of Church and State*. In a multicultural society
where there are different religions, each with deep roots in social groups,
that label needs to be modified. The present UK government has courted
what it calls 'faith communities', it has sought to give them special access to
national and local government, and it has targeted them for particular
attention in public consultations. It has provided increased state support
for 'faith' schools, and has promoted plans to give 'faith communities' an
enhanced role in the delivery of public services. Secularism in my first sense
is the rejection of this trend, as well as the rejection of longer-established
practices such as the role of the monarch as Head of the Church of England,
the use of Anglican forms of worship for state occasions, and reserved
places for bishops in the House of Lords. My main concern, then, is to
defend secularism as a criticism and rejection of all such practices. We can
call it *secularism as a preferred model of society*. It can be summarized as the
view that there should be *no privileged place for religion(s) in the public life
of society*.

Secularism in this first sense is often run together with a second normative view: what we could call 'secularism as an individual way of life'. By this
I mean a view of the world and a way of life based entirely on non-religious
beliefs and values. This is not the same as atheism; they are likely to overlap,
but it is perfectly possible to have a theoretical belief in the existence of a
God and for this nevertheless to play no significant role in how you
interpret the world or how you live.

I emphasize the distinction between these two senses of the word 'secularism' in order to make the point that secularism as a model of society does

not depend at all on any commitment to secularism as a way of life. One can be a committed Christian or adherent of some other religion, but reject any privileged position for one's own religion or other religions in the institutions of society. Many religious believers do indeed take such a position. Conversely it is a mistake to run together, as some people do, criticism of secularism as model of society and criticism of secularism as a way of life. The two may be linked in some way, and I shall consider that possibility in a moment, but they are not the same thing.

Finally, both versions of secularism are something different again from the *secularization thesis* as a sociological claim about our society – the claim that religious belief is in decline. That factual claim is distinct from the defence of either of the normative positions which can be called 'secularism'.

My aim is to defend secularism in the first sense. I begin by considering two examples of criticism of it. They are instructive because they run together all three of the positions which I have just been distinguishing. Consider first this interview with Cardinal Cormac Murphy-O'Connor, the Catholic Archbishop of Westminster, in the *Guardian* on 2 April 2008:

> The leader of Britain's Catholics claimed yesterday that 'Judaeo-Christian values' were the only thing binding British society together . . . Speaking to the *Guardian*, Cardinal Cormac Murphy-O'Connor hit out at representatives of an 'aggressive secularism' that he believes is gaining ground in the UK . . . 'People are looking for a common good in this country. A very large number of people are saying, "What is it that binds British people together?"' the cardinal said. 'There is no other heritage than the Judaeo-Christian heritage in this country.' To abandon this or to put in its place a 'totally secular view of life' would lead the nation down 'a very dangerous path' . . . Did he mean that Christian faith leaders should have a privileged position when it came to making interventions in public policy? 'Yes. I don't see why not.'[1]

This is a statement which links all three of the positions which I distinguished above, and especially the first two. Secularism as a way of life is said to be a danger, because it erodes the shared values and shared heritage which 'bind British society together'. To ensure that people continue to be bound together by that shared heritage, the leaders of religious institutions should have a privileged position in public life. So on the strength of a rejection of secularism in my second sense, Murphy-O'Connor is committed also to the rejection of secularism in my first sense. He does not specify what particular institutional arrangements he would wish to defend, but he

---

1   Accessible at http://www.guardian.co.uk/world/2008/apr/02/religion.catholicism.

clearly wants Christianity to continue to have an entrenched position in the life of this country, and he wants the institutions of our society to have a built-in bias towards Christianity.

A similar case was made, at about the same time, by Bishop Michael Nazir-Ali, Bishop of Rochester, in an article in the magazine *Standpoint*. The process of secularization, he said,

> . . . has created the moral and spiritual vacuum in which we now find our-selves . . . [In] deep and varied ways the beliefs, values and virtues of Great Britain have been formed by the Christian faith. [These values are] not free-standing . . . they cannot indefinitely exist in a vacuum . . . the danger, rather, is that we are living on past capital which is showing increasing signs of being exhausted.[2]

It is not entirely clear what the Bishop is looking for as a remedy. He says: 'To argue for the continuing importance of [Christian beliefs and values] is not necessarily to argue for the privileging of any Church.' But, he adds, 'faith should have a role in public life . . . Government will have to be increasingly open to religious concerns and to make room for religious conscience, as far as it is possible to do so.' We need to consider what this means, if it is not a 'privileging' of Christian religion.

From these two statements, and from many similar attacks on 'secular-ism', we can distil four claims which form a logical sequence:

1. A society needs to be held together by shared values.
2. The shared values capable of holding a society together need to be located within a shared tradition.
3. In our society these values have to be Christian values, because they are derived from the Judaeo-Christian tradition.
4. The Judaeo-Christian tradition should therefore enjoy a specially entrenched position in the life of our society.

I shall consider each claim in turn.

Do we need shared values?

I agree with claim 1. A society does need shared values to hold it together. Why is this? It might be said that modern pluralistic societies do not need that degree of social cohesion. Can't such a society function perfectly

---

2 Michael Nazir-Ali, 'Breaking Faith with Britain', in *Standpoint*, June 2008, accessible at http://www.standpointmag.co.uk/node/85.

adequately as long as its members are prepared to accept their differences and live side by side, in their different cultural communities, with mutual tolerance and respect?

In principle yes, but in practice we need to remind ourselves of what we have learned about the fragility of societies. We need to look at what happens when societies fall apart, as has happened in cases such as Northern Ireland or Yugoslavia. They demonstrate that tolerance and mutual respect are difficult to sustain in the absence of any stronger sense of what people have in common. A stable society needs to be more than just a 'union of social unions', it needs effective 'social glue'. And it is better to look not to artificial contrivances such as flags and anthems for this social glue, but to those things to which people are naturally and spontaneously committed. The search for sources of social cohesion is not incompatible with the acceptance of a healthy diversity. Different cultural traditions and practices can be embedded in a society in which people still have core values in common.

What should these shared values be? I have suggested that they need to be more than just the procedural values of tolerance and respect for diversity. They have to be more substantive values – and these are not hard to find. The values of caring and co-operation, of respect for life and respect for individual autonomy, of fairness and honesty, are very widely acknowledged in our own society, even if people often fail to live up to them, and the deeper the commitment to them, the more people can see themselves as working together for a common good.

I want to add a further reason why the sharing of such values is important. Only if the members of a society see themselves as united by common values and a common good will they be prepared to accept as legitimate those policies which are not in their immediate self-interest, including in particular the measures of economic redistribution which any modern society with a modern system of taxation is committed to.

Do shared values require a shared tradition?

I turn to claim 2. The shared values which I have mentioned so far do not appear to be specific to a particular historical tradition or heritage. There is a case for regarding them as universal human values. That indeed is a merit of them – that they are capable of holding a society together without excluding other societies, that they are potentially extendable to larger communities and to the global community. Why then talk of the importance of a specific social heritage or tradition?

It is important because the values which I have mentioned are very abstract and general. For them to come alive and to motivate shared activities, they need to be seen as embodied in a shared past to which people can refer and which provide concrete examples and precedents. Although plausibly universal, they are values which are transmitted by specific cultural traditions and histories.

I want to propose also a more specific reason why a shared moral tradition and a shared history are important: the problem of incommensurability. There is an irreducible plurality of values, which may conflict with one another in particular situations, and there is no algorithm which can resolve the conflicts. When values conflict, we have to decide which value is the more important in the particular case, but how are we to do so? What we have to do is to appeal to examples and precedents. Consider the ongoing tradition of thinking about war. War is a great evil, but perhaps there are worse evils, and we sometimes have to face the question whether going to war is the only way of averting a worse evil. We might then refer to the First World War, especially in the light of subsequent war literature, as a touchstone to bring home the horror and futility of war; but we might also invoke the Second World War as a reminder that there may be worse evils which only war can overcome. How great does the evil have to be to outweigh the evil of war? There is no way of measuring the relative evils. We can only compare cases. Hence since 1945, faced with the dilemma of whether to resort to war, people have often invoked the comparison with 1939 and the threat of Nazism. They did so at the time of the Falklands War, when General Galtieri was compared to Hitler, and again with Iraq and Saddam Hussein. Of course the comparison did not settle the argument. It was open to debate whether the cases were comparable, and the opponents of war were able to argue that the precedent was misleading, but the point was that a shared history and a shared tradition of moral decision-making provided a common standard by which to debate the new dilemma.

I do not want to overstate the case for the importance of a moral tradition. Some values and some applications of them are so fundamental that they are obvious without the need to invoke any culturally specific tradition. Slavery for instance was condemned not because it was at variance with a particular tradition of moral thought, but because it was quite simply inhuman, and the recognition of this required no more than basic human sympathy and sensitivity. Even so, that response needed to be articulated specifically in terms of the Christian tradition in order to answer opponents who themselves appealed to that tradition. In the debates of the late eighteenth and early nineteenth centuries the defenders of the slave trade invoked the authority of the Bible. General Gascoine, MP for Liverpool, speaking in the parliamentary debate of 1806, quoted the famous passage in Leviticus 25:

Both thy bondmen and thy bondmaids, which thou shalt have, shall be of the Heathen, that are round about thee; of them shall you have bondmen and bondmaids. And thou shalt take them as an inheritance for thy children after thee to inherit them for a possession, they shall be thy bondmen for ever.

Wilberforce responded as follows:

It is impossible not to perceive, in the very tone and manner of his allusion to the sacred writings, that their authority has not been adduced by him for any purpose of grave and serious argument . . . It seems therefore unnecessary for me to disprove the allegation, that Scripture gives any countenance to the Slave Trade . . . Indeed, among the many various signal proofs of the purity and excellence of the religion we profess, it is not the least remarkable that not only is the practice of the Slave Trade forbidden, and the principle on which it proceeds held out for our abhorrence; but it is specifically denounced as the worst of robbery, those concerned in it being branded as 'the stealers of men'. Besides; the criminality of this practice is put on plain and universal principles, clear in their meaning, and reasonable in their application; principles which both pointedly interdict the indulgence of vicious and mercenary wishes, and require us always to act on motives of love and kindness, and good will to man.[3]

So a superficial appeal to religious authority is here answered by the assertion that that appeal is contrary to, and a distortion of, values which are more deeply embedded in that religious tradition.

The Judaeo-Christian tradition?

That example conveniently brings me to claim 3. Is it indeed the case that the specific tradition in which the shared values of our own society are located is the Judaeo-Christian heritage? As a historical claim this seems undeniable; the Judaeo-Christian tradition has been the dominant moral tradition for 14 centuries and has been deeply built into our moral culture. It might be objected that the claim is *merely* a historical one, and talk of 'the genetic fallacy' might be invoked at this point to suggest that even if our values are derived from a Christian past, they are now free-standing and need no longer be located within that context. That, however, would be too

3 *The Debate on Abolishing the Slave Trade* (London, 1806, reprinted 1968 in The Colonial History Series, ed. D. H. Simpson), pp. 29–30.

simple a response. If what holds a society together is indeed a shared *tradition* of values and more generally a shared past, then the nature of that past history must continue to exercise its importance.

I want also to argue, however, that to characterize that tradition as *simply* the Judaeo-Christian tradition is equally over-simplified. We need to look more closely at the nature of that tradition, what makes it a distinctive tradition, and how it has developed. I shall argue that the case for secularism depends crucially on a proper understanding of what a shared moral tradition is.

What is the identifying feature of Christian values? A plausible answer would be that the distinctive moral contribution of Christianity is its emphasis on the value of generalized benevolence. It is love for one's neighbour, where the question 'Who is my neighbour?' is answered by the parable of the Good Samaritan: your neighbour is not necessarily a fellow-member of your own community, but any human being who needs your help. This value of generalized benevolence stands in contrast with, for instance, the lists of cardinal virtues offered by Plato and Aristotle.

However, this shift to universalism was not unique to Christianity. The classical tradition did not end with Plato and Aristotle, and the value of generalized benevolence and of duties to all our fellow human beings is equally characteristic of the Stoics, with their ideas of world citizenship and human brotherhood. This value is not unique to any one body of thought, but emerges as a response to the demise of the city-states and the emergence of the Hellenistic empires and then the Roman empire. In other words, we might say, it is a product of globalization and multiculturalism. The classical influence is as strong a strand in our moral tradition as is the Christian, and rather than speak of the Judaeo-Christian heritage we could more accurately talk of a Judaeo-Christian-Romano-Hellenic heritage. It is, in short, a multicultural heritage.

Moreover, Christian values could come to be translated into political ideas and institutions only when they were allied with ideas from the classical tradition. The value of love for one's neighbour tells us, by itself, virtually nothing about how to organize our social life and institutions. The early Church Fathers, when they came to apply the gospel ethic as a basis for public life, drew on sources such as the Stoics and Cicero, and the classical influence can be seen again in the application of the Christian tradition to the political debates of the modern (post-Renaissance) world.

To defend this claim, I want look at the case of the relation between liberal-democratic values and the Judaeo-Christian tradition. I am not a historian of ideas, I am not advancing any original historical claims here; I simply want to use this historical example to illuminate the nature of a moral tradition.

Consider this earlier statement by Bishop Nazir-Ali which anticipated his *Standpoint* article:

> British society is based on a Christian vision and Christian values. Its institutions, its laws, its customs, all these arise out of a Christian vision ... For instance, the dignity of all human beings is clearly drawn from the Biblical idea that human beings are made in God's image. Or it might be the question of equality, or it might be liberty, freedom of expression ... Unless people know what the springs are that feed our values, the whole thing will dry up ...[4]

Human dignity? Equality? Liberty and freedom of expression? It would be difficult to find any of these in New Testament Christianity. Perhaps, though, this is where the idea of an ongoing and developing *tradition* becomes important; modern liberal-democratic values *grow out of* the Judaeo-Christian heritage, as it evolves and is applied in new circumstances. In a sense, that is indeed what I want to say, but I want to look at what it tells us about the nature of a moral tradition.

A key period is the seventeenth century, when liberal-democratic values began to take shape in a recognizably modern form. One of the first systematic presentations of the case for democracy was the platform of the Levellers in the Civil War, as exemplified in the Putney Debates of 1647. The historian Tristram Hunt has said of the debates:

> ... the Levellers were not simply secular democrats in prototype: the Putney debates were more a mass prayer meeting than constitutional symposium. Every day the soldiers sought God's guidance in their search for a political solution to the civil war and a post-monarchical settlement. While the likes of Christopher Hitchens and Richard Dawkins might find it uncomfortable, the story of British democracy is intimately bound up with the theology of Protestant Christianity.[5]

Up to a point, this is obviously true. All moral and political debates of the time took place within a Christian framework and against a background of Christian beliefs and values, and the Putney Debates were no exception, but it is instructive to look at just what role such beliefs and values played in the debate. Precisely because the Christian framework has been all-encompassing, it has featured on both sides of every such debate. Earlier in the seventeenth century it was invoked in support of the Divine Right of Kings, as in this address by James I:

---

4 Interview on the *Today* programme on BBC Radio 4, 6 November 2006.
5 The *Guardian*, 26 October 2007.

The state of monarchy is the supremest thing upon earth. For kings are not only God's lieutenants upon earth, and sit upon God's throne, but even by God himself they are called gods . . . In the Scriptures kings are called gods, and so their power after a certain relation compared to the divine power . . . I conclude then this point touching the power of kings with this axiom of divinity: that as to dispute what God may do is blasphemy . . . , so is it sedition in subjects to dispute what a king may do in the height of his power.[6]

So the first point that I want to make is that the values within a shared tradition are not unequivocal. In providing a common framework for moral and political life, they are typically invoked by both sides in what may be deep conflicts.

My second point is that a tradition of values develops in a new direction because it encounters new events and new situations. We can see this too in the case of the Putney debates and the ideas of the Levellers. It was only when the Parliamentarians found themselves having to act against the king as a result of his recalcitrance, and then later having to find a justification for the authority and legitimacy of the new regime, that they found themselves having to make a principled case for new political institutions and liberal-democratic values. It was not that the values were there ready made and waiting to be applied.

Furthermore, when the tradition comes to be applied to the new situation, it again generates conflicting interpretations. In the Putney Debates, the Christian framework of debate is invoked as a justification both by the advocates of universal franchise and by the advocates of a continuing restricted franchise.

Consider these famous words of Thomas Rainsborough:

. . . really I think that the poorest he that is in England has a life to live as the greatest he; and therefore truly, sir, I think it's clear that every man that is to live under a government ought first by his own consent to put himself under that government; and I do think that the poorest man in England is not at all bound in a strict sense to that government that he has not had a voice to put himself under.[7]

---

6 'A Speech to the Lords and Commons of the Parliament at White-Hall', 1610, in David Wootton (ed.), *Divine Right and Democracy* (London: Penguin Books, 1986, and Indianapolis: Hackett Publishing Company, 2003), pp. 107, 109.
7 Andrew Sharp, ed., *The English Levellers* (Cambridge: Cambridge University Press, 1998), p. 103.

The first clause, though not using explicitly religious language, is recognizable as a statement of Christian universalism. Rainsborough sees it as leading to the principle that the authority of government must rest on consent. This conclusion, however, does not obviously follow, and there is nothing distinctively Christian about it. Where does it come from?

One possible source is Richard Hooker, the authority who would later be regularly quoted (as 'the judicious Hooker') by Locke in his *Second Treatise of Government*. Hooker's *Laws of Ecclesiastical Polity* (1594) had the aim of providing a justification for the authority of the monarch as both head of State and head of the Church. The situation did not allow a simple appeal to tradition, since the break with Rome was a fundamental break with tradition. A new basis for both secular and ecclesiastical authority was needed, and it was in this context that Hooker argued that the authority of all human law rests on consent:

> . . . to supply those defects and imperfections which are in us living single and solely by ourselves, we are naturally induced to seek communion and fellowship with others. This was the cause of men's uniting themselves at the first in politic Societies, which societies could not be without Government . . . [S]trifes and troubles would be endless, except they gave their common consent all to be ordered by some whom they should agree upon: without which consent there were no reason that one man should take upon him to be lord or judge over another . . .[8]

Hooker intends no radical conclusions to be drawn from this, but the doctrine of government by consent is one which the Levellers will draw on. It appeals to a story about the origins of society, and though Hooker bolsters it with references to Genesis, it is Genesis read in the light of the social contract tradition deriving from classical sources, for example the sophists of the fifth and fourth centuries BCE, such as Protagoras as represented in Plato's *Protagoras*. This, then, is the conceptual framework essential to sixteenth- and seventeenth-century debates about authority, government and democracy: the tradition of theories of natural law and of natural rights deriving from a state of nature and underpinning a social contract.

This framework is apparent in the exchange at Putney between the Levellers and their most articulate opponent, Henry Ireton (Cromwell's son-in-law). In response to Rainsborough's proposal that the franchise should be extended to 'the poorest he that is in England', Ireton says that 'if you make this rule, I think you must fly for refuge to an absolute natural

---

8 Richard Hooker, *Ecclesiastical Polity* (London: Everyman, 1907, originally published 1594), First Book, section X, pp. 188–90.

right and you must deny all civil right'. What does 'deny all civil right' refer to? Ireton's fear, he says, is that once the idea of a natural right for all is invoked, it will undermine property rights:

> Now I wish we may all consider of what right you will challenge that all the people should have right to elections. Is it by the right of nature? If you will hold forth that as your ground, then I think you must deny all property too, and this is my reason. For thus: by that same right of nature (whatever it be) that you pretend, by which you can say that one man has an equal right with another to the choosing of him that shall govern him – by the same right of nature he has the same equal right in any goods he sees: meat, drink, clothes, to take and use them for his sustenance. He has a freedom to the land, to take the ground, to exercise it, till it; he has the same freedom to anything that anyone does account himself to have any propriety in. Why now I say then, if you, against the most fundamental part of the civil constitution (which I have now declared), will plead the law of nature . . . – if this be allowed (because by the right of nature we are free; we are equal; one man must have as much voice as another), then show me what step or difference there is why I may not by the same right take your property . . .[9]

Ireton's own view is that the franchise should be limited to those who own freehold property, or are freemen of corporations, and as such have a 'permanent fixed interest in this kingdom'.[10] If the right to vote is not based on this 'permanent interest', then any 'foreigner coming in amongst us' would have to have just as much right to a vote.

Rainsborough rejects Ireton's argument that invoking natural rights would overturn all property rights: 'And, sir, to say because a man pleads that every man has a voice by right of nature, that therefore it destroys by the same argument all property, this is to forget the Law of God. That there's a property, the Law of God says it – else why has God made that law "Thou shalt not steal"?'[11]

At this point in the argument, then, the authority of the Judaeo-Christian tradition is being explicitly invoked, but I think it is fair to say that this is an ad hoc move. The core argument is conducted in the language of natural rights, and the core issue is that of the relation of natural rights to property rights. Rainsborough does not have an answer to that problem, which is why he has to resort to the ad hoc move.

---

9 Sharp, *The English Levellers*, pp. 108–9.
10 Ibid., pp. 103–4.
11 Ibid., p.109.

It is a dispute which Locke will later try to resolve by arguing that the rights which men enjoy in a state of nature are not only a right to life and a right to liberty, such as was invoked by the Levellers, but also a natural right to property. Like the Levellers, Locke uses the apparatus of natural law and natural rights to argue for government based on consent, and the principle of majority rule. But he also insists that 'the great and chief end ... of men's uniting into commonwealths, and putting themselves under government, is the preservation of their property'.[12] Consequently 'the supreme power cannot take from any man any part of his property without his consent'.[13]

Locke, like the Levellers, locates the ideas of natural law and natural rights within a Christian framework. By the time the doctrine of natural rights comes to have its maximum impact a century later, however, it has outgrown any specifically Christian background. Here is the classic late-eighteenth-century formulation by Thomas Paine – a deist and, in his book *The Age of Reason*, a relentless critic of Christianity.

Every history of the creation, and every traditionary account, whether from the lettered or unlettered world, however they may vary in their opinion or belief of certain particulars, all agree in establishing one point, *the unity of man*; by which I mean that man is all of *one degree*, and consequently that all men are born equal and with equal natural rights.[14]

The reference to 'every traditionary account' is intended by Paine to include, but not be confined to, the biblical account of creation. He is quite explicit that he is not relying on the truth of the biblical account, or on 'any sectarian principle of religion', but is spreading his net wider: 'It is also to be observed that all the religions known in the world are founded, so far as they relate to man, on the *unity of man* as being all of one degree.'[15]

To sum up: the idea of human rights is employed by the Levellers and their opponents, and by Locke, within a context of Christian belief, but it owes at least as much to classical ideas of the emergence of human beings from the state of nature. Paine, as a deist, loosens the link to specifically Christian doctrine. His book is one of the main routes by which the idea of human rights is transmitted to the modern world, and as Christian doctrine comes to be less and less taken for granted, the idea of human rights takes on an independent life, so that in modern statements such as the *Uni-*

---

12 John Locke, *Second Treatise on Civil Government* (1690), ch. IX, para. 124.
13 Ibid., ch. XI, para. 138.
14 Thomas Paine, *The Rights of Man*, in Bruce Kuklick (ed.), *Political Writings* (Cambridge: Cambridge University Press, 1989, originally published 1791), p. 77.
15 Ibid.

versal Declaration of Human Rights, it requires no particular religious basis. What does this example tell us about the working of a shared moral tradition?

1. Any such tradition is an *evolving* tradition, not a set of timeless principles. As it encounters new situations and new dilemmas, it takes on new shapes. In my example, the Parliamentarians find themselves having to adapt the Christian moral tradition to the new situation of a challenge to the authority of the king and the need for a new justification for the authority of parliament.
2. The tradition, when it encounters new dilemmas, evolves by *interacting with and drawing on other traditions.* The Levellers and Locke, needing to articulate an egalitarian view of natural rights, cannot find all that they need in Christian religious belief and need to draw on the classical tradition.
3. A shared tradition, just because it is shared, incorporates *internal conflicts.* When it encounters new situations, there is bound to be dispute between different views of how the tradition should be interpreted and applied. So the Christian tradition, in the seventeenth century, provides a context for the radical conflicts between the upholders of the Divine Right of Kings, the moderate parliamentarians, and the Levellers.

A privileged status?

In the light of this account of the nature of a moral tradition, I turn finally to claim 4. I have acknowledged the importance of shared values, and of shared traditions within which these values are interpreted and applied. I have suggested, however, that a shared moral tradition is not a history of consensus. It is something evolving, and internally diverse, and incorporates conflict within it. It is essential to the life of a tradition that this evolution, this internal diversity and conflict, and creative interaction with other traditions, should continue. There is therefore no case for isolating one particular strand of the diverse tradition of shared values in our society and propping it up by giving it an artificial prominence or privileged position. We cannot hive off a moral orthodoxy and preserve it in aspic.

Nazir-Ali implies that if we do not give some special prominence and protection to the Christian faith, our shared values will be left in a moral and spiritual vacuum and will accordingly collapse. This is nonsense. Values like human dignity and equality and freedom may, as I have accepted, owe something important to the Christian tradition in which they have been articulated and handed down, but they do not need to be artificially sustained by propping up a Christianity which, it is implied, would otherwise decline. Such values are built into innumerable practices and institutions of our society, formal and informal, political and social. These shared ways of life are more resilient than particular doctrinal creeds.

I said earlier that it is not clear what Nazir-Ali wants. He certainly argues for a continuing role for 'Christian discourse' in public life. I have no quarrel with that. No one would want to prevent the Church of England and the other Christian churches from contributing to public debates, and secularism does not seek to ban it. The question is, as he says, 'What kind of role should it have?' His allusion to the situation in the United States is ominous: 'It is quite possible to imagine a situation where there is no established Church, but where Christian discourse remains important for public life. For better or for worse, the United States is a good example of such a situation.'[16]

That example seems to me to be very much 'for the worse'. A society with genuinely shared values is not at all the same as one in which religious institutions are able to exercise disproportionate clout in virtue of their organized ability to deliver votes and money in elections. Religious groups can and should contribute to public debate, but it must be genuine debate, and we need to be clear what that means.

Genuine debate requires a shared language. Shared values as I have understood them here can play that role – furnishing a shared language for moral debate, while being open to conflicting interpretations and applications. They are what W. B. Gallie, 50 years ago, called 'essentially contested concepts'.[17] Consider the cases of debates about embryo research, say, or legalisation of assisted dying. Genuine debate is possible if the different sides bring to the debate shared concepts such as the dignity of the human person, or respect for human life. What makes these genuinely shared concepts is the fact that we can agree about their application to uncontroversial cases – the wrongness of murder, of slavery, and so on. They provide a language with which we can then address disputed cases. Would voluntary euthanasia represent an application of, or a violation of, the value of respect for the dignity of persons? Would respect for human life favour or prohibit the use of embryo research to find treatments for life-threatening diseases? Though the disagreements run deep, the appeal to a shared vocabulary of values at least makes it possible for opponents to see one another's positions as 'reasonable'.

This is quite different from taking a position in a moral disagreement which is simply an appeal to authority. It is no contribution to public

16 Nazir-Ali, 'Breaking Faith with Britain'.
17 W. B. Gallie, 'Essentially Contested Concepts', in *Proceedings of the Aristotelian Society*, Vol. 56 (1956), pp. 167–98.

debate simply to assert that assisted dying, or embryo research, or abortion, is incompatible with the authority of the Bible or of some other sacred text, or is forbidden by the authority of the Church, and is therefore unacceptable. It is no contribution to public debate simply to say 'Our consciences cannot accept this, and you have to respect our consciences.' More controversially, I suggest that it is no contribution to public debate, in our society, to present a case in exclusively religious language. Consider the debate around proposals to legalize assisted dying for the terminally ill. If church leaders say, as they sometimes do, 'We believe that life is a gift from God, and the legalization of assisted dying is therefore unacceptable', this position has to be translated into a shared language, and shown to be a plausible application of the shared value of respect for life, if it is to be part of a genuine public debate. That clearly is essential if the churches want to be seen to be upholding the shared values which bind us, rather than simply fighting their corner. This is where the plain facts of secularization and multiculturalism become relevant. However much the values that have informed public life in our society have derived from the Christian tradition, they can no longer be tied to the body of Christian belief if they are to perform the role which, as I have argued, it is important for shared values to perform.

Conclusion

I have agreed that, historically, Christianity has furnished a major part of our moral tradition and values. That fact, however, is no argument against secularism; it is consistent with the form of secularism which I set out to defend. Christianity – the Christian churches and individual Christians – are, like other faiths, welcome to play a continuing part in shared public life, but it should not be a privileged role, not an exclusive or entrenched role. It is important to acknowledge the historical facts about the tradition we have inherited, and important that education should make people aware of their shared history and traditions – but aware of them in all their complexity and diversity. A tradition, I have argued, is a living thing, continually developing through interplay with experience, through interaction with new situations and with other traditions. The lesson to be learned from the past is that we should continue and encourage the further development of a tradition of shared values, not try to preserve artificially one particular component of that tradition.

My conclusion is analogous to the position taken by Michael McGhee in his contribution to this volume. He argues that, without endorsing religious belief, we can still recognize religious traditions as valuable 'repositories of human wisdom', and draw on them for insights into the human condition.

My position could be seen as the social analogue of that suggestion. As someone who was brought up as a Christian and is now an atheist and a humanist, I recognize what I owe to my Christian upbringing. While rejecting Christian beliefs, I can acknowledge that my having grown up in a culture with a predominantly Christian past has made me who I am, and that the values by which I try to live have been partly shaped by that past. At the same time I am aware that, in a society which is increasingly diverse and in which religious belief continues to decline, that tradition can no longer play an exclusive role but must be enriched by interaction with other traditions, both religious and non-religious, to make possible the shared ethical discourse and the shared values which we need.[18]

---

18 This chapter is based on a lecture given at the London School of Economics and Political Science in June 2008, as part of the 'Secularity and Value' lecture series organized by the Forum for European Philosophy.

15

Religion in Public Life

ANTHONY O'HEAR

The thesis I want to develop in this essay is prescriptive. That is, as will become evident, it is based on how I conceive the State and the political, and also on what I think religion ought to be. Having said that, my conclusion is one which has some basis in Christian history, as I shall demonstrate at the end, and it is intended to have some relevance to the current situation which obtains in Western democracies. I take this situation to be one in which churches are the preserve of minorities, within societies which are predominantly secular and pluralist. So I want to suggest ways in which in this context religions(s) might relate to the wider society in general and to the political in particular.

My title ('Religion in Public Life') is really too broad, as I will show. There are many religions and many ways they might connect with public life. Indeed, the phrase 'public life' is itself very broad. It certainly will include the political, but there is or should be much more to the public realm than the political. That is to say, it is a deformation of public life if everything public is political. There are many areas of public life which should be seen as independent of politics, as producing a counterbalance to the political through the autonomous institutions spawned in and by those areas. These areas should include the law, the arts, sport, the military, education and much else besides, including, as I will argue here, religion. In the modern world much blurring of boundaries goes on between the political and the rest of public life. This is objectionable for all sorts of reasons which would have seemed obvious to nineteenth-century thinkers such as J. S. Mill, and should be obvious to us for different reasons, following our experience of twentieth-century totalitarianism, totalitarianism being precisely the move on the part of the State to bring everything within its own control and direction.

Although I am presupposing a view of society in which there will be many areas of life autonomous of the State and outside the political, the State and politics are necessary and desirable even as providing a framework in which people can lead peaceful and orderly lives, taking responsibility for what is rightfully theirs, pursuing their own projects and seeking their own salvation. Action by the State through the political process is also necessary on occasion to remove obstacles to liberty and opportunity, and also to give some legal backing to what the society as a whole regards as the basic conditions necessary for living together as a society. Of course, putting things like that may be consistent either with a great deal of State activity and regulation or with very little, but my position is a pluralist one in which the State and politicians should exercise far more care than they normally do in taking on themselves what is better seen as the prerogative of individuals, of their families and of autonomous institutions and organizations.

The view of politics and the political I am sketching is thus pluralist in two directions. There should first be a plurality of sources of power and influence in a society. This is the autonomous institutions point. But then, second, it is pluralist in a more fundamental sense. While each of us might want to defend a particular view of life as being the right one or the best (for all, even), I believe that no one has such a comprehensive monopoly of wisdom as to have the right to impose that view on everyone else; this follows in part from a belief in human fallibility, which can be expressed in either secular or religious terms. So within what I have just referred to as the limits imposed by the very fact of a group of people living together, my view is that individuals should be free to follow and develop their own philosophies of life, including religious ones.

What those limits to freedom might be will no doubt vary from one society and from one mentality to another; and even within the broadly liberal conception of society I am presupposing here, there will at different times and in different societies be differing conceptions of the limits of the acceptable. But I would also stress at this point that in the very conception of a society which is in some sense liberal and pluralist there will be some very specific limitations on what people might be allowed to do, which will stem directly from a joint acceptance of the very pluralism I am advocating, and which is precisely what will allow groups and individuals to pursue their own higher level philosophies of life. In other words, there will have to be a degree of 'live and let live' on contentious issues arising from competing philosophies of life, which would condemn and even legislate to prevent actions which conspire to undermine the liberties enjoyed by all. So, to take some specific examples, we should condemn the bombing of abortion clinics (even if we are fiercely opposed to abortion); we should ensure that novels and cartoons can be published without fear of reprisals, even though we find them offensive and some find them blasphemous; and we should be on our guard against creeping censorship through the implicit acceptance that some areas are off limits to academic enquiry.

In what follows I will be taking 'the public' to refer to those aspects of life which go on outside the privacy of the home and outside the inner sanctum of a person's relationship with his or her god. Most of what will follow in this essay will be devoted to the clarification of how we might think about religion, and also to the drawing of important distinctions, which are too often glossed over in discussions of this sort. As will become apparent, while I think that religion certainly has public aspects, it is important not to lose sight of the extent to which religion, in the sense I am interested in it, is at its heart private.

I think that what I have to say in a positive sense will commend itself to a broad swathe of Christians. If this turns out to be so, it will not be sur-prising, because what I say derives from a specific reading of the Christian tradition, and from attempts within that tradition to find a *modus vivendi* with the secular world. However, I will not be too disturbed if some modern Christians disagree with my conclusions, because there are trends within Christianity which strike me as misguided from a religious point of view, indeed as part of that very swallowing up of everything in the political which I was criticizing a couple of paragraphs ago.

A core element of religion is the relationship between the believer and God; indeed I am tempted to say that this is the key element, at least in the type of religion I am interested in discussing here. So what I say here will not apply to conceptions of religion, such as that proposed in at least part of the Old Testament, where the focus is on a chosen people rather than on saved individuals, and even less to that expounded by Durkheim in which, when primitive peoples worship their god, what they are actually worship-ping is the tribe itself. Obviously in such essentially communal interpreta-tions of religion there will be different accounts of religion and public life and also of the relationship between the individual believer and his god from the one I am here developing. With this clarification, we can say that what is ultimately at stake in religion as I am taking it is the care of the indi-vidual soul, the turning of the soul away from fantasy and towards reality, and in Christian (as in Platonic) terms the soul is understood as having a destiny which transcends this life. In Christian mythology Jesus proclaimed the kingdom of God, to be sure, but the kingdom was not of this world. It was hidden, like a mustard seed, and grew in the hearts and in the commu-nity of believers. Jesus' kingdom was distinguished in that respect from the kingdoms and communities of this earth.

I cannot comment in any detail on the notion of the kingdom as it appears in the New Testament. This is a huge topic in its own right and I am not in any case competent to say anything on it from an exegetical point of view. It is, though, interesting to note that in the nineteenth century some famous exegetes followed a broadly Kantian approach: that the kingdom which Jesus preached and inaugurated was in some sense an ideal ethical community (Kant's kingdom of ends, perhaps) which might be realized on earth. In the twentieth century, by contrast, an apocalyptic view gained more favour: that the kingdom was something to be realized in a revelation at the end of time. There seems to be something of a consensus now that neither of these approaches is adequate to what Jesus and the New Testament actually taught. The kingdom of the New Testament was not a regime on earth at all, neither a Kantian kingdom of ends realizing itself now or in the future, nor an end time apocalyptic utopia. It was rather an assertion of the way God, as a transcendent reality, is acting in and through Christ and the Church, even now, to save his chosen people; but, I would judge, with the emphasis on transcendent, real and within us to be sure, but, equally, not of this world. It is both now and not yet, but not of this world and never of this world.

There are undoubtedly public and social aspects to the gospel: that is, it matters to our own spiritual development how we treat other people, and we are to treat other people as we would treat Jesus himself (as we are told in the Beatitudes and the Sermon on the Mount). But this is primarily because of the sacred worth there is in each of us individually, and as seen by God breaking in on us from outside secular history. On my understanding of Christianity, religion has all sorts of public implications in the sense that it imposes on us social duties, but these duties arise from the sacredness of each of us as individuals and from the individual transcendent destiny of each of us. It is because other people are sacred, individually, that we have duties to them, and because I am sacred, individually, that I have responsibilities to myself and others. In this sense, religion is not essentially social in a worldly sense, and should not be seen as attempting to produce a political settlement on earth. From the point of view of the believer it is essentially individualistic, not in the sense that it is selfish but in the sense that it is primarily concerned with the worth and fate of each of us as individuals, and how each of us responds to God's transcendent self-revelation breaking in on us from outside time. Each of us, as an individual, needs faith and repentance as the basis of the religious life. Each of us enters the world alone and leaves alone, and religion must focus on these moments of ultimate loneliness, particularly the last, as the point at which, *pace* John Donne, each man is very much an island, confronting in his nakedness his Maker. Religion is about the turning of the soul in preparation for this moment, and that is something each one of us has to do alone, even if it can be done only with the help of divine grace and from within a Christian community, and even if, once turned, we are helped by the community of the Church militant, journeying with that Church in the hope and expectation of ultimate membership of the Church triumphant.

To turn now to public life in a more general sense, the ethic which largely underlies contemporary Western societies is, given a certain variability from one regime to another, that of liberal individualism. Some would see this philosophy as essentially secular, as arising in the eighteenth-century Enlightenment. No doubt the prevailing political philosophy today tends to be a somewhat uneasy agglomeration of Enlightenment notions of human rights and of a broadly utilitarian approach to ethical and political questions. For all their differences, both utilitarianism and human rights philosophies, by taking the individual (individual rights, individual pleasure and pain) as their starting point, feed naturally into the politics of liberal democracy, and in this politics the conflicting strains of both rights-based philosophies and utilitarianism are very apparent. In their secular forms, anyway, both utilitarianism and theories of human rights will differ from religious views in making no appeal to any transcendent source of value or of any notion of the sacredness of the individual which cannot be analysed in terms purely of this world.

By contrast, as with Socrates in his prison, the religious view of life which I am developing will see life as a journey through this life to a better world, provoked and borne up by intimations of transcendence on the way. While this view is not essentially communitarian, as I have already argued, the individual on his or her pilgrimage through the secular world will need to be supported by communities in various ways. First, there will need to be a religious community which transmits and develops the religious message, and supports the believer on the journey, but there will also need to be the secular community within which the religious quest takes place. It is here that we see an important role for the state or political authority, even from the religious point of view. For, according to the Western-liberal concept of politics which I am relying on here, a key role of the State is to provide security for those who live within it. This, of course, means protection of life and property within and defence against threats from without. From the perspective of the religious life, the State will be seen as necessary to provide a settled and secure order within which the religious life and community can flourish and develop.

But there is also a potential tension between Church and State, especially if the State is secular. The religious perspective, being transcendent and appealing to a divine and timeless authority, will also provide a yardstick by which other institutions, regimes and customs can be judged. Christ's authority is not of this world, and because it is not of this world but of a higher authority altogether, it stands in judgement over this world. In particular, it will judge the actions of the secular State unfavourably if these are seen as compromising or undermining the sacredness of the individual, if the State in any way seems to be seriously abusing individuals for its own ends. From the point of view of Christianity, it is never expedient that one man dies for the people.

So is it ever expedient that one terrorist is tortured or sent back to where he is likely to be tortured? Is it ever expedient that an old person is quietly and gently disposed of, or a disabled foetus aborted, or embryos produced, manufactured indeed, for research? Obviously these areas will be of central importance to religious moralists, and may well bring them into disagreement with a prevailing public ethic of utilitarianism and the prevailing politics of administrative convenience. Conflict of this sort should not seem surprising when one reflects just how demanding the idea of the sacredness of the individual is, nor should we be shocked that others find this ethic inconvenient. What would be more shocking would be a religious collapse in the face of contrary public opinion, or perhaps better, in the face of the convenient pragmatism so easily favoured by legislators and bureaucrats; though what, in a secular, pluralist State not collapsing might entail is not always easy to determine.

As I have already suggested, it should not involve bombing abortion clinics even if we think abortion is wholly wrong, because living in a free society, as well as affording all of us freedoms, does, as part of its dispensation, part of the social contract, if you like, impose restrictions on what individuals can do to others in their society, even for what might seem the best and morally most urgent of reasons; on the other hand I am not at all clear what someone wholly opposed to embryo research on religious grounds should do if he or she were invited to go on the Human Embryology and Fertilization Authority – unlikely, I admit, and liable to happen only through some oversight on the part of the appointers – but if it did happen, should it be seen by that individual as a chance to prevent some harm or rather as collusion in what should not be given any support or credibility at all?

But this is a practical question, which does not impinge on the right and duty of the Church to speak out clearly against what it believes to be seriously wrong, though even here there might be disagreements about just how this speaking out should be pursued; one might think here of what strikes critics of the Catholic Church as pusillanimity or worse in Nazi Germany, but what might more reasonably be seen as a degree of prudence which did not actually comprise the Church's underlying stance which had been very clearly set out in the encyclical *Mit brennender Sorge* (written, incidentally, by Pacelli before he became Pope). However, whatever we might think are the practical implications in specific cases, it is clear that a religious standpoint is one from which we will judge other values and decisions. The religious citizen or subject will see rulers as themselves under a higher law. This higher law – maybe in the medieval sense natural law – is one to which we are all subject, whether in the political sense we are rulers or subjects.

In this understanding the religious person will take issue with the Roman view of the State, that in which the emperor is the sole source of law and divinely endorsed, and also with legal positivism, in which there is no law other than that which is determined according to correct constitutional procedures. It would also stand aloof from the more sophisticated form of legal positivism of some contemporary American theorists of law, who want to judge actual decisions of the courts and actual legislation in terms of what they, the theorists, take to be those principles which can be seen as best explaining the rights and liberties enshrined in American and British law; from the point of view of a religious thinker, the spirit of these laws (assuming we can identify what is meant) is itself a human artefact, and may be found wanting from a timeless, transcendent perspective. This sense of being found wanting will only be increased when it emerges that the spirit in question, as discovered by the theorists, turns out to be precisely that of the contemporary secular progressivism which religious people often find lax on questions of fundamental human values.

The sense that the religious community has values which are not necessarily identical with those of the secular power, and which in any case derive not from *raisons d'état* but from a different source altogether, allows us to rule out from the religious point of view a number of possible relationships between religion and State. One, which we may call Kemalism (after Kemal Attaturk, the founder of modern Turkey) would be where the Church (or mosque in this case) is allowed to exist, but where its role is conceived as being essentially to support the secular power. We may indeed have problems with fundamentalist Islam (to which we will turn shortly), but one can hardly quarrel with devout Muslims who find Kemalism objectionable. If this is what living in a secular State is to mean, it is not surprising that religious people might reject secularism. Staying in that part of the world, we might also glance at the Orthodox notion of the Turkokratia. This was a doctrine developed during the time of the Ottoman Empire, when it seemed to the Orthodox hierarchy that survival depended on what amounted to collusion with the Turkish authorities. Again, there may have been reasons for this; but one cannot help reflecting on the way in which the Orthodox hierarchies in communist days were prepared to collaborate with the authorities (even to the extent of endorsing Ceausescu in Roumania only days before his fall). All this may have been a legacy from the spirit of Turkokratia, and one which may by no means be extinct even after the fall of communism.

But Kemalism and Turkokratia are by no means the only ways religions can be compromised in their dealings with the State. A more difficult example, and one which may in practice take us closer to home, might be the way the Catholic Church in general and, according to their enemies, the Jesuits in particular were, to put it bluntly, prepared to condone scandalous behaviour from Louis XIV and his court in order to give the Church an easy ride in France. Of course, it wasn't put quite like that. The argument was that allowing the king concessions on sexual matters which would not be allowed to ordinary believers would be the means to the salvation of many thousands of those ordinary believers whose religious practice could thus be secured by maintaining the position of the Church in France. It has to be said this was ultimately a self-defeating practice even from the pragmatic point of view; for the Church, having compromised its sexual morality to suit the monarch, was then in a weak position when it came to commenting adversely on the pointless and utterly immoral wars which disfigured the later parts of Louis' reign (ironically at a time when, once married to the formidable and formidably pious Mme de Maintenon, Louis actually began to behave far better in his personal life). But, this example aside, maybe it could be asked whether there is not a degree of Jesuiticalness in the behaviour of the churches today in Britain, in the sense of a too easy acceptance of the nostrums of secular morality. Observers quickly gain a sense that many church leaders are relativistic and flexible about moral matters, while those who stick to what they conceive of as timeless truths are made to seem obstinate and unfeeling.

It is easy to understand and, up to a point, to sympathize with the tendency of religious people to seek accommodations with the secular world. After all, even within an institution claiming divine guidance, doctrine does develop, and not all insights from the secular realm are misguided, even from a religious point of view. There is always indeed the very real possibility that some of what religious people take as being divinely inspired is itself simply an aspect of contemporary and local practice. In fact there may be a far worse temptation for the religious person thinking about the relationship between the Church and the world than engaging in casuistry or attempting to sympathize with or reach accommodations with the better and more humane elements of the secular world. It is what, on the face of it, seems to be the opposite position; instead of making religion consonant with the world, one tries to make the world in the image of religion by setting up some form of theocracy, in which the rules and practices of the public realm are themselves determined by religious edict.

There have, of course, been theocracies in Christian history, notably the Geneva of John Calvin and the Munster of Thomas Muntzer. There are also the attempts to set up Islamic states, run by religious authorities, such as those of the early caliphates and those in Iran and Afghanistan today under the Taliban; the very notion of the Dar-al-Islam, central to Islamic thought, envisages a pure society run on Koranic lines, in which there are no distinctions, except of administrative divisions of labour, between the religious, the legal and the political. During the Christian Middle Ages and for some time subsequently the papacy itself was a secular ruler (though it is not clear to me that there was any very rigorous attempt there to set up a theologically inspired regime).

I will use the term 'theocracy' to refer to a political set-up in which the government is in the hands of religious leaders by virtue of their being religious leaders, who then attempt to impose a theologically inspired regime on the people. It would doubtless be said by its advocates that such a regime would be the best, because its precepts and aims would be pure, unworldly and inspired by transcendent values and insights. To go back to the kingdom of the New Testament, could we not, by political means, achieve a society founded on the virtues of the New Testament and inspired by the spirit of the Beatitudes and of the Sermon on the Mount? In such a society people would be more just, more humane, more equal, more virtuous and more compassionate; oppression would be absent, and the people, freed by the nature of the regime from the pursuit of selfish ends, would do what was best from a timeless point of view, because, encouraged by the politico-cum-religious authorities, they would see that it was the best and because they felt happy in its pursuit.

What is involved in theocracy as so defined has a striking resemblance to Plato's Republic, ruled by philosopher kings in the interests of virtue and with an eye on the ideal world above. Theocracy, as we are understanding it here, would not, of course, involve the rigid class stratification we find in Plato, but even without that it would still suffer from many of the defects of Plato's vision, the best once more being the enemy of the good. Even if we are religious, we should be careful here, and we should be particularly careful not to be seduced by the perennial excuse offered by advocates of utopian visions from Plato himself onwards (assuming for the moment that Plato was actually arguing in favour of his republic): that when, as inevitably happens, a utopian project ends in tears and worse, the fault is not with the vision but with a specific, flawed attempt to implement it. Thus, even though there were undoubtedly abuses in, say Calvin's Geneva or in Khomeini's Iran, these are incidental to the project itself, and would be avoided in a more perfect implementation of the vision.

They will not be. The theocratic vision is itself fatally flawed, and flawed in the first instance for a good theological reason, namely that of original sin. Human beings are imperfect and so are human institutions, manned and used as they are by human beings. This fundamental fact experience has shown us to be universally the case even aside from the actual doctrine of original sin, and the point ought to be granted even by those who do not accept original sin in its theological sense. Even if an institution is founded in the name of faith or virtue, and enshrining within itself the highest principles and standards, it will not be immune from corruption. This point applies to churches as well, as history amply demonstrates. Looking at history and considering the point about original sin, the wonder is not that the Catholic Church today, say, is imperfect in all sorts of ways; the wonder rather is that it has moved away from some of the really gross imperfections visible in the medieval Church.

In fact, leaving aside a theological belief in the divine guidance of the Church, we might be able to offer some sort of purely historical explanation for the morally improved state of the Catholic Church now, compared to the fifteenth century, say, an explanation relevant to our general theme. For much of the medieval period the Church was a powerful secular ruler as well as the religious authority, and monasteries and bishoprics were often politically powerful and rich in their own rights. As institutions of power they gave those heading them careers of immense wealth and prestige, and all that went with wealth and prestige. So the Church itself and its major institutions became prizes to be seized and fought over (much as the big State bureaucracies are in our own day). In being prizes to be seized and fought over, by men (and women) who were interested to a large degree in the prizes, they easily got diverted from their ostensible aims, and became run mainly for the benefit of those running them, as we saw with the papal states (and as we see in today's National Health Service). In short, the medieval papacy itself became an Italian princedom, in behaviour little different from the other States of central Italy, though actually having a bigger influence throughout Christendom than its neighbours, owing to its universalist religious pretensions and its claims to a divine mandate, and to the wealth which arose from the donations of the faithful.

The Church, once a secular power, was potentially more dangerous than a merely secular State, precisely because of the divine authority it claimed for itself, and its consequent power and mission. It gave its adherents and leaders an extra tool, so to speak, in the furtherance of their ambitions. And this extra power and extra tool were sure to attract to its ranks people whose own ambitions were far from those of the Church in its pure state. To take another example, people are sometimes surprised that the Taliban and the Iranian theocracy, or perhaps more accurately, people acting in their name, indulge in great cruelty. They should not be; the power claimed by these theocracies in the name of Allah makes it inevitable that psychopaths of all sorts will be attracted to them, in much the same way that a communist system will reveal and release hundreds of little Lenins in every village and commune, and a fascist system similar outgrowths of little Hitlers. And worst of all, once a church has been subsumed into a theocracy, it will cease to perform the essentially critical role it has in society when it is clearly separate and independent. Theocracy, far from being the greatest role for religion to play in our imperfect world, is actually its greatest temptation.

The point I am making here may well have some foreshadowing in Augustine's doctrine of the two cities. The city of God is not of this earth and will not be found in its pure form short of the Last Judgement. It may be defeasibly identified with those currently en route for eternal glory, but in all actual human institutions, including the Church itself, there is an inextricable mingling of the elect and the reprobate, of the two cities in other words. In this life, due particularly to the corruption of human nature after the Fall, there is need for a political State in order to establish the conditions of relative peace and security which individuals should work out their salvation (or otherwise). But the State cannot actually legislate or coerce so as to promote the salvation of individuals, nor should we expect it to.

More precisely, though, the position I am here developing can be found in Dante, and in the poet's changing attitude to the Guelphs and the Ghibellines of his time. The Guelphs were the party in Italy (and Florence) who were broadly in favour of the papacy and its power, while the Ghibellines favoured the establishment in Italy of rule by the emperor. Dante, as a Florentine leader, was initially a Guelph, but it is fair to say that his experiences in Rome and Florence and then in exile convinced him that a politically powerful papacy would inevitably suffer from all the defects we have been sketching above. Not for nothing are a number of popes, including his arch-enemy and contemporary Pope Boniface VIII, consigned to hell, precisely because they used the papacy and its power as if it were a secular princedom. But secular power, which is bound to corrupt the Church and compromise its mission if it is entwined with the Church, does have a positive role to play in stopping wars and in ameliorating discord and crime, and could do so under a wise and powerful sovereign. It was because Dante had hopes that Italy might fall under what he believed might be the beneficent rule of the putative Emperor Henry VII of Luxemburg that he moved towards the Ghibelline cause after his exile from Florence. These hopes were dashed with Henry's death, but Dante's own experiences allowed him to develop in *The Divine Comedy* a picture of the clear separation of the roles of Church and State, the Church being concerned with salvation (only) and the State with providing the conditions of peace and security which we (and the Church) all need in our journey through the world.

Actually there was nothing very new in Dante's political vision. Writing on the papal reforms instigated by Hildebrand (Gregory VII) in the eleventh century, in which there was an attempt to sever the close relationships which then existed between Church and State, the historian Reginald

Lane Poole wrote (in 1884) 'It is perfectly clear that if the church was to exercise that sway which all Christians agreed it ought to exercise over the consciences of men, it must be as free as possible from those ties which bound it to the secular state.' Further, as Gregory regarded civil government as a human institution deeply polluted by its sinful origin, there could be no preferred type of regime, such as monarchy for example (so much for the divine right of kings). Indeed, 'granted only the superiority of ecclesiastical power, there was no concession she (the Church) would not make in favour of popular rights';[1] and we find in the writings of Manegold of Lautenbach, a follower of Hildebrand, as eloquent a statement of the theory of the social contract as any in the seventeenth or eighteenth centuries.

To try to bring these reflections together in some sort of conclusion, I can record that when I originally started thinking about the relationship between religion and the public world, it was because of a degree of unease I had been feeling about what struck me as an aggressively strident secularism, lambasting what is referred to as religious fundamentalism. I was thinking of attacks on what are called faith schools, whether Christian or Muslim, and also of the British government's use of charity and equality legislation to coral the activities of religious charities, such as adoption agencies, into its own vision of the good life. I will make a few brief remarks on each case in conclusion, so as to explore what seem to me to be the implications of what I have been arguing thus far.

To take the question of faith schools first, at the most general level the question raised here is that of the responsibility for the education of children. Where does this primarily lie, in the hands of parents, or is it vested in the State? We can all follow Mill[2] in agreeing that the State has a duty to ensure that education actually takes place, while insisting, like Mill, that the responsibility for carrying out and directing that education ought to be that of the parents who have brought their children into the world. Like Mill, one could argue, on broadly liberal grounds, that 'a general State education (would be) a mere contrivance for moulding people to be exactly like one another . . . (and that) in proportion as it is efficient and successful, it (would) establish a despotism over the mind, leading by natural tendency to one over the body'.[3] It would be inappropriate here to go into any detail on these matters, so I will simply record my impression that as the State has directed and regulated education more and more (particularly since it

---

1 Reginald Lane Poole, *Illustrations of the History of Medieval Thought and Learning* (1884), (New York: Dover Publications, 1960), pp. 198–203. I owe this reference and the general point to Leonard Liggio.
2 John Stuart Mill, *On Liberty* (1859), quoted from Mill's *Utilitarianism* (ed. Mary Warnock) (London: Collins/Fontana, 1962), ch. 5.
3 Ibid., pp. 239–40.

nationalized the curriculum and exams 20 years ago), what Mill says has been largely borne out in experience. The State clearly has no monopoly of wisdom (or even no wisdom at all) on educational knowledge, which is Mill's point. And one could add to Mill's refreshing pluralism here, the more specifically religious conviction (which I share) that children do not belong to the State or its agencies.

I would further add that if the State insists on funding education in such a way as to put private education out of the hands of the vast majority of the population, then it will have to countenance not just the existence of religious schools and schools of all kinds; it will have to fund them too, if there is parental demand. After all, families of Catholics, Mormons, Muslims and Scientologists all pay taxes just as much as the families of agnostics, atheists and secularists. What, though, if some of these schools teach Islam or creationism (whatever that means)? I am inclined to ask simply, What if they do?, and leave it at that, uncomfortable as it no doubt is to many. But just how deep does our liberal pluralism go?

Of course, I am assuming here that there are limits to what is tolerable, given what I said earlier about mutual tolerance, so if a school was manifestly abusing children physically or psychologically as part of a supposed religious ritual, or urging its pupils to train as terrorists, then action should be taken, swiftly and firmly. But teaching that Islam is the only true religion and that ideally its remit should include the political or that the world began a mere 10,000 years ago hardly fall into those categories. Do they in any uncontentious sense amount to abuse at all? Maybe they do, but rather than the State issuing lists of doctrines proscribed in all schools, it seems to me that we will do better just to accept that there may be at the margins a degree of irresolvable conflict here between religion and the prevailing ethos (which seems to hold not just that science is true, but also that the teaching of scientific truth as the only truth is so important as to trump all other considerations). Actually I suspect that with mutual goodwill all sorts of reasonable compromises are possible in this area, and that they will in the main be made (after all, children of creationist parents will mostly do public exams in science, and there are plenty of Muslims prepared to live under the Dar-al-harb and to engage in its political processes). So the discomfort which many of us might feel in the area of schooling can in the main be ameliorated. But where compromises do not seem to be possible, a genuinely pluralist, liberal society ought to act permissively towards religious dissidents, just as I argued earlier that religious people should act permissively towards the existence of abortion clinics.

On the question of whether Christian adoption agencies should be forced to accept homosexual couples as prospective adopters, the situation seems to me to be clearer. The State seems to be simply abusing its power in forcing religious people either to act against their principles or not act at all, where what they want to do compromises no one's freedom. After all, homosexuals are not being barred from adopting through non-religious agencies, so if it is a question of equality, the State has already secured that. But I think that actually the case sets a wider and worrying precedent, in that in it the State is using the law to enforce a code of ethics which is in itself contentious and goes too far beyond what I described at the beginning of this essay as reflecting any general consensus on what is required for us as a society to live together to be a justifiable case for legislation.

Throughout this essay I have defended a pluralist view of society and of political organization, in which religion certainly has a role to play, but one distinct from that of the secular power or sovereign. Anticipations of this view can be found in the Middle Ages, as we have just seen, though of course neither Hildebrand nor Dante had their visions realized, or not for any length of time. What I have myself proposed stipulates a clear role for religion in public life, but a role different from that arising from some of the other religious positions we have surveyed. It would, though, be fascinating to think that the limited, pluralist state of Western democracy, which is the perspective from which I have been writing, is itself in some ways a descendant of a powerful strain of medieval Christian thinking, that represented by Hildebrand, Manegold and Dante, at least in the limited role that strain accords to religion in the political realm. And given this, and given the two contemporary examples we have just looked at, it would not be entirely unfitting if in these post-religious days religion itself becomes a guardian or advocate of the classical liberal State and of its proper limits.

16

Religion and Theology

GORDON GRAHAM

It was long a commonplace among preachers, amounting almost to a platitude, that the Christian religion is not a theory but a way of life. The contemporary debate (or dispute) between Christian believers and secular humanists is generally conducted by both parties on the assumption that this is false, that what is at issue between the two sides is primarily cognitive, a matter of conflicting beliefs rather than contrasting behaviour. In accordance with this assumption, contributions to the science/religion debate either pit scientific theories against theological doctrines, or seek to reconcile the two in some way. They never compare, say, the merits of chemical analysis with the value of hymn singing, even though these activities differentiate science and religion also.

The most straightforward version of the cognitive difference between religionists and their opponents takes it to be a debate between theists and atheists, that is to say between those who believe that God exists and those who believe that there is no God. Yet, though this equation is generally treated as almost a truism, it rules out an interesting possibility, one suggested by the author of the book of James, who tells his readers, 'You believe that there is one God. You do well. Even the demons believe – and tremble!' (James 2.19). If this passage makes any sense (as it seems to), there must be logical space for theistic belief that is not religious, for a personal conviction in the existence of God that does not result in worship. The Dutch theologian Herman Bavinck makes the point this way: 'Demons have no religion; they are no doubt convinced that God exists, but the thought of God moves them only to fear and hatred.'[1] Such demons, we might say, are *irreligious* theists, to be contrasted with *religious* theists who expressly engage in the practice of worship – prayer, praise, sacrifice, incantation and so on. These are activities that secular humanists deliberately eschew, certainly, but what the possibility of theistic demons shows is that the

---

1 Herman Bavinck, *The Philosophy of Revelation* (Grand Rapids: Eerdmans, 1953), p. 142.

secularists' rejection is a second kind of difference between the two groups, a difference in behaviour *distinct from* any difference in belief.

Now since this difference between the religious and the secularist is at least as evident as any difference in propositional belief, the commonplace assumption must further suppose that the cognitive component to the dispute is the more important of the two, that though religious believers and secularists do live their lives differently, at the heart of religion are theological beliefs that secularists don't share. In other words, they must tacitly suppose that though Christianity is indeed a way of life, it is a way of life founded on a theory. The main purpose of this essay is to ask if this is a supposition there is reason to accept, a question that can only be answered by a philosophical exploration of the relation between belief and practice in religion. The dominance of Christianity has made explicit discussion of this topic relatively rare in the philosophy of religion, because down the centuries highly articulated (and contested) theologies have been formulated for Christianity's most distinctive practices – notably baptism and Holy Communion – thereby suggesting that the role of theology is to explain and justify practice. However, the tendency to think in this way is reinforced by a more widespread philosophical prejudice about the relation of belief to practice, a prejudice, I shall argue, that has distorted our understanding of what is at issue in a properly critical reflection on the significance of both religious faith and its rejection.

The concept of 'faith', however, itself raises further complications. Often 'faith' is taken simply to be another word for 'belief'. This is not, in my view, a plausible identification. I understand by 'faith' a distinct *attitude to* a composite of belief and practice. When we speak, for example, of having (or lacking) faith in the democratic process, we express an attitude towards something that is neither a set of political beliefs and principles nor a mere institutional procedure, but some combination of the two. So too, Christian faith is related to, but not to be equated with, believing the theological doctrines characteristic of Christianity. No doubt a better understanding of the relation between belief and practice in religion will also enable us to understand better the nature of religious faith. However, it is the belief/practice relation with which I am concerned here, and in particular a widely held conception of it.

I shall call this common conception the 'doxastic model'. It is frequently assumed to be correct in the context of theology and religion, but its deployment is by no means confined to this context. The relation between political philosophy and political practice, for example, has often been assumed to have this character. Even more commonly, the relationship between science and technology is generally understood in this way. In all three cases, the doxastic model has two components. The first is the idea that belief explains behaviour, the second that justified belief rationalizes practical action. Since in a democracy 'majority opinion' is more likely to be appealed to as the standard of justification than 'true' political beliefs of a Platonic kind, the doxastic model is less persuasive in the context of modern politics than it once was. By contrast, the same model goes virtually unquestioned when applied to the relationship between modern science and technology.

In this third context it both generates and sustains the following picture. Technology is to be characterized as the use of techniques derived from scientific theories. Belief in the truth of these theories explains why the particular techniques are widely used. Their use is rationally justified just insofar as the theories from which they are derived are indeed empirically verifiable. In this way scientific theory underwrites technological practice, and truth in theory is the route to success in practice.

It is easy to see how the same model finds application in the case of religion. If we suppose that religious people engage in practices derived from their theological beliefs, then we can say that the theological beliefs explain their behaviour. Moreover, the rationality of their behaviour can be assessed in terms of the warrant they have for holding the theological beliefs they do. If those beliefs are false (or at any rate poorly grounded when compared with empirical science, say) as secularists contend, then their religious behaviour is irrational, no better than superstition in fact. This is what makes theological 'theory' fundamental to religious 'practice', and thus makes a religious 'way of life' derivative from its 'theology'.

Science and technology

This doxastic model of belief and behaviour has a powerful hold on our thinking, and requires some equally powerful rebuttal. The most compelling argument against it, in my view, will be one that shows it to be erroneous even with respect to science and technology, and the strongest possible version of such an argument will show that it cannot be sustained even with respect to medicine, which is the most plausible example for the model within the whole sphere of science and technology, initially at any rate. Its plausibility arises from a widely held belief that, in contrast to magical spells and folk remedies, the mark of modern medicine lies in its having abandoned tradition and convention in favour of cures and treatments based upon an extensive and detailed knowledge of anatomy, physiology and biochemistry – knowledge that we owe to the investigations of medical science. Medical practice, in other words, is applied medical science, and further improved treatments can be expected just so long as the application of scientific methods produces advances in human knowledge.

It seems to me probable that most people regard this understanding of what makes modern medicine different from traditional 'healing' as quite uncontroversial, and yet even with respect to well-known examples drawn from the history of medicine, the relationship between theory and practice is not so simple. For instance, the eighteenth century witnessed huge advances in anatomical knowledge, and for the first time people came to understand the function of different organs properly. But it was over 100 years before the sort of surgery that made effective practical use of this knowledge was developed. Conversely, penicillin, perhaps the single most powerful remedy to disease ever discovered, owed more to chance than to scientific theories current at the time of its discovery.

Neither of these familiar examples fits the doxastic model very well, but let us set them aside and assume that, by and large, modern medicine is indeed a highly plausible example of how the model connects theory and practice, belief and action. Even if it is, we would not be warranted in inferring from this that *in general* practices of healing are related to the beliefs associated with them in the same way. Consider, for example, homeopathic remedies. Proponents of conventional medicine tend to be sceptical about homeopathy. However, for the most part they base their doubts on the absence of any clinical evidence that clearly demonstrates the efficacy of homeopathic remedies. They do not much concern themselves with the theoretical adequacy or inadequacy of Samuel Hahnemann's vitalistic 'law of similars' with which homeopathy originated. More importantly, from a logical point of view, if, contrary to this scepticism, satisfactory clinical evidence *were* to emerge in favour of homeopathic practice, this would do nothing to restore vitalist theory because the success of the remedies would give us no reason to affirm the truth of Hahnemann's 'law'. *A fortiori*, evidence of their effectiveness could not be undermined by a demonstration of vitalism's falsehood. The 'law of similars' might completely fail to explain the nonetheless demonstrable success of homeopathic remedies.

The point applies quite generally to folk remedies. Being the outcome of human experience, folk remedies are not infrequently effective. But in times past the 'theories' by which their efficacy was 'explained' were invariably both *ex post facto* and fanciful. What this reveals is that practice and theory may be divorced, rationally speaking, thus making it possible for successful practitioners to claim this success as support for the bogus theories to which they subscribe. The same divorce can be found the other way round. The truth and explanatory value of Harvey's theory of the circulation of the blood did nothing to validate the practice of blood-letting that was so prevalent in the medicine of his day. Similarly, lithium has proved to be effective in the treatment of (some) bi-polar depression, even though medical science has as yet been unable to show that it has any biological function in the human body.

In short, the doxastic model does not fit modern medicine very well, and insofar as it does, this gives us no reason to extend the model to the general human practice of healing. Once, on the strength of these doubts, we go on to consider technology more broadly, the plausibility of the model recedes yet more rapidly. Great technological innovators such as Thomas Edison and Alexander Graham Bell had virtually no scientific education, and their innovations owed nothing to the ground-breaking work in electromagnetic theory that James Clerk Maxwell was doing around the time of their invention. While making this point, however, we need not deny that there are areas of technology in which relevant scientific knowledge on the part of engineers is indispensable. Genetic engineering is one striking instance, and is the sort of example that gives powerful support to the doxastic model of belief and practice. But genetic engineering – like computer science – is both new and unusual. In general, science and technology can operate quite independently, and this shows that even in the most plausible of the three applications the model is mistaken with respect to both of its components. We are rationally justified in using a technique that has proved effective regardless of the truth or falsehood (or even existence) of any theoretical explanation we can offer for its effectiveness. Conversely, the truth of a theory cannot in itself secure the effectiveness of the techniques it suggests. In other words, even when it comes to science and technology, true belief and rational action are not related in the way the doxastic model supposes.

Style and meaning

The conclusion to be drawn from the preceding section is that only in some relatively rare cases is practical action derived from or rationally underwritten by theoretical beliefs or principles. Science is thus detachable from technology, even when there is a contingent association between the two. If theology is detachable from religion in a similar fashion, then the 'religion versus science' debate seems misconceived. Assume it to be the case that, for example, 'creationism' is a theological explanation in competition with evolutionary biology. It follows that 'science' is at loggerheads with 'religion' only if creationism (or some such belief) importantly underwrites the practice of religion. But if, as the foregoing argument suggests, a practice can be rationally engaged in irrespective of the cogency of the theories associated with it, then the inadequacy of any particular theology will imply nothing about the degree to which religious practices are warranted. Praising God in the words of Psalm 19 ('The heavens declare the glory of God and the firmament shows his handiwork') does not require us to believe that the world was created 10,000 years ago, complete with species fully differentiated. Nor is the act of praise more 'rational' for those who believe these claims than for those who do not.

It might be replied that there is an important hiatus in the argument here. Even if the doxastic model does misrepresent the relation between science and technology, it cannot thereby be concluded that it equally misrepresents the relation between theology and religion. This is because there is a crucial difference between the two cases, a difference that becomes more evident when we look at the example of homeopathic medicine again. In 1810, on the basis of his 'law of similars', Hahnemann published *Materia Medica Pura*, a collection of 65 remedies. Let us suppose that a few of these remedies substantially improved the health of those who used them, and further suppose, as is widely agreed, that the vitalism on which he based them is false. The reality of any improvements in health brought about by Hahnemann's successful remedies is unaffected by this, because the existence of a 'vital force' is not crucial to their efficacy. By contrast, however, prayer and praise is wholly *vacuous* if there is no God to which it is actually being addressed, not because it is ineffectual, but because it is meaningless. Frequently, attempts are made to 'prove' the efficacy of (petitionary) prayer. The results are rarely impressive, but such attempts are in any case wrongheaded. Insofar as we could produce empirical evidence of a systematic improvement in the psychological well-being, family relationships or economic prosperity of people who say prayers together regularly, this would not show that *prayer* had been effective, only that reciting words in a certain way can have beneficial effects. Imagine a comparable case. A very solitary person might genuinely experience an improvement in her mental well-being by sitting down once a week and writing letters to 'a friend'. But if in reality there is no one at the other end of this correspondence, it is the act of putting pen to paper, not human contact, that is having this effect. She may feel less lonely, but she is still alone.

What these observations suggest is that, in contrast to science, and hence contrary to the arguments of the previous section, the theological content of religious practice is not separable in the way that the 'scientific' content of homeopathy might prove separable from its recommended remedies. One way of stating this point more succinctly is to say that while the only thing that matters about a medical remedy is its *effect*, what matters about religious practice is its *meaning*. The effect of a remedy is what it is, irrespective of any theory about what makes it effective, but an action is meaningful only if the attitude from which it arises is intelligible.

This reference to the intelligibility of human action is of the first importance, in my view, but on closer examination it will serve to show that in some contexts the divorce between theory and practice is even more radical. That is because the intelligibility of a practice may require no 'theory' at all.

A 'way of life', let us agree, is in part composed of actions that are severely practical in just this sense: their purpose is to serve basic human needs – securing food and shelter, dealing with disease and danger, satisfying sexual desire, assisting procreation, and so on. Now the extent to which the practices that a given society has developed in its attempts to meet these needs do truly serve them, is indeed a matter for critical scrutiny and empirical inquiry. There are undoubtedly many instances in which widely held but false beliefs have sustained injurious practices (the belief that female circumcision is a necessary condition of female fertility, for instance), though sometimes false belief can generate and sustain beneficial practices as well. In this sense empirical beliefs, often of a general or 'theoretical' kind, can properly be said to underwrite social institutions and patterns of human action. Some work well, some do not. Often the difference is best ascertained empirically, and there is no reason why empirical work of a sophisticated theoretical nature cannot be required.

Nevertheless, it is also characteristic of human beings that their ways of life are marked not just by functional utility, but by *style*. This is true for the greater part of human life, in fact. For example, dress has a utilitarian function – to keep the body warm (or cool) and dry. Some materials are highly effective to these ends, and others less so. Consequently, an important part of the history of dress is the invention of materials that are better, functionally speaking. But universally, human beings have also valued *beautiful* fabrics, and there is no necessary connection between the functional and the beautiful.

The example of dress is just one aspect of what is sometimes called 'the aesthetics of everyday life'. This aesthetic component, however, should not be thought of as merely 'surface decoration'. Human beings do indeed decorate their bodies, and this too is part of the aesthetics of everyday life. But dress styles are not like face paint or jewellery; they are ways in which human beings *realize* the important functions of keeping warm and dry. In a similar way, style in the preparation and serving of food is *formative*, a matter of proper nourishment and not just attractive garnish. Style determines the composition of the cake, we might say, and not just the appearance of the icing on it.

Food that has little or no nutritional value gains nothing in that respect by being stylishly served. But the truth of this proposition lends no support to the crudely utilitarian view that nutritional value is all that matters. Style also matters. For present purposes, however, the point to be emphasized is that while there can obviously be a science of nutrition, there can be no science of style. It is a common prejudice to conclude from this that style is simply a matter of subjective preference or 'liking', with the implication that assessments of nutritional value are true or false, while in matters of style anything goes. Outside of the philosophy classroom, hardly anyone really believes this. People choose, recommend, relish, award prizes to, and generally treat matters of style as though they admit of being better or worse in just the way functional remedies do. But if there is no *science* of style, what determines better and worse?

This is of course a very longstanding, and vexed, question in aesthetics that cannot be fully explored here. So I shall simply make some reasonably uncontentious observations in order to make progress in this context. First, even though there can be no factual inquiry into or empirical theories of style, and therefore no scope for the concepts of truth and falsehood perhaps, matters of style can still be matters of *judgement*. Some people have a better eye for colour than others, a better sense of dress, a more subtle nose, a more accurate ear, and so on. As a result, their opinions on matters of style have an authority that the opinions of people without these aptitudes do not. It is this that gives reason and intelligibility a foothold, even though there is no scope for empirical 'evidence' or proof.

Second, the fact that these judgements of right and wrong are not demonstrable in the way that empirical assessments are, does not license the (common) inference that they are essentially contestable. As Kant observes in the case of beauty, such judgements aspire to universal agreement, and frequently command common consent. People do disagree about what is and is not beautiful, but by and large, especially over time, there is a remarkable degree of consensus. This is why something's being judged beautiful (or the reverse), generates reasons for action in a way that personal preference would not. My preference for wine over beer gives you no reason to prefer it, but my claim that a particular wine is specially good does give you reason to prefer it to others. In this respect, judgements of style are 'practical' in a way that factual judgements are not. 'Come and see this *green* dress' does not connect with practical reason in the way that 'Come and see this *beautiful* green dress' does. Similarly, 'This building is so ugly it ought to be demolished' has a rational authority that 'This building is so square it ought to be demolished' lacks. In short, and in general, judgements of style provide reasons for action, and this further connects them with considerations of rationality and intelligibility.

Third, judgements of style are made possible by distinctively human sensibilities, sensibilities that other animals do not have and which some human beings lack. In aesthetics this is what the eighteenth century called 'taste', but there is no need to restrict it to the perceptual apprehension of beautiful sights and sounds that lies at the heart of Kant's *Critique of Judgement*. Some people have sensibilities that are exhibited *directly* in action – in cookery, or photography or singing or storytelling for instance. Such sensibilities enable them to choose the right amount, the right angle, the right speed, the right timing, where other people are more likely to get it wrong.

Fourth, these judgements of right and wrong are always directed at the particular, and for this reason cannot be deduced from general principles. Yet there is still scope for reasoning and reflection of a general kind. This is a point to be returned to at greater length when the question of theology's relation to religion is taken up again. For the moment, it may be sufficient to remark that the drawing of parallels, analogies and connections between particulars can be illuminating in this context. There can be organized thought which is neither explanatory nor deductive, but nonetheless systematic and reflective, reminiscent of the way in which botany differs from physics perhaps.

Fifth, and relatedly, it is this possibility that allows style to convey meaning. For example, there are funereal and celebratory styles of dress. Architectural style can be exhibited equally well (or equally badly) in both public buildings and private dwellings: castellation on a large mansion is impressive; on a small terraced house it is absurd. Decorative styles can be extravagant, economical, restrained or ostentatious. Dress and make-up can be used to make personal appearance elegant, seductive, aggressive or ridiculous (sometimes deliberately so of course, as in the case of clowns). And so on. This gives individuals non-arbitrary choices between styles (often equally *stylish*), and these are choices which also admit of right and wrong. Ridiculous dress is right for a clown, wrong for a lawyer. Both adequately serve a function – covering the body – but each *says* something different, and it is this that enables us to speak of the *language* of style.

Theology as grammar

The argument so far may be summarized as follows. If we take as our starting point the claim that religion is a way of life rather than an explanatory theory, it seems that we must construe the religion/science debate rather differently from the way in which it is normally interpreted, namely as a potential conflict of belief. Presupposed in the commonplace interpretation is a certain idea of the relation between theology and religion according to which the latter is based upon the former. This is an idea that accords with a quite general conception of the relation between belief and practice which I called the doxastic model, a model that seems least controversial when applied to science and technology. But even here, I have argued, it misrepresents the relation between theory and practice. Science and technology can be importantly related, but the relationship is nonetheless a contingent one; there is no necessary conceptual relation between the two. Similarly, it seems, there is no necessary connection between theology and religion.

Even when we observe, correctly, that religious actions necessarily have meaning as well as practical purpose, this does not imply any foundational role for theological belief or doctrine, because meaning can be generated by 'style' no less than by intellectual interpretation. Furthermore, meaning generated in this way is not any less subject to judgement and reason than is the choice of causally effective means to given ends.

So far, however, my explication of 'style' has been confined to the aesthetics of everyday life and to the sensibility (or lack of it) that enables individuals to make intelligible choices between styles of acting and living. A sense of style, though, is just one of a number of important sensibilities by means of which the life of the species *homo sapiens* rises above simple sense experience and is made distinctively human. Among these sensibilities we can include a sense of humour, a sense of occasion, a sense of history, and a sense of adventure – examples that have the advantage of being less contentious than the idea of a 'moral sense' to which some philosophers (notably in the eighteenth century) have appealed. In the present context, however, the question naturally arises as to whether there is a *religious* sensibility properly so called.

Some such concept is familiar in the philosophy of religion at least since Schleiermacher's *Speeches*,[2] where it was invoked in a sustained attempt to resist the common reduction of religion to either speculative metaphysics or ethics. It was brought to still greater prominence by Rudolph Otto in *The Idea of the Holy*[3] with his celebrated notion of the *mysterium tremens*. Like the moral sense, though, a religious 'sense' is a contentious concept. On the one hand, some people suspect that (in both cases) an occult 'sixth' sense is being called into existence for dubious epistemological reasons, while others, bearing in mind (for instance) the distinction between a sense of humour and mere tendency to laugh, regard the alternative account – simple identification with projected 'feelings' – as seriously impoverished.

Some of this contention arises, I think, because all such sensibilities seem to hover uncertainly between the realist/anti-realist distinction that philosophers have such a strong inclination to draw. It seems incontestable that something's being a joke has to be internally connected with the actual stimulation of subjective amusement among human beings. On the other hand, it seems equally evident that people can be amused by jokes that are 'not really' funny, and that humourless people can fail to be amused by jokes which really are. Similarly, something's being beautiful is necessarily

---

2 Friedrich Schleiermacher, in Richard Crouter (ed.), *On Religion: Speeches to its Cultured Despisers* (Cambridge: Cambridge University Press, 1988, 2006).

3 Rudolph Otto, *The Idea of the Holy: An Inquiry into the Non-rational Factor in the Idea of the Divine and its Relation to the Rational*, tr. John W. Harvey (London: Oxford University Press, 1950).

connected with its ability to draw the attention and admiration of people who encounter it, and yet people can also admire kitsch and be attracted by the pornographic. Nor can this difference be captured in terms of the conventional. It makes no sense to ask whether saying 'Thank you' is 'really' polite, for instance, because politeness is *constituted* by such gestures. Humour, by contrast, is *not* constituted by amusement or laughter.

In other contexts, the dual aspect of these sensibilities has been called 'quasi-realist'. Whether this is helpful terminology or not, it points to something crucially important, namely, that the mind's *engagement with* reality is necessarily different from the mind's *contemplation* or *explanation of* reality. Accordingly, taking seriously the suggestion that religion is a way of *being in* the world rather than a system of *thought about* the world, inevitably gives it this *quasi*-realistic character. Sometimes, just in virtue of this fact, the same suggestion awakens a suspicion on the part of orthodox theists that 'religion' is being emptied of its theological content. This is evidently a very important issue, but it is possible to suspend its examination if we are careful to distinguish between 'the sacred' and 'the supernatural'. A sense of the sacred is a practical attunement to the world, and as such, part of what has been called 'the natural history of religion'. By definition the supernatural (if such there be) is that which *transcends* the natural, including natural religion.

Once sacred and supernatural have been distinguished, it is possible to see that while theology is almost invariably assumed to be a systematic study or account of the supernatural, there is conceptual space for an alternative, namely the theology of the sacred. This is connected, I think, to Wittgenstein's parenthetical (and somewhat gnomic) remark 'Theology as Grammar' (*Philosophical Investigations* §373), provided we take the parallel that remark invites us to draw rather strictly. For the most part, speakers of a natural language, even those who have a special 'feel' for the language, make judgements about what is and is not grammatically or syntactically correct in application to particular instances while being unable to articulate the grammatical rules covering all these instances. So, too, it is plausible to think, people with a finely attuned sense of the sacred may be unable to articulate any conceptual structure in which their judgements of what is and is not sacred are made coherent. In the grammatical context, we are unlikely to hold that articulation of this kind is either impossible or redundant; grammar books exist, and people learning languages find them useful. So, too, we might say, theology as the 'grammar' of the sacred is both possible and valuable. In the space remaining, I shall make a few brief remarks about the 'grammar' of the sacred, before returning (even more briefly) to the relation of the sacred to the supernatural.

There are common human practices that fall uncertainly between practical purpose and ritualistic action. Ablutions are a striking case. Nowadays the practice of taking a shower first thing in the morning is invariably justified in terms of personal hygiene; that is to say, in terms of its causal efficacy for human health. It is not at all clear, however, that this is the truly operative reason. Only a tiny proportion of the people who regularly engage in the practice have any well-founded empirical beliefs about what the causal connection could be, and yet as a human practice it is very widely observed. We could infer from this that advertisers have tricked the vast majority of people into pointless activity, but that would be to miss the essential point; this is the way people in the developed world prepare for the start of a new day. It is not because of what a hot shower *does*, but because of what it *means* that people act in this way.

It is practices like these that give shape to the day. In a similar fashion, meals mean more than nutrition. Among many other things, meals are ways in which the day is punctuated and family bonds made tangible. The point can be extended. Weekends shape the week; birthdays, religious festivals and public holidays shape the year. Birth, maturity, marriage and death rituals shape lives. Without 'shaping' of this kind, the passage of time would be an indistinguishable 'flow' – just one thing after another – and human beings would 'live' in the way that dogs and trees live: an organic existence with beginning and end. They would not lead lives as we commonly understand the expression.

I shall call the things that shape our lives, including relations between people, 'markers'. Some markers are dispensable and some are negotiable, but some are neither. They are, we might say, 'absolute' and it is our sense of the sacred and our moral sense (if there is such a thing) that enable us to distinguish the absolute from the preferable and the interchangeable. Distinctive attitudes separate moral and religious absolutes, however, the latter being most naturally characterized by the language of veneration and desecration. This difference enables us to explain the following sort of example (which I owe to Nicholas Wolterstorff). If circumstances were to bring it about that you were driven to steal from your mother, it is sufficient (perhaps) to explain the wrongness of doing so in terms of quite general moral obligations and prohibitions and/or her well-being. But suppose you are invited to trample on a photograph of your dead mother. What exactly is objectionable about this? There is no obviously moral dimension – since no right is violated and you could not be doing her harm in any obvious sense. Perhaps, indeed, it would give great satisfaction to those who had greatly disliked her, thus making it a good opportunity to give other people pleasure. Yet, at a minimum, most people would be deeply reluctant to do this, and need some very strong reason to counter this reluctance. Anyone who finds such reluctance puzzling and thinks there is no real objection because 'It's only a picture', reveals themselves as oddly inhuman and lacking (for instance) any understanding of the difference between a treasured family photograph and a photo ID. To this extent they lack any sense of the sacred; which is to say, while they can judge what is useful and beneficial, they have no place for the *veneration* of things. Alternatively, consider a quite different kind of picture – realistically representational but entirely imaginary depictions of children as sex objects for adults – which someone pores over in secret and furtively passes around like-minded acquaintances. Anyone who can see nothing objectionable in this behaviour on the grounds that no real child was actually subject to sexual abuse in the making of them, may care about harm and detriment, but has no use for the concept of desecration.

Veneration, idolatry, desecration, sin, innocence, purity and impurity are all key concepts for the grammar of the sacred. In everyday thought and conversation these actual words may occur relatively rarely. Yet only a tiny minority of human beings have no use whatever for the judgements that they express, judgements that are necessarily 'quasi-realistic' as that term was used earlier. It is the task of the grammar of the sacred, I suggest, to make articulate the ways in which judgements that use or imply such concepts fit together into a coherent manner of existence; how, we might say, they *inform* a human life and make it something other than the biological existence between birth and death that people have in common with plants and animals.

We are now in a position to think of religion as primarily a way of living life, letting it be shaped by a desire to avoid idolatry, venerate the sacred and protect it from desecration. Interpreted as the grammar of the sacred, theology has a role in systematizing and making coherent the judgements upon which such shaping depends. But in doing so, it is not providing the underlying 'theories' that the religious life 'applies'.

This question arises however. If we characterize 'the sacred' in terms of *absolute* requirements and prohibitions, it appears that something more needs to be said about the authoritative nature of these absolutes. Since 'absolute' here contrasts with dispensable or negotiable, and nothing that arises from human will or inclination alone – including the will or inclination to shape life this way or that – is non-negotiable, we need some further step that makes *submission* of the will intelligible. In most religions the further step is evident, because encounters with the sacred are encounters with a divine or supernatural realm, a different order of reality that is (in some sense) beyond or greater than the natural world of human pleasure and welfare. Anyone who wishes to retain sacred value while abandoning the supernatural must therefore explain what it is that enables the sacred to *require* veneration, to *forbid* desecration and so on: to explain, in short, what prevents it from collapsing into a mere *affirmation* of the Ubermensch, in itself groundless and without implications for others (as Nietzsche acknowledged). We can interpret Kant's *Groundwork*[4] as an attempt to attach veneration to morality (through 'reverence for the moral law') and this is a move that contemporary thought often makes in its assertions that human life is 'sacred' and human rights 'inviolable'. Importantly, though, having largely abandoned traditional religious metaphysics, in the second *Critique*[5] Kant gives the veneration of morality a transcendental grounding in the necessary suppositions of God, freedom and immortality. This reveals, I think, that the secular aspiration to retain sacred value without supernatural warrant has more work to do. And though it is a topic for another essay, my suspicion is that any purely naturalistic account of the sacred will reveal a philosophical instability that can only be resolved when the supernatural is invoked as its ground.

---

4 Immanuel Kant, *Groundwork to the Metaphysics of Morals*, tr. H. J. Paton (London: Hutchinson, 1785/1948).
5 Immanuel Kant, *Critique of the Power of Judgment*, tr. Paul Guyer (Cambridge: Cambridge University Press, 1790/3, 2001).

17

Wisdom and Belief in Theology and Philosophy

SIMON OLIVER

There are, indeed, things that cannot be put into words. They *make themselves manifest*. They are what is mystical.[1]

Have you noticed that religious beliefs are frequently described in the media as 'deeply held'? Within a late modern culture which struggles with political apathy, the dissolution of shared values and our supposed failure to commit to anything beyond self-interest, this description could express an admiration for the resilience and dedication which is frequently exhibited by the religious and their communities. At the same time, describing religious beliefs as 'deeply held' might also suggest a degree of dogmatism, inflexibility and the absence of pragmatic reason. Such views are apparently held by 'faith' (a private matter) which is opposed to 'reason' (which is apparently neutral and publicly shared). How are such 'deeply held religious beliefs' to be weighed and valued in debates concerning, for example, biomedical ethics or laws regarding incitement to religious hatred? Without any apparent means of evaluating publicly the truth of particular religious claims (because religion is assumed to be a private matter which does not submit to neutral reason), beliefs pertaining to those claims are protected largely because their infringement might be injurious to the individual believer, thereby constituting a violation of human rights. This latter characterization of religious belief is exploited by the so-called 'new atheists' who have attacked religion so vehemently in recent years.[2] The religious are described as dogmatic, uncommonly certain, irrational, pernicious and the subjects of unwarranted privilege in political and public life.

Is religious belief really like that? It is certainly true that the new atheists

---

1 Wittgenstein, *Tractatus Logico-Philosophicus*, 6.522.
2 For a characterization of 'new atheism', see Tina Beattie, *The New Atheists: The Twilight of Reason and the War on Religion* (London: Darton, Longman & Todd, 2007).

usually attack a particular *kind* of religious belief, namely the fundamentalist variety which many theologians and anthropologists identify as a peculiarly modern phenomenon.[3] Moreover, the fundamentalist religious beliefs
attacked by the new atheists usually represent a mirror image of their own
dogmatism or scientific fundamentalism.[4] It is perhaps significant that
those who attack religion on scientific or historical grounds usually admire
the religious fundamentalists as 'true believers' who at least have the
courage of their allegedly flawed and even deranged convictions. There may
be more than a degree of ironic mutual appreciation between the opposing
sides in this debate.

The nature of belief in general is, of course, an enormously complex field
of philosophical and theological study, and belief's relation to knowledge is
much contested.[5] However, the characterization of religious belief as *either*
dogmatic and fundamentalist *or* liberal to the point of being reducible to
culture or dispensable, *or* lying on a spectrum somewhere between these
two poles, presents the matter in a fashion which many theologians recognize as too modern and broadly dualistic. Religious belief is frequently
regarded as simply a variety of a wider and more general form of belief. So
belief that God exists, or belief in God, is treated as if it were concerned with
just one more being alongside others who might or might not exist. Evidence for the existence of this being must be produced in the same way that

---

3 See, for example, Malise Ruthven, *Fundamentalism: The Search for Meaning* (Oxford: Oxford
University Press, new edn, 2005) and Harriet Harris, *Fundamentalism and Evangelicals*
(Oxford: Oxford University Press, 1998).

4 For comments on the fundamentalist character of some scientific atheists, see Simon
Conway Morris, *The Crucible of Creation: The Burgess Shale and the Rise of Animals* (Oxford:
Oxford University Press, 1999); ibid., *Life's Solution: Inevitable Humans in a Lonely Universe*
(Cambridge: Cambridge University Press, 2004); Alister McGrath, *The Dawkins Delusion?:
Atheist Fundamentalism and the Denial of the Divine* (London: SPCK, 2007); John Cornwell,
Darwin's Angel: An Angelic Riposte to The God Delusion (London: Profile Books, 2007).

5 A distinction is often made between 'belief *that*' and 'belief *in*'. For example, I may hold the
belief *that* it is currently raining outside, while I believe *in* my friend's ability to use her talents
to transform the lives of other people. The belief *that* something is the case may elicit our
assent to a fact which we suppose is demonstrable or at least likely, while the belief *in* something or someone will provoke our commitment, trust and faith. While religion may certainly
concern belief *that*, say, God exists, this will frequently be expressed in the form of belief *in* a
certain way of life or the purposes of God. We may think that a clear rationalist approach
would restrict us to 'belief *that*'. Why? Because 'belief in' something has the whiff of faith or
trust beyond the immediate and literal implications of the evidence to hand. However, a mil-
itantly atheist scientist may believe *that* natural selection is the means of the evolution of
earth's species, while believing *in* science's ability to provide the exclusive and fundamental
account of the nature of reality. It would be difficult to find any sphere of human enquiry that
did not involve the interweaving of 'belief *that*' and 'belief *in*' and, by implication, the blend-
ing of faith and reason. See H. H. Price, 'Belief "In" and Belief "That" in Basil Mitchell (ed.),
The Philosophy of Religion (Oxford: Oxford University Press, 1971), pp. 143–67.

I might produce evidence for the existence of an unseen planet on the far side of the galaxy, or evidence for the designer of the machine lying before me. Little account is given of precisely what is meant by 'God' and, given a particular account of 'God', what might constitute belief in such a God, or knowledge of God.

Much contemporary philosophy of religion finds a comfortable home within this characterization of religious belief. The understanding of God in this field of study is remarkably similar to that proffered by the new atheism.[6] Over the past 30 years the most prominent philosophers of religion have espoused the design argument with enthusiasm as a properly scientific inductive demonstration of the high probability of God's existence.[7] At the same time, we have seen a striking confidence in the ability of theological language to furnish us with substantial information about God while theodicy continues to provide *reasons* for that which the pre-modern tradition regards as inherently *unreasonable*, namely evil. On the face of it, one might expect theologians and religious communities to be delighted with such fulsome support from a good number of prominent theistic philosophers. However, it is not only striking that philosophy of religion has negligible impact on the religious and the agnostic, but also that the impact among theologians is frequently negative. Theologians go out of their way to point out that the God of modern theistic philosophy is not the God of orthodox Christianity. They continually maintain that the business of Christian *doctrina* (teaching) is rather more interesting and complex than the cognitive propositions treated by philosophers of religion.[8]

In the context of this debate concerning religion and God, there appear to be three options. First, one might adopt a position of outright atheism. Alternatively, one could espouse a cognitive propositional certainty regarding God's existence which tends to be rationalistic (based on reason divorced from the *particularities* of a religious tradition and its revelation, sometimes known as 'natural theology') or fideistic (that is, dependent on faith devoid of reason). In some sense, as Denys Turner points out, atheism and theism thus construed are mirror images of each other and share at least this in

---

6 See Richard Dawkins, *The God Delusion* (London: Black Swan, 2006), p. 52; Richard Swinburne, *The Coherence of Theism* (Oxford: Oxford University Press, 1989), p. 1.
7 See, for example, Richard Swinburne, *The Existence of God* (Oxford: Oxford University Press, rev. edn, 1992), ch. 8.
8 See, for example, the work of Sarah Coakley, *Powers and Submissions: Spirituality, Philosophy and Gender* (Oxford: Blackwell, 2002), chs 6 and 7; 'Does Kenosis Rest on a Mistake? Three Kenotic Models in Patristic Exegesis', in C. Stephen Evans (ed.), *Exploring Kenotic Christology: The Self-Emptying of God* (Oxford: Oxford University Press, 2006), pp. 246–65; George Lindbeck, *The Nature of Christian Doctrine: Religion and Theology in a Post-Liberal Age* (London: SPCK, 1984), pp. 16ff. See also the remarkable epilogue to Rudi te Velde, *Aquinas on God: The Divine Science of the Summa Theologiae* (Aldershot: Ashgate, 2006) in which the author demonstrates that Aquinas is not a 'theist'.

common: they agree on what they are denying or affirming, namely on what they mean by 'God'.[9] Finally, one could adopt a position somewhere in the middle, namely a thoroughgoing agnosticism or a broader scepticism which is characteristic of the liberal theology of the 1970s.

For those of us who work at the interface between theology and philosophy under the influence of pre-modern thought and particularly the apophatic and mystical tradition of Christian theology, a different approach might seem possible. For the patristic and medieval theologians, the grammar of the word 'God' goes hand-in-hand with what might constitute belief in God. The Christian tradition begins with the view that, if we are going to talk about 'God' at all, we must not predicate of God anything which belongs to creation *as such*. Why? Because if God were to possess any characteristic which belongs properly to creation (for example, temporality), then God would be part of *creation* and therefore not the *creator*. We would be talking about a creature, and therefore an idol. So the mystical tradition begins by talking about what God is *not*: God is not another aspect of creation, or a kind of being – one among others. God is unknowable in himself because our finite, created minds are orientated and fitted to the knowledge of the finite and created. It is always easier to say what God is *not* rather than what God *is*, and revelation is not a packet of information delivered independently of all other modes of human knowing.[10]

It is therefore the task of the theologian to be very careful concerning how one uses the word 'God'.[11] For St Thomas Aquinas, for example, theological language is an extremely delicate matter.[12] Only perfection terms can be predicated positively of God, but we do not understand the *full* meaning and implications of such speech, for we do not know God in himself. What seems to be at issue is not only whether we can speak literally of God, but whether literal speech is possible at all because there does not seem to be a readily identifiable and accessible locus in which we can anchor meaning. Meanwhile, doctrine is understood as what Nicholas Lash calls 'protocol', namely that Christian teaching (*doctrina*) which is 'the least bad way' of speaking about the transcendent, thereby forming a guard against the ever-present threat of idolatry.[13] Doctrine is not *straightforwardly* propositional

---

9 Denys Turner, 'How to be an Atheist', in *Faith Seeking* (London: SCM Press, 2002), pp. 9–10.

10 See John Montag SJ, 'Revelation: The False Legacy of Suárez', in John Milbank, Catherine Pickstock and Graham Ward (eds), *Radical Orthodoxy: Suspending the Material* (London: Routledge, 1999), pp. 38–63.

11 See Nicholas Lash's contribution to this book.

12 St Thomas Aquinas, *Summa Theologiae*, Ia.13; David Burrell, *Aquinas: God and Action* (Chicago: Chicago University Press, 2008).

13 See Nicholas Lash, *Easter in Ordinary: Reflections on Human Experience and the Knowledge of God* (Notre Dame and London: University of Notre Dame Press, 1990), pp. 257–65.

(simply delivering facts or information), but forms a structure for our speech about God whose primary role is to help us worship more truthfully. 'To worship more truthfully' in this context means the avoidance of idolatry, or the worship of ourselves. Far from being dogmatic and credulous, the tradition of Christian theology viewed from this perspective looks particularly reticent and careful.

Having first studied modern philosophy and prior to encountering the depths of the Christian tradition and particularly its mystical or apophatic character, I was always attracted to a liberal and sceptical approach to theological issues and questions of religious belief. My sense of the debate, however, remained within the modern terrain I sketched earlier. Aside from scepticism, the other option seemed to be a kind of rational cognitive (believing or non-believing) certainty concerning God which treated God as a kind of thing. However, reading about the genesis of Christian doctrine and its very positive encounter with ancient Greek philosophy while I was studying for a second degree, this time in Theology, I encountered a striking alternative. In the first centuries of Christian thought, belief, knowledge and God were understood in a very different way when compared to modern and late modern conceptions. While the mystical and apophatic traditions were reticent, their approach to God did not seem to be sceptical in quite the modern sense. The traditional reticence of Christian theology is born of the sense that our knowledge is a dim reflection of truth which, although faint, is not thereby 'off the mark' and untrustworthy. It is therefore this earlier tradition of theology and philosophy to which I would like briefly to explore in this essay, focusing first on the understanding of 'wisdom' as a goal and virtue which is common to both. What I would like to point to is quite straightforward and risks stating the obvious, namely that in pre-modern thought theology is apophatic or at least thoroughly restrained, and that it finds this stance mirrored in the most prominent contemporary philosophical tradition. This apophaticism is crucial to the philosophical method understood as the love of wisdom, where wisdom consists in what Nicholas of Cusa (1401–64) calls *docta ignorantia*, or 'learned ignorance', namely realizing first and foremost what one does *not* know. Before examining why this more traditional theology and philosophy might inform our understanding of religious belief, I would like to begin with a very brief examination of two texts which stand at either end of a long tradition of philosophy as the wisdom of 'not knowing', namely Plato's *Symposium* and Nicholas of Cusa's two short treatises entitled *De Sapientia*.

Plato on eros and the philosopher

In Plato's *Apology*, an associate of Socrates named Chaerephon asks the Delphic oracle if there is anyone wiser than Socrates.[14] The Pythian priestess confirms that Socrates is the wisest person. However, Socrates is aware only of his lack of wisdom. He therefore seeks a person among the poets, artisans and politicians of the city who is obviously wiser than he so that he can demonstrate the oracle's utterance to be wrong. Realizing that these people think they know everything but in fact know nothing, Socrates comes to the conclusion that he is the wisest because he neither knows, *nor thinks that he knows.* On leaving a rather irate politician whose ignorance Socrates has just demonstrated, he says to himself, 'I am wiser than this man; for neither of us really knows anything fine and good, but this man thinks he knows something when he does not, whereas I, as I do not know anything, do not think I do either.'[15]

This is the understanding of knowledge and wisdom which is echoed throughout the Platonic corpus, from the aporia of learning in the *Meno* to the love of wisdom in the *Symposium*. As Pierre Hadot points out, it is the basis of irony in Plato's dialogues in which Socrates assures his interlocutor that he, Socrates, knows nothing and has nothing to impart before proceeding to demonstrate that his interlocutor is ignorant of that which he thought he knew. Knowledge is not a commodity which one can 'pour' from one mind into another as the Sophists thought, but is a process of awakening the soul to recall what was already latent within. This Socratic-Platonic understanding of wisdom is expressed in an important way in the middle dialogue *Symposium*.

The *Symposium* is the account of a banquet given by a poet named Agathon. At the party, each of the guests gives a speech in praise of Eros. Throughout the dialogue, the figures of Socrates and Eros become increasingly confused, most especially in the speeches of Diotima and Alcibiades. As Hadot points out, the reason why the figures become so intertwined is that Eros and Socrates personify the figure of the philosopher, the former mythically, the latter historically.[16]

How is the similarity between Socrates and Eros understood? Principally, through the myth of the birth of Eros which Socrates heard from a priest-

---

14 Plato, *Apology*, tr. Harold North Fowler (Cambridge, MA: Harvard University Press, 1999), 21a ff. See Pierre Hadot, *What is Ancient Philosophy?*, tr. Michael Chase (Cambridge, MA: Harvard University Press, 2002), ch. 3. I am greatly indebted to Hadot's reading of the Platonic tradition.
15 Plato, *Apology*, 21d.
16 Hadot, *What is Ancient Philosophy?*, p. 1.

ess named Diotima. According to Diotima, Eros is not a god because Eros exists relative to something which it lacks: love is focused on that which is not yet, or not fully, attained. Rather, Eros is an intermediary (*daimōn*) between the mortal and the immortal, between human beings and the gods. This is explained by means of the following mythical story.[17] On the occasion of the birth of Aphrodite, the gods hold a celebratory banquet. Penia (signifying poverty or penury) comes to beg at the end of the meal. Poros (meaning 'wealth' or 'resource', the son of Metidos or 'cunning') was drunk on nectar in Zeus's garden and had fallen asleep. Seizing an opportunity and being herself without means, Penia lay with Poros and bore Eros. Being conceived on the birthday of Aphrodite, this is why Eros has always been the attendant of beauty. However, Diotima explains that Eros, in being the offspring of Penia and Poros, is a strange and unclassifiable being. Taking after his mother, Eros is ever poor, and is a hardened barefoot wanderer. But from his father, Poros, Eros takes the ability to scheme cleverly for all that is beautiful and good in a brave and impetuous manner. He has a degree of know-how. We are told that 'Love is at no time either resourceless or wealthy, and furthermore, he stands midway betwixt wisdom and ignorance.'[18]

The similarities between Socrates and Eros are apparent through the remainder of the *Symposium*. For the moment, we can see that the figure of Socrates-Eros is the figure of the philosopher. As the child of Penia, the philosopher is poor and deficient, lacking knowledge. Yet as the child of Poros, the philosopher is also resourceful. Eros is halfway between ignorance and wisdom. His father is clever and inventive (*sophos*); his mother is *en aporiai*, senseless. The philosopher Eros has a 'learned ignorance'.

According to Hadot, this becomes programmatic for the tradition of Platonic philosophy as 'the love of wisdom' becomes simultaneously ironic and tragic. The true philosopher will always be *en aporiai*, knowing that he does not know, neither sage nor non-sage. He belongs neither wholly within the realm of humans nor in the realm of gods (who do not practise philosophy because they are already wise). The philosopher, like Eros and Socrates, has no home and is unclassifiable. The tragic element of philosophy, according to Hadot, lies in the philosopher's desire for that which exceeds her, but which she loves. Like Kierkegaard, the one who wanted to be a Christian but realized that only Christ is a Christian, the philosopher knows that he 'will never be entirely that which he desires'.[19] There is

---

17 Plato, *Symposium*, tr. W. R. M. Lamb (Cambridge, MA: Harvard University Press, 1996), pp. 203b ff.

18 Ibid., p. 203e.

19 Hadot, *What is Ancient Philosophy?*, p. 47.

therefore an insurmountable distance between philosophy and wisdom. 'Philosophy', explains Hadot, 'is defined by what it lacks – that is, by a transcendent norm which escapes it, yet which it nevertheless possesses within itself' in some fleeting way.[20] This is reflected in the aporia of learning in the *Meno*. Even of that of which we are ignorant, we already know something: that we are ignorant of it. This is why the Socrates of the *Symposium* is at one and the same time someone who claims to have no wisdom and is a figure of praise and admiration. The philosopher is not only an unclassifiable being 'in the middle', but is also a mediator between the gods and humans. What the philosopher first and foremost reveals to humans *is that they are not gods*.

Nicholas of Cusa's *De Sapientia*

At the far side of the Platonic tradition lie two short treatises on wisdom by Nicholas of Cusa which represent a rather similar view of the philosopher to that which we glean from the *Symposium*. Like Plato, Cusa writes of the intense desire for wisdom in the form of a dialogue between someone with no formal education – the *Idiota* – and the apparently wise and learned *Orator*. The *Idiota* points out that the *Orator* claims to be wise, but is in fact ignorant of his own ignorance. The two retire to a barber's shop to discuss the matter, whereupon the *Idiota* uses a number of characteristically Cusan examples to explain his position.

Wisdom, says the *Idiota*, proclaims itself in the streets and declares that it dwells in the highest places. So the *Idiota* looks to the streets, to the marketplace, and points out that one can see money being counted, goods being weighed and oil being measured out. By the reasoning of counting, weighing and measuring, human beings discriminate by means of a single unit. One is the beginning of number (all subsequent numbers are multiples of 1), the smallest weight is the beginning of weighing, and the smallest measure the beginning of measuring. For the sake of argument, the *Idiota* takes the smallest weight to be the ounce, the smallest measure to be the inch. Every number is constructed by means of the 1, every weight by means of the ounce, and every measure by means of the inch. But by what, asks the *Idiota*, do we attain to the 1, to the ounce or the inch? Oneness is not attained to by number, because number is subsequent to the 1. Likewise, the ounce is not attained to by means of weight, nor the inch by means of measurement.

What is Cusa's point here? It is that the composite cannot be the measure of the simple, or that what is subsequent to an origin cannot be the measure

---

20 Ibid., p. 47.

of its origin. Take the example of creation in Christian theology: the creative act cannot itself be a natural process, for natural processes are subsequent to creation and cannot 'measure' creation. This is the basis for the Judaic, Christian and Islamic conviction that God creates *ex nihilo*. As Cusa writes, '. . . the Beginning of all things is that by means of which, in which and from which whatever can be originated is originated; and, nevertheless, [that Beginning] cannot be attained unto by any originated thing. It is that by means of which, in which and from which everything that can be understood is understood; and nevertheless, it cannot be attained unto by the intellect.'[21] Again, this is another expression of the Platonic conviction that, for example, the Form of horse is not itself a horse.[22] Moreoever, particular horses do not 'measure' the Form 'horse', but rather the reverse. Thus that which is the origin of measure is not itself a measure, that which is the origin of weight is not itself a weight, and that which is the origin of being is not itself *a being*.

Cusa thereby defines 'supreme wisdom' in the following way: 'that you know . . . how it is that the Unattainable is attained to unattainably'.[23] This is a characteristically Cusan paradox. What does this mean? Cusa is pointing out that the means by which we attain knowledge, namely by comparison and measuring one thing in terms of another by means of a proportion, cannot be the means by which we attain that which is simple and the measure of all things. In other words, whatever means we use to attain knowledge of creation or the natural world, we cannot use those same means to attain knowledge of the origin of creation or the natural world. Why not? Because this would be to treat that origin as part of the order it is supposed to measure – in other words, as an object among other objects. In fact, in *De Docta Ignorantia* ('On Learned Ignorance'), Cusa goes further and states that wisdom is the realization that God is beyond all distinction – potency and act, motion and rest, lesser or greater, light and dark, maximum and minimum – and in God all opposites coincide.[24] Why? Because the absolute simplicity of God measures these spectra. It is not that God lies at the extreme end of, say, the act–potency or rest–motion spectrum. This would be to conceive God through a kind of proper proportionality, and such speech about God would in fact be speech about a

---

21 Nicholas of Cusa, *De Sapientia* I.8, in Jasper Hopkins (tr.), *Nicholas of Cusa on Wisdom and Knowledge* (Minneapolis: Arthur J. Banning Press, 1996).
22 This interpretation of Plato's metaphysics of the Forms refers particularly to its later expression in the *Theaetetus*.
23 Op. cit., I.7.
24 See Nicholas of Cusa, *Selected Spiritual Writings*, tr. H. Lawrence Bond (New York: Paulist Press, 1997). All translations from *De Docta Ignorantia* are from this summary edition of Cusa's works.

creature. The crucial point for Cusa is that there cannot be a proportion between finite and infinite. The finite world is not simply a smaller version of the infinite. Rather, the infinite comprehends within itself all finitude because it is not itself just a very big finite thing.

This has implications not only for our knowledge of God, but for the nature of our knowledge in general. For Cusa, we attain knowledge by the comparison of one thing with another. Moreover, human perception is always from a certain perspective, and only God views each object from an infinite number of perspectives at once and therefore knows each thing as it is in itself. In *De Docta Ignorantia*, Cusa puts it this way:

> A finite intellect . . . cannot precisely attain the truth of things by means of a likeness. For truth is neither more nor less but indivisible. Nothing not itself true is capable of precisely measuring what is true . . . So the intellect, which is not truth, never comprehends truth so precisely but that it could always be comprehended with infinitely more precision . . . Therefore, the quiddity of things, which is the truth of beings, is unattainable in its purity, and although it is pursued by all philosophers, none has found it as it is. The more profoundly learned we are in this ignorance, the more closely we draw near to truth itself.[25]

This has led some commentators to see in Cusa a proto-modern scepticism, particularly concerning empirical knowledge. Is this the case? What we certainly do not find in Cusa is anything like the division between the phenomenal and the noumenal, or Locke's primary and secondary qualities. Our knowledge or perception of things is merely a partial knowledge which can be infinitely perfected. The being of what we know exceeds infinitely the phenomenologically given. However, this does not mean that our knowledge is untrustworthy; rather, it can become ever more precise and is therefore reticent and provisional. It is more *ignorantia* than *scientia*.

So why are Cusa and his Neoplatonic forebears not sceptics in the modern sense of the term? This is a complex question relating to the history of philosophy, but broadly we can point to the tradition of knowledge as 'illumination' to explain the character of Neoplatonic knowing as we find it in a figure such as Cusa, and contrast this with knowledge understood as 'representation' which emerges for the first time in the late Middle Ages. It is therefore to illumination and representation that I now turn.

---

25 Nicholas of Cusa, *De Docta Ignorantia*, I.3; *De Sapientia* II.38.

Knowledge as illumination and representation

In Plato's dialogue *The Republic*, Socrates famously describes knowledge and the nature of the Good metaphorically with reference to the illumination provided by the sun.[26] He points out that the sun provides light, warmth and therefore sustenance to the creatures and objects around us, and also illuminates the world to make things visible and therefore knowable. This becomes a metaphor for the illumination provided by the Good within the visible realm which we inhabit. For Plato, the Good makes things knowable, and it is by participation in the Good that things come to be and are sustained. What does Plato mean? A crude but straightforward example might refer to the mug in front of me on my desk. I can identify this object as a mug and not, say, a dish because it performs the functions I associate with mugs particularly well. It would not, however, make a very good dish. So the fact that this object is a *good* mug makes it knowable as a mug rather than a dish. However, the object in front of me may be barely recognizable as a mug if it does not perform the functions of a mug very well; it might be cracked, for example, or be unsuitably small. In this case, my knowledge will be less clear. The object in front of me does not seem to be anything very specific; it could be any one of a number of things, and is therefore less knowable. It is not a very *good* anything. Its being – what it is – is relatively undetermined.

The crucial point for Plato is that we can participate in the Good with more or less intensity. Moreoever, fact and value are not in any way dissociated: something is knowable – and something *is* – to the extent that it is good. My intellect can be more or less intensely illuminated by the Good, and the visible realm which I attempt to know will be more or less knowable according to the intensity of its share in the Good. So knowledge can be more or less bright. At its darkest edges, however, in the faint shadows, knowledge will be dim but will still share in the light of truth.

This notion of knowledge as illumination became highly influential within early Christian thought both East and West, particularly through Neoplatonism and Christian mysticism. God is the light which illuminates all creation, sustaining creation in being and making it knowable by intellective creatures. Both being and knowledge can be more or less intensely illuminated by God. Using light as a metaphor for God is quite common and deliberate. Why? Because light is not something we can point to as just another object in a room, but is something 'other' which saturates us and makes our surroundings visible and knowable. Thus God, understood through the metaphor of light and illumination, is not 'just another being',

---

26 Plato, *Republic*, VI.508a ff.

or something which competes with other objects for our attention; God is that which makes knowledge and belief possible. Crucially, however, whatever we perceive, however dimly, our knowledge is not to be distrusted. It is not 'off the mark', but is simply a partial indication of a truth which can be more intensely known. At the limits of our knowledge, when we attempt to gaze directly at God as the source of being and knowledge (the 'sun'), we are blinded by the intensity of the light. Darkness and light become indistinguishable.[27] This is expressed in the eleventh century by St Anselm in his *Proslogion*:

> [My desiring soul] strives so that it may see more, and it sees nothing beyond what it has seen save darkness. Or rather it does not see darkness, which is not in You in any way; but it sees that it cannot see more because of its own darkness. Why is this, Lord, what is this? Is its eye darkened by its weakness, or is it dazzled by Your splendour? In truth it is both darkened in itself and dazzled by You . . . It is, in fact, both restricted by its own limitedness and overcome by Your fullness.[28]

This tradition had a broad influence on Christian belief and practice leading up to the high Middle Ages. To believe in God was not to believe in just another object within our metaphorical visual field, but to believe that our knowledge is made possible by something wholly other to which creation points. Yet this belief and knowledge was not thought to be untrustworthy and therefore a source of scepticism, bur rather partial and susceptible to ever greater illumination and clarity of vision. As Cusa put it, our knowledge is capable of ever greater precision. Most importantly, true wisdom is thought to begin in realizing the dimness of one's own perceptions, or one's *ignorantia*.

How is this tradition of knowledge as illumination superseded in modernity? One figure to whom scholars have recently returned in examining the origins of modern thought is the Franciscan John Duns Scotus (1265/6–1308). While aspects of Scotus' thought are highly contested and complex, few would deny that he understands knowledge in terms of representation rather than illumination.[29] What does this mean? Imagine I am gazing at a tree. According to knowledge understood as representation, my knowledge

---

27 See Denys Turner, *The Darkness of God: Negativity in Christian Mysticism* (Cambridge: Cambridge University Press, 1998).

28 St Anselm, *St. Anselm's* Proslogion, tr. M. Charlesworth (Notre Dame: University of Notre Dame Press, 1979), p. 135.

29 The most scholarly treatment to date of this aspect of Scotus' thought is Olivier Boulnois, *Être et Représentation: Une généalogie de la métaphysique moderne à l'époque de Duns Scot* (Paris: Presses Universitaires de France, 1999).

of a tree is rather akin to my mind taking a snapshot of the tree as if my mind were a camera. Whereas for an earlier tradition the form of the tree would come to reside in the intellect in such a way that there is an intimate connection between knower and known, for this later tradition what I know is not the tree itself, but *only a representation of the tree*. This is significant for two reasons. First, representations can be the cause of mistrust. In other words, my representational knowledge of the tree can be called into doubt because it is only a representation – a picture or snapshot, if you like. Understood in this way, the knowledge which comes from our senses can be the object of suspicion and doubt, and hence knowledge as representation is often regarded as the beginnings of a peculiarly modern form of scepticism. A corollary of this provides the second reason why knowledge as representation in Scotus is important. Because knowledge is now somewhat problematic, the focus for philosophy shifts from *what* we know (in which ontology (the what) and epistemology (the knowledge) are intertwined) to *how* we know what we know. This therefore marks the invention of an autonomous and particular variant of philosophy which has become of almost exclusive concern in the modern period, namely epistemology – the study of how we know what we know. With knowledge understood as representation, created beings are known without reference to a transcendent and simply are as they *appear* to be to us in our representation of them (this being the beginning of the long road to the modern philosophies of thinkers as diverse as Kant and Locke). We do not know things in themselves (however falteringly or partially), but only *representations* of those things. What we see of creation is rather like flicking through a family album of holiday snapshots rather than being on holiday in person. In some forms of modern philosophy (one thinks particularly of Descartes), the central project therefore becomes exclusively epistemological: the assuaging of scepticism and radical doubt by the attainment of certain or foundational knowledge.

Knowledge as representation further influences theological discussions in early modernity. The Christian tradition had long held the view that we can name God from creatures (metaphorically or, in some sense, analogically) according to an especially nuanced understanding of the Neoplatonic teaching that an effect (creation) will resemble its cause (God). However, if one's knowledge of the effect – creation – is a mere 'appearance' or 'representation' and not indicative of things in themselves, then naming God from creatures, in however attenuated a sense, would become increasingly problematic and untrustworthy. Thus Christian theology comes to find refuge in a much more positivistic understanding of a bounded 'revelation' which is regarded as a packet of information arriving in a fashion that is unmediated by creation.

Conclusion

The parody of traditional religious belief as dogmatic and credulous which we often encounter in contemporary debates between atheism and theism does not reflect the affinity between a more traditional theology and philosophy which begins with *docta ignorantia*, or learning what one does not know. This 'way of negation' informs the genesis of Christian teaching in the early Church because it provides a guard against idolatry and the tendency to think that we know what we are affirming or denying when we speak of 'God'. As Denys Turner points out, the job of belief or unbelief might be somewhat more interesting and challenging than the contemporary theist versus atheist debate suggests.[30]

However, are we thereby left merely with agnostic doubt, or a scepticism which might in the end lead only to indifference? While this might be the result should one believe that our knowledge of God is based upon a representational knowledge of creation, this need not be the case with knowledge understood as a more-or-less intense illumination in which we begin with learning what we do not know, and continue in the conviction that such wisdom is indicative of the true and the good. The task of the Christian thereby shifts from the apologetic defence of a system of cognitive propositions concerning God and the world towards the task of delineating, clarifying or bringing into greater focus the meaning and implications of a particular vision of creation and its origin.

There is a tendency in both modern philosophy and distinctively modern theology to believe rather a lot, and to pit this knowledge against others who know and believe enough to discount the existence of God. Atheism is not humanity's default setting from which we are moved by proofs of certain propositions, and it is most certainly not a kind of 'negative' knowledge in the tradition of Socrates-Eros or Nicholas of Cusa. After all, atheism asks us to deny an awful lot in order to arrive at a highly determined and essentially positive conclusion: God does not exist. Moreover, it is not that atheism or secularism leave the cleared ground unoccupied. As a number of theologians have recently pointed out, secularism and atheism are positive inventions. One version of what arrives as a kind of pseudo-theology to fill secularism's void asks us to believe that we are our genes, that evolution 'measures' being itself, and that the processes of the reproduction of a virus among biological life-forms is univocal with the practice of religion in human communities. That is quite a lot to sign up to, and it's rather more than the view that what we know is a partial but beautiful shard of that which can only be wholly other, that which a long tradition names 'God'.

---

30 See Turner, *The Darkness of God*, pp. 9ff.

18

Provocation

HARRIET A. HARRIS

Faith seems to come neither as the outcome of debate nor of the stifling of reason. The triggers and seeming grounds of faith have a fleeting nature, so I move away from debates which test their efficacy and soundness. In the following reflections I explore aspects of gaining and losing faith, and of living by faith, to see what they suggest about the dynamics of faith in relation to the tasks that reason performs.

My faith has changed over the years. As a child I had what would best be described as evangelical conversion experience(s). I went to evangelistic rallies by such people as Elvis Presley's half-brother and ex-New York gangster, Nicky Cruz. I went up at the altar-call every time, because the atmosphere was so emotionally charged and the call to be saved was so pressing. I was probably saved about five times. I was nine or ten years old when I started going to church, and my father, who is a Jewish intellectual agnostic, and largely unsympathetic to religion, said to one of his friends: 'What do you do when your daughter decides to freak in?'

At the time, the things that were most important for my faith were the encouragement and enthusiasm of my older brother, testimonies of other people, a quite intense and happy experience of God's acceptance, the truth of the Bible (which I took in a rather rigid way), and the way in which other Christians live. Some of these were clearly triggers for my faith. Could some of them count as grounds upon which to base faith?

This I have come to doubt. Most of the seeming grounds for faith can fall away: for example, when the experience of others seems alien, when God seems non-communicative, scripture itself shatters every attempt to read it straightforwardly; or when feeling let down by the behaviour of religious people, or disillusioned with one's own religious life. All of this can happen while faith remains. One's faith can change to a point where its initial triggers are no longer effective, and its seeming grounds have become like quicksand (although another ground may have presented itself).

If asked why I have faith, at the bottom line I'd say that it is provoked in me. I get needled into faith. I suspect this experience resonates with follow-ers of all the world's faiths, including those, such as the majority of Buddhists, who do not believe in a god. People who have faith, have faith because they would be too restless without it.

In saying this I am putting to one side the supposition that people have faith because they are born into and raised with a particular faith. We live in a context in which people commonly move away from the practices, beliefs and non-beliefs of their elders. If they stay with the faith of their family, they conceive of themselves as having at some stage made that faith their own.

I suspect it has always and everywhere been so. That in ages gone by, and in parts of the world, and indeed in parts of the UK, today, people are raised in communities of faith neither undermines nor strengthens what I say about provocation. By analogy, people may be brought up with music and encouraged to play an instrument, and such an upbringing will educate them musically. But whether or not people take to music, make the playing of an instrument their own, or reject the musical heritage of their upbring-ing, seems not ultimately to be determined by the musicality (or lack of musicality) of that upbringing.

In following the Christian faith, I understand faith as coming from and being grounded in God. The restlessness I allude to makes sense to me in the words of Augustine, 'You have made us for Yourself, and our heart is restless until it finds repose in You.'[1] In this essay I am not fleshing out the theology or confessional articulation of my faith, but I regard faith as continually accompanied by provocation, including the provocation to think and speak truthfully, and to unite integrity of thought and integrity of action. Confessional aspects of faith are the fruit of such efforts. I have come to regard God as the provoker of faith and to find sense in theology that expresses this.

At the same time, I believe that many dynamics of faith are generic across and outside of particular religions. I try at the end of this essay to relate some thoughts on living by faith to an a-theistic position, hoping what I say can be regarded as truthful there. I have chosen Buddhism, about which I am no expert, but in respect of which I can rely on my colleague Michael McGhee for correction. I have found that some philosopher friends who follow no religion, but regard themselves as having some sort of faith, relate to what I say about restlessness.

---

1 *Confessions*, Bk I, ch. 1.

Gaining and losing faith

People have faith, don't have faith, or lose faith for so many different reasons. If we accept the many and diverse testimonies about faith, some people come to God intellectually, others emotionally. Many come to faith through social interactions. Some of the arguments or experiences that trigger faith may also seem to provide grounds, and philosophers debate whether religious experience or facts and interpretations of the natural world can count as evidence for faith. Yet, as suggested above, people can arrive at points where the intellectual reasons for believing in God leave them unmoved, and where emotionally God seems to be absent, and yet they find that they cannot live without faith.

A possible way to express this is to say that faith is what is left over when all else falls away. But conceptually this would sever faith from its rational, experiential, bodily and social expressions – all of which, in many circumstances, contribute to its tenacity. It is more fitting to say that provocation or restlessness remain, which may reignite faith and push one again along the path of reflecting on one's experiences (which now include new experiences of loss), and rebuilding an integrated vision and life – one in which one's thinking, experiences and actions do not contradict each other.

When an American Roman Catholic priest, Vincent Donovan, went to the Masai people in Africa, and found his faith being shattered, he said, 'I did not hurt in my head. I hurt all over.'[2] Before he had gone through this experience, he had regarded his faith as primarily cerebral, a matter of giving intellectual assent to certain claims about God and Christ. But when his faith was severely challenged, partly by experiencing how distorting and inauthentic it was to impose Western styles of Church upon Africans, and he came to 'doubt the very message of Christianity',[3] it was not his mind but his whole self that was at stake.

Faith is not apart from reason; reason is taken up in the development of faith. By this I mean that as faith develops in form and content (for example, through learning practices of confession, learning to live as one who is forgiven and forgiving, believing in a God of mercy), it transforms our way of seeing and being in the world. Faith develops into bodily expression – corporate in both a physical and a social sense – precisely because it transforms our way of being in the world. Reason itself is subject to this shaping. At the same time, reason, although shaped by the developing faith, is also its critic. We trust reason in this role, whether or not its judgements

---

2 Vincent J. Donovan, *Christianity Rediscovered: An Epistle from the Masai* (London: SCM Press, 1978, 1982), p. 62.
3 Ibid., p. 62.

are sound, because reason is what we rely upon when thinking as hard as we possibly can.[4]

If reason leads to the shattering of faith, the pain is felt throughout the body: 'I ached in every fibre of my being.'[5] If reason leads in the opposite direction, this can restore the body: 'Life would rise up within me and I would *feel* the possibility and joy of living', wrote Tolstoy.[6] Biblical images of God lightening your face, or Christ lifting the load off your back, refreshing you like water, feeding you like bread, evoke the full-bodied impact that faith can have. Paul wrote to Philemon, asking him, as the Authorized Version puts it, to 'refresh my bowels in the Lord' (Philemon 1.20). The bowels, not the heart, were considered the centre of the emotions: in other words, your deepest insides. We reflect this when we say that we are 'churned up', or 'gutted'. Being stirred up in faith and losing faith both 'churn us up inside'.

Living by faith

Indeed, the demands of faith, its regular provocations, churn people up inside: the provocation to give and seek forgiveness, to have hope in the face of despair, to admit and face failure, to overcome pride, to have courage, to champion justice, to defend mercy. The argument that if we had full knowledge of God there would be no room for faith, seems beside the point. If we had full knowledge of God, we would still struggle with forgiveness, hope, failure, pride, courage, justice and mercy. Living by faith is not like trying to convince oneself of something, but of living with risk in the context of trust. Many of the demands of faith are not primarily intellectual.

That said, when the intellect is not sufficiently engaged in matters over which we feel provoked, little integration is achieved (and this is specifically a matter of integrity, not of intelligence). Bad theology is an expression of disintegration, duplicity; in other words, the diabolical, where we compartmentalize ourselves and justify a thought or action in one area that we would not tolerate in another. Here is evidence of the lack of truthfulness, and it can issue in harmful practice and violence. As we know too well, religious people do violent deeds.

In the face of religious violence, I propose that the proper role of the intellect is an integrative and not necessarily a moderating one. Too often

---

4 Cf. Linda Zagzebski, *Philosophy of Religion: A Historical Introduction* (Oxford: Blackwell, 2007), p. 230

5 Donovan, *Christianity Rediscovered*, p. 63.

6 Leo Tolstoy, *A Confession and Other Religious Writings*, tr. Jane Kentish (Harmondsworth: Penguin, 1987), p. 64.

people respond to violent religious extremism by extolling the virtues of religious moderation – which is like water off a duck's back, or even grist to the mill, for extremists. It is misleading to suggest that the provocations of faith are only moderate, and never extreme. While moderation may often be called for, sometimes it specifically is not.

'Who stands firm?' Dietrich Bonhoeffer asked:

> Only the one for whom the final standard is not his reason, his principles, his conscience, his freedom, his virtue, but who is ready to sacrifice all these, when in faith and sole allegiance to God he is called to obedient and responsible action: the responsible person, whose life will be nothing but an answer to God's question and call.[7]

Being provoked beyond parameters that one might have thought were reasonable or realistic is a feature of having faith. It is one of the ways in which faith effects transformations both in people's apprehensions of the world, and in social action.

Consider Jesus telling his disciples that unless they hate their fathers and mothers, wives and children, brothers and sisters, and even life itself, they cannot follow him (Luke 13.26). The Semitic people of his day used the language of love and hate to talk about choices. They would have understood Jesus as saying: if you are to be my disciple, you must choose me over and against your family – you must prefer me. As put by Jesus, this is a very exacting call. Jesus is warning his followers that to be his disciple means precisely not to hold anything else more dear. Probably he is saying, you cannot follow me, you cannot go where I am going – to die on a cross – if in fact your attachments lie elsewhere. The point is to provoke his followers beyond what they had imagined, to test and improve their preparedness for what lies ahead.

In the subsequent verses, in the Gospel of Luke, Jesus says, 'Whoever does not carry the cross and follow me cannot be my disciple. For which of you, intending to build a tower, does not first sit down and estimate the cost, to see whether he has enough to complete it? Otherwise, when he has laid a foundation and is not able to finish, all who see it will begin to ridicule him, saying, "This fellow began to build and was not able to finish"' (Luke 13.27–30).

If you start to build a tower, but cannot afford to finish it, it will be worse than not having embarked on the project in the first place. The practice of being a Christian – the cost of following Jesus – is to carry the cross, which

---

7 Dietrich Bonhoeffer, *After Ten Years: Letters and Papers from Prison*, enlarged edn, Eberhard Bethge (ed.) (New York: The Macmillan Company, 1971), p. 5.

means to bear the sins and burdens of our brothers and sisters (meaning our worldwide family, our fellow human beings, our neighbours in the broadest sense of neighbour), to be driven like a scapegoat from the gates of the city – as have the Buddhist monks protesting in Myanmar/Burma. Of course, they are following the teachings of the Buddha rather than of Jesus, but the same point applies. If they embarked on their protest but then couldn't see it through, they would have made only half a protest, and that would be worse than no protest at all. Their cause would have been harmed.

Each of these monks will have made choices in his own way, choosing his path of peaceful resistance at the cost of family, friendships and personal safety. In some cases, it has been to the cost of their own lives.

Of course, I am in no position to speak for them, but I find them immensely impressive, and see parallels in their courageous acts of compassion, and what Jesus demands of his followers. In a kind of virtuous circle, my faith is encouraged by the realization that it takes such moral strength to be faithful. As I understand the teachings of Buddha and of Jesus, being faithful requires us to make our own selves an end to oppression, hatred and violence. It is more natural to deflect pain by hitting out or griping at others, or by fleeing the situation that caused it; but marching peacefully under persecution, and carrying the cross, involve absorbing pain and violence in our own bodies and souls, and not letting any of it run out the other side. This is why Jesus gave such stark warnings about how costly it is to follow him. The question is whether one can see it through.

Taking up the cross brings with it the possibility that one will be brought to the point that Jesus was brought to, and which Bonhoeffer experienced and expressed so profoundly; where reason and virtue are not one's final standard, but 'in faith and sole allegiance to God [one] is called to obedient and responsible action'. Hearing that call to obedient and responsible action is a matter of seeing the moment, and understanding what kind of a moment it is, and what one's part in it must be. Answering that call is not a matter of falling into irrationality. In Kierkegaardian terms, such crises require a temporary suspension of ethics and rationality. Reason has played an integrating role. It has enabled the logic of one's faith to develop with integrity, such that one understands how costly the demands of one's faith may be. And, by that logic, reason must at the right moment let one go.

Summarizing reflections

I have not made a distinction between 'faith-in' and 'faith-that', because this distinction comes in and out of view as integration wanes or waxes. Where would one draw the line between the two supposedly different forms of 'faith', for example, in understanding Bonhoeffer's acceptance of the cost of discipleship? I apologize for committing a philosophical sin in speaking of 'faith' and 'reason' without defining them. I am not sure that such longer-hands as 'religious disposition' and 'critical reflective thinking' would help. By 'faith' I mean everything from the least developed response to needling, to a well-developed confessional position in which 'reason' plays an integrating role, for which it remains a critical voice, and with respect to which it sometimes stands aside.

Index